NO WAY TO PICK A PRESIDENT

ALSO BY JULES WITCOVER

85 Days: The Last Campaign

The Resurrection of Richard Nixon

White Knight: The Rise of Spiro Agnew

A Heartbeat Away: The Investigation and Resignation of Vice President

Spiro T. Agnew *(with Richard M. Cohen)*

Marathon: The Pursuit of the Presidency, 1972–1976

The Main Chance *(a novel)*

Blue Smoke and Mirrors: How Reagan Won and

Why Carter Lost the Election of 1980 *(with Jack W. Germond)*

Wake Us When It's Over: Presidential Politics of 1984

(with Germond)

Sabotage at Black Tom: Imperial Germany's Secret War in America, 1914–1917

Whose Broad Stripes and Bright Stars? The Trivial Pursuit of the Presidency, 1988

(with Germond)

Crapshoot: Rolling the Dice on the Vice Presidency

Mad As Hell: Revolt at the Ballot Box, 1992 *(with Germond)*

The Year the Dream Died: Revisiting 1968 in America

NO WAY TO PICK A PRESIDENT

Jules Witcover

FARRAR, STRAUS AND GIROUX
NEW YORK

Farrar, Straus and Giroux
19 Union Square West, New York 10003

Distributed in Canada by Douglas & McIntyre Ltd
Printed in the United States of America
Designed by Lisa Stokes
First edition, 1999
Library of Congress Cataloging-in-Publication Data
Witcover, Jules.
No way to pick a president / Jules Witcover. — 1st ed.
p. cm.
Includes bibliographical references.
ISBN 0-374-22303-3 (alk. paper)
1. Presidents—United States—Election—History.
2. Electioneering—United States—History. 3. United States—Politics and government—20th century. I. Title.
JK524.W58 1999
324.973′092—dc21 99-34933

For Peter, Corin, and Macey

Acknowledgments

A book drawn from more than forty years of reporting and writing on presidential campaigns and elections owes a profound debt to hundreds of colleagues, politicians, political professionals, voters, and friends made and maintained along the way. In the manuscript's early stages, sage advice came from my old friend the late John Chancellor. Many interviews helped me form and flesh out my ideas, particularly those with presidential candidates Lamar Alexander, Bill Bradley, Bob Dole, and Phil Gramm; vice presidential candidate Jack Kemp; former Republican National Chairmen Haley Barbour and Frank Fahrenkopf; former Democratic National Chairmen Don Fowler and Paul Kirk; and Charlie Black, Hal Bruno, James Carville, Kent Cooper, John Deardourff, David Doak, Sam Donaldson, Charles Lewis, Dick Morris, Mike Murphy, Joe Napolitan, the late Matt Reese, John Sears, Bob Shrum, Terry Smith, Stuart Spencer, Bob Squier, Lesley Stahl, Ray Strother, Bob Teeter, and Fred Wertheimer. My thanks to each of them.

In the solitude of the book's writing, the list narrows and the debt deepens to a few who provided unwavering support and encouragement. These include my incomparable editor at Farrar, Straus and Giroux, Elisabeth Sifton, and my indomitable agent, David Black. Most of all, my fellow writer-in-residence and endlessly cheerful, loving, and much-loved wife, Marion Elizabeth, lightened the burden by creating a warm and placid cocoon from which to work, as well as constructive criticism softened always with a radiant smile.

Jules Witcover

Contents

"Do not run a campaign that would embarrass your mother."

—Senator Robert C. Byrd of West Virginia, 1987

"The hardest thing about any political campaign is how to win without proving that you are unworthy of winning."

—Governor Adlai E. Stevenson of Illinois,
Democratic presidential nominee, 1956

"The voters have spoken—the bastards."

—Representative Morris K. Udall of Arizona, after losing the Democratic presidential primary in New Hampshire, 1976

NO WAY TO PICK A PRESIDENT

INTRODUCTION

Then and Now

One early evening more than forty years ago, in my first professional involvement in presidential politics, along with perhaps twenty other reporters, I boarded President Dwight D. Eisenhower's campaign train at Union Station in Washington. We were bound for Philadelphia, where the president was to speak in pursuit of a 1956 reelection victory over the Democratic nominee, Adlai E. Stevenson of Illinois.

En route, White House and campaign aides circulated texts of Eisenhower's speech so that we members of the traveling press could meet early morning-edition deadlines. The aides strolled through the small compartments of the train, answering reporters' questions or just passing the time. As we clacked away on our noisy and cumbersome portable typewriters, Western Union clerks moved through the train collecting parts of our stories, page by page—"takes," in the jargon of the precomputer news business—for wire transmission to our newsrooms around the country.

It was all very low-key, although to a neophyte like myself it seemed a glamorous exercise of the sort that in those days drew young reporters to the craft of journalism (then seldom called either a craft or journalism). Legendary figures like Merriman Smith of United Press—"Smitty" to his contemporaries in the press corps and on the White House staff, but an unspoken "Mr. Smith" to an awestruck me—toiled with sleeves rolled up past their elbows and cigarettes dangling from the corners of their mouths, in a scene out of a Hollywood movie, wisecracking as they wrote.

Four years later, in 1960, in my first exposure to a presidential primary campaign, I strolled down the Main Streets of small mining towns in West Virginia accompanying, with only three or four other reporters, Senator John F. Kennedy of Massachusetts as he canvassed for votes. He would pop into local stores, shake hands with storekeepers and customers, and somewhat deferentially identify himself as a candidate for the Democratic nomination, asking for their consideration on primary day.

As Kennedy moved from town to town, he would often share his car, driven by an aide, and his thoughts with a reporter or two. And as primary day approached, the candidate would ride in a single bus with his campaign staff and reporters, sometimes sitting up front talking with a selected reporter he knew from Boston or Washington, other times sauntering to the back of the bus to banter with groups of us relaxing there, sipping beers or harder stuff, always in adequate supply. At day's or night's end, the candidate would join us in a nightcap, discussing the day's events or anything else that came into his mind, or ours.

Kennedy seldom felt it necessary at these times to stipulate that what he was saying was off the record, or "on background," and none of us tried to take notes or make a tape recording of our conversations. This was a time for the candidate to relax and for the reporters to get to know him a little better—not necessarily in the details of his thinking or actions that day, but in making an informal assessment of the man himself with his hair down.

Much has changed in presidential politics in the intervening time since the Eisenhower campaign of 1956, beyond the mode of campaign transportation and the replacement of reporters' typewriters with laptop computers. And the easy access and relationship to the candidate that reporters enjoyed in the Kennedy campaign of 1960 is largely a nostalgic memory today. Presidential campaigns have become marathon exercises in complex logistics, and except for the longest long shots in the early primaries, presidential candidates are often remote and inaccessible to the traveling press attempting to take their measure for American voters.

Candidates and presidents harmed by news-media disclosures of their personal peccadilloes and shortcomings of character have learned to be more protective of themselves. A new generation of reporters, grown more skeptical or even cynical toward politicians in the wake of the deceptions of the Vietnam War period and the Watergate scandal, has adopted more demanding standards for them than those of earlier journalistic generations.

In Kennedy's time, the yardstick for reporting on the personal behavior of candidates and presidents was whether such conduct appeared to affect the performance of their official duties. Now, in the era of gossip-sheet journalism, the Internet, and all-scandal-all-the-time radio and cable television, it appears that almost anything that can be learned is fair game for disclosure. Much is made by younger reporters today of the fact that Kennedy's womanizing before and after he entered the White House was not reported at the time. They assume that his behavior was widely known among the press corps, but that was not so, at least in my case and among my circle of reporter friends. It was not difficult for a sitting president to keep such things secret. Even if it had been known, however, it probably would not have been reported, given the journalistic standards of the time.

Today's presidential campaigns as a whole are as different from the campaigns of 1956 and 1960, or of 1952 for that matter, as the supersonic jet is from the horse and buggy. Eisenhower in 1952 and John Kennedy in 1960 each started campaigning openly and in earnest only after the campaign year itself had begun; each ran in only a handful of primaries to achieve the nominations of their parties. Each had only a few political strategists whispering in his ear; they relied largely on party chieftains around the country to generate support. Television and public-opinion polling were only beginning to become important to their campaigns, and the cost of running was a mere fraction of what it was to become.

The political parties, and voters' loyalty to them, played much greater parts in the 1952, 1956, and 1960 campaigns than they do today. Now, the explosion of television channels enables both Democratic and Republican candidates to reach many more voters, though at an astronomical cost, and polls help the candidates' strategists read the voters' minds in more refined ways, also at considerable expense. At the same time, the Internet has emerged as a huge campaign tool for direct communication with voters, bypassing the news media, not only to propagandize but also to recruit, organize, and even solicit money. Meanwhile, party loyalty has disintegrated so much that no presidential campaign goes by today without the presence of several independent or third parties to challenge the old two-party fortress. Poll after poll reports a widening public yearning for more choices, a fact fed on by Ross Perot in creation of his Reform Party in 1996.

Yet, for all that, the system by which Americans choose their president today still does resemble in essential ways the one that elected Eisenhower in 1952 and 1956, Kennedy in 1960, and every president thereafter. Major-party candidates still have to compete for public support in state primaries, though in many more of them, and (except for the self-financing Steve Forbes in 1996 and 2000) they have to raise money to pay their expenses in those primaries. They have to accumulate convention delegates in various ways in all the states. And those who win their party's nomination have to collar a majority of votes in the electoral college to claim the presidency.

The results of this system since the days of Eisenhower and Kennedy—the presidencies of Lyndon Johnson, Richard Nixon, Jimmy Carter, Ronald Reagan, George Bush, and Bill Clinton—have not been particular testimonials for it. Of these men, only Nixon, Reagan, and Clinton were deemed by the voters effective enough to warrant a second term. At that, Nixon was forced from office early in his, in the worst political scandal in the nation's history, and Clinton had to survive House impeachment and a Senate trial. With each succeeding election year, millions of Americans have demonstrated their loss of confidence and interest in the system and in the candidates it produces, boycotting the voting booths in droves.

Also, more and more distinguished Americans have turned their backs on seeking the presidency, including heroes like General Colin Powell in 1996 and longtime political figures like Governor Mario Cuomo of New York in 1992 and Senator Bill Bradley of New Jersey and former representative Jack Kemp of New York in 1996—men to whom attainment of the White House might have been expected to be their Holy Grail.

In Kemp's case, he did agree finally to be the Republican vice presidential nominee, but he had to endure only the two-month general campaign in the fall, paid for in full by taxpayers. As the year 2000 campaign geared up, Bradley decided that the time was right for him, but the road to the White House is no less daunting. It has indeed become such a wrenching ordeal, exacting such a high price in time, money, reputation, and personal and family privacy, that many of America's best real or prospective leaders decline even to consider subjecting themselves to it. Among the early dropouts from the 2000 campaign were Senators Bob Kerrey of Nebraska, John Kerry of Massachusetts, John Ashcroft of Missouri, and Paul Wellstone of Minnesota (for health reasons) and House Minority Leader Richard Gephardt of Missouri.

Now, as the United States marks its first presidential election of a new century, one deplorable fact has become crystal-clear: the process by which the nation chooses its leader has been hijacked—by money, ambition, and, yes, the ingenuity of the men and women who practice the art of politics in all its forms.

It is an art that, over the span of fifty-three presidential elections, has come to resemble not an exercise of civic-mindedness but rather an orgy of no-holds-barred warfare. It is fought out first in a relentless pursuit of campaign money, then state by state in the trenches of primary elections and caucuses, and finally nationwide through the new high-tech weapons of mass communication, increasingly under the generalship of mercenaries. From beginnings when no political parties existed, no presidential primaries, caucuses, and national conventions were held, and candidates seldom spoke publicly in their own behalf in brief campaigns, the process has evolved into a seemingly endless partisan, highly structured, and bitterly personal combat for the presidency.

Over the 209 years since George Washington took the oath of office as the first president, a complicated and tremendously costly obstacle course to the White House has been constructed. It has required ever-increasing commitments of time, energy, and money not only from the candidates but also from their friends, family, and, more and more, armies of political professionals generating profit and celebrity for themselves in their involvement.

Candidates by and large have become self-selected, deciding to seek the presidency as much out of personal ambition as personal and party achievement and acclaim—even to the point, as the billionaires Ross Perot and Steve Forbes demonstrated, of buying their way into the process.

Joining the campaigns, and often replacing high-minded individuals devoted to a single candidate in a single election, have been "hired guns" who may or may not have a close attachment to the candidate and who are driven primarily by the lure of influence, money, or notoriety, or all three. The time when campaigns were run by one-horse jockeys—friends or professional associates of the candidate motivated by devotion to him and his ideas and involved only so long as he is involved—is largely gone. Now we live in the era of the political technocrat—the hired campaign strategist, pollster, media consultant, fund-raiser—who auctions off his expertise to whichever candidate offers the most money or the best chance to wield influence and gain celebrity. What the candidate himself stands for may not matter; more and more, these hired guns are like geography teachers who can lecture that the world is round or flat, provided the price and potential for success and prominence are right.

Hand in hand with this attitude comes a campaign mentality that preaches that anything goes. Whatever it takes to win is done, the only caveat being that one's tactics should not be so egregious that they backfire, and even that caveat is often ignored. What it takes to cause a backlash against sleazy campaigning seems to increase with every election. Negative politics, which candidates and campaign managers once shunned as self-destructive except in the most dire circumstances in the waning days or hours of a campaign, have often become the first tactic to be used, to throw the opponent on the defensive at the outset. In the process, generations of young Americans, drawn into politics by good intentions, are witnessing and learning the dark underside of a calling that not too long ago was regarded with at least a measure of high purpose and public service. Under the tutelage of the growing breed of win-at-all-costs political operatives, idealism is a casualty.

These highly paid political technocrats have become more and more visible and vocal, not only in shaping the candidate's strategy and persona but also in speaking for his campaign. As the technocrats build their reputations as political magicians, they are in greater and greater demand, not only to run campaigns but to work the lucrative celebrity circuit in lecture halls and television studios. Responsibility for the tone and content of a political campaign, let alone a presidential one, which should rest with the candidate, is shifted to his professional handlers, often to his ultimate political detriment and to the public's.

Campaign finance laws, originally intended to clean up presidential politics, are riddled with loopholes and instead have lengthened the obstacle course and the price to run it, widening the opportunity for the political technocrats to gain profit and fame. The clock starts running twelve months before the presidential campaign year, when a politician must build his qualifications for the available federal campaign subsidy, so candidates go into a campaign mode then. They stump the states holding the earliest primaries and caucuses, and states where big fund-raisers can be found, and the news media follows them as they crisscross the country. This means that the spotlight focuses on them at a time when complaining voters are still recovering from the last inundation of politics in the previous presidential election.

Even an incumbent president like Bill Clinton in 1995–96, with no primary opponent in sight, worked the early money circuit assiduously. Indeed, his fund-raising proclivities, indulged in on an unprecedentedly avaricious scale, were a persuasive discouragement to any fellow Democrat who might have been toying with the prospect of challenging him.

Individuals of great wealth like Perot in 1992 and 1996 and Forbes in 1996 and 2000 can circumvent the federal campaign finance laws and the considerable burdens imposed by them by spending millions of dollars of their own money. Such blatant attempts to purchase the presidency—or at least gain entry into an election process that their personal experience would never otherwise have earned—further undermine the credibility and integrity of the system.

In the first half of 1999, one Republican presidential candidate, Governor George W. Bush of Texas, accumulated so much campaign money in an unprecedented fund-raising effort involving wealthy and well-placed friends—$37 million—that he too was able to duck federal spending restraints imposed on other candidates, placing them at further disadvantage.

As states compete for larger shares of the publicity and financial benefits of staging early caucuses and primaries, the obstacle course has become unduly demanding in terms of time, money, and endurance. In 1996, a record forty-two Republican state primaries were held, nearly three quarters of them in the first three months of the year. For 2000, the calendar was accelerated even more, and forty-six Republican and at least thirty-seven Democratic primaries were scheduled. Because of the early start in fund-raising, the presidential campaign remains at least a two-year marathon, often a longer one, and now also requires a built-in wind sprint from January through March of the election year. The pace is exhausting for the candidates and puts an additional premium on early money; for the voters, the task of assessing the candidates and digesting the rush of information about them is equally exhausting and confusing.

The party conventions that follow have become mere confirmations of decisions reached in the frenetic caucuses and primaries. And the general-election campaigning is essentially a competition for crowds and television evening news coverage, rather than a revealing debate on the key issues facing the country, except in formal debates that also have their shortcomings. The result more often than not is voter disgust and, by election time, apathy, resulting in abysmally low turnouts. In recent presidential elections, only about half of all eligible Americans voted, a performance worse than that in most other advanced countries, including those in the former Soviet bloc. The winner goes to the White House as the choice of perhaps one in four voters who could have had a say.

In all this, the news media that traditionally played watchdog, holding the candidates (and their handlers) to account for what they say and do, has been reduced to being either bystander or accomplice in the artful manipulation of politics by the hired guns. At the same time, the advent and proliferation of radio and television talk shows have encouraged the phenomenon of the celebrity journalist, whose participation often undermines his credibility in reporting on presidential politics and the credibility of his whole profession, already the target of wide public skepticism.

Weighing in as well are burgeoning political action groups and other special-interest groups from big business to labor, and an assortment of single-issue advocacy movements that with money or other political pressure try to influence and even control the candidates for their cause. And as we saw in 1996, foreign contributors either are sought by the major parties or insinuate themselves into the American electoral process to gain influence at the highest levels of government.

Is this any way to pick a president? Does the road to the White House have to be a disreputable trial by ordeal for the candidates and also for the public, who must endure its length, its noise level, its corruption, its divisiveness, and its cost, not simply in money but in the price it exacts in public incivility? Just as important, does the existing process discourage the best potential presidents from seeking the office? The roster of presidents going back at least to the end of World War II has not been particularly distinguished, and public respect for the office has steadily diminished. The intellectual and character flaws of its occupants and aspirants have been unveiled by news organizations that have helped to convert the election process from the educational exercise it should be to a running exposé of the worst in American public life. Campaign managers occupy themselves in "damage control" for their candidates and in damage proliferation against their opponents. The result sheds little light on the critical issues before the country or on the ideas the candidates have about how to deal with them.

This depressing state is not what our Founding Fathers envisioned. They never foresaw the election of the American president evolving into an all-consuming competition for campaign funds to feed a political technocracy dominated by people whose first and often only loyalty is to themselves—to their own influence, power, celebrity, and greed. Examining how this money-driven technocracy in all its manifestations emerged, how it has come to have a stranglehold on presidential politics, and what can be done about it is the objective of the following pages.

1 Me for President

Every American mother likes to think that her son (or, nowadays, her daughter) can become president. Although it isn't likely to happen, the long odds don't prevent a fair number of Americans who have attained the constitutional age of thirty-five from trying. Many don't seem to have much else in the way of qualifications for the job, but that doesn't stop them.

It's said that when John F. Kennedy first thought about seeking the presidency, he looked around the United States Senate, saw a number of his colleagues who were being mentioned as prospective candidates, and asked himself: Why not me? Kennedy at that time was forty-two years old and had served six years in the House of Representatives and seven in the Senate. Many others who have reached for the White House have had much less experience to recommend them, but if they're old enough, are native-born, and have resided in the United States for fourteen years, as the Constitution also stipulates, nothing but good sense prevents them from reaching for politics' shiniest brass ring.

Long service to one's political party does remain important, however, particularly in the Republican Party. In recent years, a sort of pecking order by longevity has been established, with only occasional intrusions by candidates with sufficient celebrity to breach that order. General Dwight D. Eisenhower, for example, brushed aside the party stalwart Senator Robert A. Taft of Ohio in 1952, and Ronald Reagan barged in on patient GOP foot soldiers George Bush and Robert Dole in 1980. In between, party regulars who had "earned" the nomination—Richard Nixon in 1960, 1968, and 1972,

Barry Goldwater in 1964, the short-time incumbent Gerald Ford in 1976, Bush in 1988 and 1992, and Dole in 1996—all were anointed as toilers in the party vineyards. Dole, forced to wait in the wings by Reagan, and then by his vice president, Bush, campaigned in 1996 on the argument that it was "my turn."

"It's always seemed to me," says Dole, "you should have some party experience, you should have done some legwork in the party. I don't say you earn the spot; I mean, it's never yours. But I think it's just the way it ought to work. If I want to go out and run as a Republican, I should be able to go out and tell the people in Iowa and New Hampshire whoever I've been able to deal with over the years. If I wake up some morning and say I want to be president, having done nothing in the party, but I've got a lot of money in the bank or whatever [*Steve Forbes, please note*], there's something missing there, the way I look at it. You've got to have a feel for the people you represent. You get that through experience and hard work, and defeat. In my case, I started off as a young Republican district chairman, way, way, way back. That's when you had to work your way up in the party. Now you just need sort of celebrity status or the money. Once you're sort of established, then you start doing things for the party."

On the other hand, Dole says, "I was considered by some too much of an insider, I had too much experience." Some, he recalls, "said he's been there so long, he has no ideas, he's tired. I didn't feel that way, but some people had that view: that it's good to get this fresh face, somebody who just pops out of the sky."

The imposing task that running for and winning the presidency has become, however, has discouraged many distinguished Americans from making the try. So has the knowledge that they will run in a glass fishbowl, their every word and action exposed to public scrutiny. At the same time, some of the most improbable political figures have sought the office, and a few—like an obscure peanut farmer and former one-term governor of Georgia named Jimmy Carter—have won it, encouraging others to emulate their boldness.

There was a time when the most prominent political leaders did step forward to seek the presidency, or were pushed to the fore by their peers in the famous smoke-filled rooms where party nominations were negotiated. These peers were well equipped to assess the prospective candidates on two critical aspects: their qualifications for the presidency and their prospects for election to the office. Theoretically, the chances of an untested candidate seizing the prize were minimized by the gauntlet of party elders the nominee had to run. On other occasions, the necessity of multiple convention ballots before a nominee could be agreed upon inevitably led to delegation horse trading by state and big-city party leaders, producing eventual nominees who, while prominent at the time, proved to be eminently forgettable. Typical was James A. Garfield in 1880, a former Union general and Ohio congressman, chosen to be the Republican nominee on the thirty-sixth ballot to break a deadlock between James G. Blaine of Maine and John Sherman of Ohio.

Garfield's claim on history was his assassination in his first months in office and the elevation to the presidency of an even greater obscurity, Vice President Chester A. Arthur, a former Collector of the New York Custom House. Arthur had been tapped as Garfield's running mate as a payoff to New York Republican bosses. The Garfield-Arthur ticket was a rebuke to the notion that the smoke-filled room was a reliable if undemocratic vehicle for producing effective national leadership.

So was the nomination forty years later of Senator Warren G. Harding of Ohio by the Republicans in the most famous smoke-filled-room exercise. After four inconclusive ballots, a group of fellow senators called Harding into a hotel suite and questioned him into the wee hours before determining he was sufficiently inoffensive, and anointing him. Their attempt to put another Senate colleague on the ticket, however, was rejected by the convention delegates. Instead, they nominated the benign governor of Massachusetts, Calvin Coolidge, with fateful result when Harding, like Garfield, died in office, only seventeen months after taking the presidential oath.

By this time, the power of the cigar-puffing party bosses to handpick nominees was being diminished by the development of presidential primaries to select convention delegates. By 1916, twenty-six states had adopted primary laws as part of the Progressive reform movement. That trend flagged during and between the two world wars, but it resumed with a vengeance in the 1970s, again reducing the power and influence of party kingmakers. The now-dominant primary process in effect issued an open invitation to anyone with the ambition and, in the absence of strong qualifications, the chutzpah to run.

The would-be presidents who have tried and failed rival in their near-anonymity and forgettableness our elected vice presidents. Who cannot but remember Larry Agran, John Ashbrook, Roger Branigin, Ned Coll, Phil Crane,

Lar Daly, Ben Fernandez, Lenora Fulani, Milton Shapp, Morrie Taylor, and Sam Yorty? Such long shots are often asked whether they are not really running for the vice presidency. Shapp, a nondescript governor of Pennsylvania who had won some local acclaim for settling a massive truckers' strike, was such a nonbelievable presidential prospect in 1976 that he was asked at a press conference in Washington whether he was "really running for Secretary of Transportation"!

In late 1979, a Republican senator from South Dakota named Larry Pressler, widely considered one of the Senate's and his party's lightest lightweights, threw his hat in the ring. When in only three months the folly of his initiative struck him as it had everybody else, he pulled out. But senators, as members of an exclusive club of one hundred, often consider themselves to be in the prime breeding ground for presidents, although only two, Harding in 1920 and Kennedy in 1960, were directly elected to the Oval Office from the Senate in the twentieth century. The latest example of presidential pipe-dreaming is Republican senator Robert Smith of New Hampshire, a vacuous nonentity who in 1998 indicated his intention to seek his party's nomination, hoping to use his state's first-in-the-nation primary to jump-start a national campaign. By mid-1999, his dismal progress persuaded him to quit the GOP and consider switching his doomed candidacy to an obscure third party.

Before World War I, when the United States first emerged as a world power, being governor of a state was considered the best place to prepare for the presidency. That job's administrative responsibilities made it seem like a good training ground for running the country, and much political power rested in the governorships. But as the foreign-policy responsibility of the presidency greatly enlarged, and as the election of delegates to the major parties' nominating conventions became more democratic, other officeholders and men prominent in other fields were able to project themselves into presidential contention and garner the delegates required to capture the nominations.

The mortality rate of presidents in the twentieth century eventually made it clear that a job once shunned as a dead end, the vice presidency, was in fact the best stepping-stone to the Oval Office. The deaths of four presidents—William McKinley, Harding, Franklin D. Roosevelt, and Kennedy—elevated Theodore Roosevelt, Calvin Coolidge, Harry Truman, and Lyndon Johnson;

and the resignation of Richard Nixon put Gerald Ford, the nation's first unelected vice president under the Twenty-fifth Amendment, into the White House.

While the presidency began as an exalted position to be occupied by exalted men—George Washington, John Adams, Thomas Jefferson, James Madison, James Monroe—it also in time fell prey to unimpressive and forgettable figures as well—William Henry Harrison, John Tyler, James Polk, Zachary Taylor, Millard Fillmore, Franklin Pierce, James Buchanan—before Abraham Lincoln strode onstage. Thereafter, another nine quadrennial elections passed before another giant appeared—Theodore Roosevelt, himself elevated from the vice presidency. And in the century to follow, only a handful—Woodrow Wilson, Franklin Roosevelt, Truman, Eisenhower, Kennedy, Johnson, and, in some quarters at least, Ronald Reagan—were regarded as superior.

Although some romantics like to suggest that the office seeks the man, that has seldom been true, with only a few notable exceptions—Washington, Franklin Roosevelt after his first term, and Eisenhower. Most presidential hopefuls, especially in the second half of the twentieth century, have had to go out and get the presidency if they wanted it. Even Eisenhower, sought by both parties in 1948 but unwilling, four years later at the Republican convention seized the party's nomination over Taft only after a stiff fight over contested credentials. The closest thing to a genuine draft in the Democratic Party in the last half century came in 1952, after Governor Adlai E. Stevenson II of Illinois had declined to seek the nomination, saying he preferred a second term in Springfield. Upon Truman's announcement that he would not run again, eleven hopefuls and favorite sons, led by Senator Estes Kefauver of Tennessee, joined the fray, but Stevenson was not among them. Truman himself urged Stevenson to run and a group of Illinoisans established a draft committee. Despite repeated statements declaring his unfitness for the presidency and unwillingness to seek it, by convention time the Stevenson draft had attracted key party leaders like Mayor David Lawrence of Pittsburgh. Stevenson was nominated on the third ballot but was snowed under by Eisenhower in November.

The route most candidates have been obliged to travel, however, is a torturous one. It requires them to spend a year or more before the election campaign actually starts building name recognition and raising money. They must spend month after month away from home and family, sleeping in nondescript motels and hotels, even on occasion on a supporter's living-room couch, as Mayor John Lindsay of New York did in 1972.

They must submit themselves to the company of rich fools and their harebrained ideas for making the country better or themselves richer, in exchange for campaign contributions. They must associate with local and state party hacks, many of them unsavory characters, who dangle support under their noses in return for a promised job or a seat at the decision-making table. They must attend crack-of-dawn country breakfasts where they are stuffed with huge stacks of pancakes, mountains of greasy eggs and bacon, and rivers of warmed-over coffee before embarking on another eighteen-hour day of glad-handing. Then there are dreary Kiwanis and Optimist Club lunches with local insurance salesmen and undertakers and their sappy rituals. (MC: "We're honored today by the presence of a good friend from Washington, D.C.—Jack Kemp!" All: "Hi, Jack!") And each night there is the interminable, barely edible cold chicken dinner, shaking hundreds or even thousands more hands at a reception in the local VFW hall, followed by three hours of speeches by locals running for sheriff or county supervisor. And the candidates must endure all this with frozen smiles that they must somehow fashion so as to seem genuine.

Many would-be presidents do all this while holding down a full-time job as a governor or in Congress, stealing away hours each day begging for money on the telephone or hours each night on quick plane trips halfway across the country and back. Others who do not have a full-time job make one of campaigning for president. An example is Lamar Alexander, former governor of Tennessee and Secretary of Education in the Bush administration, who spent two years seeking the Republican presidential nomination for 1996 and, having failed, started up again on a second bid almost immediately after the election. His best showings in a competitive primary or caucus in 1996 were third place in Iowa and New Hampshire, which he obviously deemed sufficient encouragement to start the trek all over again. As far as could be perceived with the naked eye, the groundswell for another Lamar Alexander presidential campaign essentially began and ended in his own head, but that is all it takes under the existing system of candidate self-selection.

For every individual who attains his party's nomination, let alone the presidency, there are dozens like Alexander who make the same debilitating and dehumanizing commitment and come up empty. And not only once, but several times. It used to be that when a presidential aspirant ran, lost badly and tried again, he was regarded as a screwball. Exhibit A was former Minnesota governor and Eisenhower cabinet member Harold Stassen, the classic hopeless candidate for the presidency more than half a dozen times. Now there is a certain method in the madness.

"Given the nature of the primary process," says the pollster and campaign strategist Robert Teeter, "you have to spend a lot time running for president—two or four or maybe ten years. And who's to say that's bad? The process tends to surface people who have been around for a long time. Certain people are seen as acceptable; you may not vote for them but they don't scare you to death because they've been around for three or four cycles—Hubert Humphrey, Ed Muskie, Bob Dole, Jack Kemp—and have gone through press scrutiny, and the public has gotten used to them. Those candidates who come out of nowhere, like [Governor Michael] Dukakis [of Massachusetts], are not successful."

But persevering is not for everybody, even ambitious politicians like Walter Mondale in the 1976 cycle. After more than a year of actively exploring a presidential candidacy, he suddenly announced in late 1974 that he was abandoning his quest because he was no longer "willing to go through fire" for the Democratic nomination. He was weary, he said, of "sleeping in Holiday Inns." But presidential ambition, once experienced, does not die easily. Less than two years later, when Jimmy Carter, the presidential nominee, was shopping around for a running mate, Mondale made himself available. Referring to his 1974 complaint, he now observed: "What I said at the time was that I didn't want to spend the rest of my life in Holiday Inns. But I've checked and found they've all been redecorated. They're marvelous places to stay, and I've thought it over and that's where I'd like to be."

After a year or more of chasing money and supporters, the candidate must go delegate hunting. From February through June in each presidential-election year, voters in state primaries and caucuses choose the delegates they wish to represent them at one of the two major-party conventions. The delegates are usually designated in these exercises according to the presidential candidate for whom they announce they will vote. The most politically active citizens in each state must be courted assiduously by the candidate to win their support and then keep it. It is a long and costly obstacle course not recommended for the faint of heart, the deficient of wallet, or the sore of feet.

In earlier days, when presidential nominees of the major parties were chosen by state party leaders in the legendary smoke-filled rooms of the national conventions, a certain peer review applied in making the selections from among men—exclusively men—prominent in party affairs, at the big-city, state, and national levels. The most likely candidates were large-state governors, prominent cabinet members, and, occasionally, members of Congress or military heroes. Rarely, an individual well established in a nongovernment field—a newspaper publisher, financier, or businessman—would be considered. Not only the perceived qualifications of the candidate to be an effective president but also the practical consideration of his chances of being elected were uppermost in the judgment of those making the choice. Factionalism and ideology also counted, with much wheeling and dealing among the parties' power brokers.

In these circumstances, the chances of a little-known candidate breaking through with little establishment backing were slim. But with much greater popular participation in the process, given the proliferation of direct primaries and party caucuses, it has become closer to the truth (yet still far-fetched) that any mother's son could become president. Increasing numbers of them tried, qualifying for a ballot position in various states, sometimes attaining it, but never getting much beyond that initial stage. As the process became more open, however, more and more candidates entered into contention, not because fellow Americans demanded their services, but because they decided to offer themselves. Seeking the presidency for many was like climbing Mount Everest—because it was there.

Others, to be sure, were propelled into the race because of their political success at another level, having demonstrated voter appeal or a superior record in administering a state, running a government department, or fighting a war. The vice presidency, once considered the equivalent of a gold watch awarded for faithful party service and a one-way ticket to political oblivion, came to be viewed differently: in seven of the last nine presidential elections, in fact, one or both of the major party presidential nominees had served as vice president.

An irony in the competition for president is that because of the physical hardships imposed and the costs of running not only in dollars but in lost privacy and in unwanted scrutiny of private and financial affairs, many of the most respected Americans choose not to run. As the bar is lowered, many less qualified or less known Americans see their own chances raised, at least in their own minds. In 1992, for example, the decision of the popular and respected governor of New York, Mario Cuomo, not to seek the Democratic nomination opened the door for a governor from Arkansas relatively unknown to most Americans named Bill Clinton. And in 1996, General Colin Powell's rejection of strong overtures from the Republican Party invited a large field of presidential contenders to challenge the old party warhorse Bob Dole.

Self-selection in deciding who shall compete for the presidency has been underscored by the recent phenomenon of wealthy men—Ross Perot in 1992 and 1996, Steve Forbes in 1996 and 2000—bankrolling their own campaigns. Rich men, certainly, have as much right to run for president as poor men. But their money enables them to bypass hurdles that presidential hopefuls without their financial resources must clear—becoming well known and posting achievements that can garner the popular and financial support required to make a respectable showing.

Candidates with plenty of money or the ability to raise it therefore take the playing field with a tremendous advantage. In today's political combat, it is not enough to be a formidable candidate. One must be supported by a vast array of political talent and foot soldiers schooled in the refinements of seeking high office in the era of television, computer technology, and mass persuasion, and one must have or raise the millions of dollars it takes to finance their efforts.

Considering the immense personal and financial sacrifices demanded of presidential candidates and their families, it is not so surprising that some of the nation's most prominent and promising public figures elect not to seek the presidency. Considering the same sacrifices, and how low public service generally has fallen in the esteem of the citizenry, it is also surprising how many do seek the job. With a true presidential draft a far-fetched prospect these days, and with the party mechanisms that once brought forth presidential nominees from the top echelons no longer functioning as of yore, the field of prospective presidents is left basically to self-selection.

The man who picks himself and then goes about the business of gathering an organization around him, like the manufacturer of a new product, sets out to find the right people to develop, shape, test, and market it, using state-of-the-art equipment if he can afford it, making up for lack of it with personal energy, ingenuity, charm, and luck if he can't. And because the needs are there for many specialized skills, the free-enterprise system brings forth other men and women who have them. Today they are known, often disparagingly, as "hired guns." They are at the heart of presidential politics, leading the parade, in Bill Clinton's favorite phrase, over the bridge to the twenty-first century.

2 The Era of the Hired Gun

The first time many Americans paid much attention to the phenomenon of the hired gun in presidential politics was in August 1996. Then, the unfamiliar name of Dick Morris burst onto an otherwise humdrum Democratic National Convention in Chicago. Lurid newspaper and television accounts told of this political consultant's antics with a prostitute, which included, among others, letting her listen in on telephone conversations with his most prominent client, the president of the United States.

At the time the story broke, Morris was riding high as the mastermind who—single-handedly, he said—had resurrected the dying political fortunes of Bill Clinton, self-styled New Democrat. Clinton's first presidential term had stumbled through a series of inept personnel decisions and a conspicuously failed major effort to reform the nation's health-care system, which the Republicans had effectively characterized as more of the Democrats' old liberal experimentation and big federal spending. A major result was the Democrats' loss of Congress to the Republicans in 1994 for the first time in forty years.

Morris, a former consultant for Clinton's gubernatorial campaigns in Arkansas who thereafter had transferred his loyalties and strategies to Republican candidates such as Senator Trent Lott of Mississippi, returned to Clinton with a plan. He convinced the president that he had to reestablish himself aggressively as the New Democrat he had campaigned as in 1992. With Clinton's adoption of more centrist positions, presented in a massive operation to sway public opinion that combined polling and television advertising before the 1996 election, the scheme appeared to work. Morris later put the cost at nearly $85 million, or more than twice what Clinton spent in the 1992 campaign. Subsequently, a study by the Pew Research Center for the People and the Press concluded that the television blitz had little effect on Clinton's recovery. But Andrew Kohut, who conducted the study, observed that nevertheless "the strategy created a tremendous change in the way we think about political spending."

As Clinton's fortunes climbed in the polls during 1995 and 1996, the Republicans began to slip, victims of unpopular overreaching by the new House Speaker, Newt Gingrich of Georgia, and other conservatives then running Congress. They slashed desired federal programs and, in a colossal political blunder, permitted the federal government to be closed for days in a stubborn showdown over budget balancing with Clinton. Suddenly, Clinton's outlook for a second term began to look brighter, and Morris' professional reputation with it.

On the day before the news of Morris' indiscretions hit the Democratic convention and the country at large, Morris and his wife had lunch with a small group of newspaper reporters and columnists in the Chicago hotel suite of the CNN anchor Judy Woodruff and her husband, Albert Hunt, the executive Washington editor of *The Wall Street Journal.* We all sat, intrigued and amused, as Morris held forth at length about how his advice to Clinton on repositioning himself away from the traditional liberal Democratic posture had brought him back to political life. The burden of his message was that Clinton was about to be renominated for a second term as a result of Morris' shrewd counsel shifting the president to the center of the political spectrum, even toward the right, preempting the Republican leaders on key issues like crime, taxes, budget cutting, and handling the economy.

The fashionable word among the political cognoscenti at the time for Morris' miracle working was "triangulation"—locating Clinton unassailably in the middle of a hypothetical triangle with the Republicans on one side of him and his fellow Democrats in Congress on the other, leaving him insulated from criticism addressed to either extreme. Morris unabashedly proclaimed his own brilliance to the assembled Washington reporters and columnists. At the end of the lunch, he excused himself and went into the adjacent bedroom, closing the door to make a private phone call. If the rest of us in the room chose to surmise from this that Morris was placing a call to the president himself, that clearly was all right with him. Later, however, some of us speculated with a certain titillation whether the call had been to someone else.

In any event, within twenty-four hours Dick Morris was a fallen angel. He was "asked" to resign from the Clinton entourage amid a major personal and political embarrassment that, for the moment at least, put a damper on the renomination of the president for whom he had labored so ingeniously—if not, it turned out, single-mindedly.

Further lurid details about Morris' dalliances with the prostitute did not begin to match the long-term damage his political advice and activities eventually delivered upon the reputations of Clinton, the Democratic Party, and, in fact, the American political process. Although Clinton was easily reelected, the manner in which he financed that reelection—at Morris' specific urging—brought scandal upon him, his party, and the election process, casting a shadow over Clinton's second term that could not be dispelled. The scope of the Democrats' fund-raising efforts, skirting if not violating campaign finance laws, was not widely understood until late in the campaign, but thereafter it became the focus of high-visibility investigations and hearings in both the House and the Senate.

An integral part of Morris' strategy for the resurrection of Clinton's political fortunes, along with "triangulation," was a massive polling and television advertising effort, designed first to discourage any potential Democratic nomination challenge and then to insulate Clinton against expected Republican attacks far in advance of the election year of 1996. This strategy, dictating an unprecedented campaign of fund-raising from within the White House itself, was highlighted by the reward of sleepovers in the Lincoln Bedroom and other astonishingly crass perquisites granted to big-money donors. Morris apparently had nothing to do with the choice of those perks, only the inspiration for the early polling and advertising, which required the millions of dollars raised from the recipients of the favors. Charges that the White House was for sale soon were being heard nightly on television evening news and in newspaper headlines from Maine to California.

Morris was not the only one of the new breed of fee-for-service operatives who reaped great personal financial reward from the whole sorry exercise. Poll takers, television advertisement writers, time buyers, and other assorted members of the new political technocracy all lined their pockets in the course of the early preemptive strikes against Clinton's critics and in behalf of his policies.

According to an analysis of federal campaign spending records made by the public-interest Campaign Study Group for *The Washington Post*, a partnership of hired guns including Morris called the November 5 Group received about $60 million in 1995–96 from either the Clinton-Gore campaign or the Democratic National Committee; another $40 million was funneled to the group by the DNC through state parties, essentially for television ads. Morris told the newspaper that the November 5 Group charged a 7 percent commission on the ads, or about $7 million, split this way: the media firm of Squier Knapp Ochs, which actually made most of the ads, got 50 percent; Morris 25 percent; the pollsters Mark Penn and Doug Schoen about 10 percent; the political consultant Hank Scheinkopf of New York about 10 percent; and a video producer, Marius Penczner of Nashville, about 5 percent. Although Morris contended that his prime motive for pressing Clinton to run extensive television advertising more than a year in advance of his reelection campaign was to resurrect the president's political fortunes, others in the consulting business saw a more mercenary reason.

Raymond Strother, a prominent Washington media consultant who once worked for Clinton in Arkansas with Morris, remembered Morris calling him in December 1995 and asking him to prepare pro-Clinton commercials to be aired in numerous communities around the country. When Strother asked him why he was starting so early, he said that Morris told him, "I need some way to get some commissions out of this." Strother declined, saying he never split commissions with other consultants, whereupon Morris reminded him, Strother recalled, that "we're talking about a lot of money." Strother still said no. "You couldn't depend on him, because he'd change; he'd always be making a deal with someone else," Strother said.

The usual commission paid by television stations on ads placed with them is 15 percent—the same amount also paid by direct-mail houses, phone-bank operatives, printers, and most other recipients of campaign business placed through consultants. On a large volume of business, the commission is sometimes negotiated down, as it apparently was in this case. "Fifteen percent of a lot of money is a lot of money," Strother noted. Perhaps Clinton got into so much trouble, he said, "because Dick Morris needed some early money" to support a lavish lifestyle that included houses and apartments in Florida and Europe. "I know it's a hard thing to say," Strother said, "but I've seen him do it in other campaigns . . . He has a voracious appetite for money. He had to produce a lot of money because his lifestyle dictated it."

Strother notes that "because virtually everything is commissionable, a campaign is a giant money cow. If you spent $10 million on a campaign, that's $1.5 million in the pocket of a consultant, usually a media consultant." Morris later told me that while commissions often amount to much less than 15 percent, his own net income from the Clinton campaign for the 1995–96 election cycle was indeed about $1.5 million. "I didn't particularly consider that exorbitant," he said. It was, he said, "not unlike what a television anchorman makes, what the head of a major advertising agency makes, what a CEO of a corporation makes."

Certainly, Dick Morris was not the first political professional to milk the system, only the most blatant example of what the process had wrought since the days when the acquiring of money was not the prime motive for men engaged in the practice of politics at the highest levels. More than a hundred years ago, a rich Ohio businessman named Mark Hanna set aside a pure accumulation of personal wealth to focus on becoming the nation's most powerful political boss. He hitched his wagon to the star of a local congressman named William McKinley, helped elect him governor of the state and then president of the United States in 1896, in the process switching from the business world to the political. Hanna easily outfoxed and outorganized a coalition of local and state Republican Party bosses in winning a first-ballot nomination for McKinley, and the national party chairmanship for himself. But he was no hired gun in the latter-day sense of political freelancing as personified by Dick Morris but, rather, a thorough political party animal.

Since then, however, and particularly since the advent of television, politically astute men and women attracted to politics as Hanna was are motivated to a significant degree, if not singularly, by the pursuit of money. A few make a great deal of it; many make a very comfortable living, others scramble on the fringes of a "profession" that is very fragmented, its financial rewards varying, depending on the skills required and the demand for them.

Even before Hanna's day, to be sure, personal aggrandizement in the guise of political influence was an important lure to men who allied themselves with presidential candidates, and that certainly was true of Hanna himself. From the early days of patronage and the spoils system, it was a generally lucrative undertaking to have assisted a presidential candidate attain the White House. The reward, if not a high government job, was at least access to information from which profitable business transactions could be made. But the notion of a blatant fee-for-services relationship in the presidential campaign itself was rare, except for the common practice of distributing "street money" or "walking-around money," which amounted to paying registered voters a few dollars to go to the polls and cast a ballot for the distributor of the largesse.

Beyond pecuniary advantage, however, people who worked at the highest levels in behalf of presidential candidates customarily did so out of commitment to party, a personal commitment to the candidate, or devotion to the causes he embraced. The early movers and shakers were men like Thurlow Weed, Thaddeus Stevens, Simon Cameron, David Davis, Zachariah Chandler, Roscoe Conkling, Thomas Platt, Matthew Quay, and eventually the legendary Mark Hanna. They all derived their payoffs not from fees in the business of vote gathering and opinion shaping, but rather from the political influence their work brought them.

Key party officials who knew their way around the national political circuit, such as it was, were the essential operatives that every office seeker needed to win. Big-city and state political machines produced men, and in time maybe a few women, with the political skill and experience to lend a hand, usually city by city or state by state. There was much more talk of political leaders "delivering" states than we hear today, and much greater prospect that they could do so. Party leaders ruled the roost. Except for a brief time in the Progressive era in the early twentieth century, delegates to the national conventions were chosen through insider caucuses and local conventions in most states, or simply by fiat of the party leader. And when the delegates got to their national convention, they usually voted as they were told to vote. The major political parties regarded selection of the nominees as, essentially, a business for their most prominent insiders and, once accomplished, they heavily depended on party loyalty to bring victory in November. The parties routinely disbursed largesse to voters, and a party's endorsement of a candidate was good enough for millions of loyalists as they trooped to the polls.

Presidential campaigns in the fall were Main Street phenomena in those days, with storefront headquarters serving as community gathering spots at which volunteers licked stamps and stuffed envelopes while debating the issues of the day, neighbor to neighbor. The limited funds available usually paid for enough campaign buttons and bumper stickers to give the candidate plenty of visibility in the neighborhood, as well as old-fashioned walking-around money to encourage turnout on Election Day.

If a candidate's chief campaign operatives were not important officeholders in his party or personal friends and associates, they often were allies in the advancement of a political objective or cause, not professional political specialists for hire. People with flexible work schedules, like lawyers and newspapermen turned press agents, often dabbled in campaigns, but the chief strategists usually were the candidate himself and his closest personal advisers, like Hanna for McKinley, Colonel Edward House and Joseph Tumulty for Woodrow Wilson, and Louis Howe and James A. Farley for Franklin D. Roosevelt. After an election, those men customarily became White House aides or cabinet members, or returned to private life but continued to function as outside advisers to the man they helped attain the Oval Office. After any election, they seldom went shopping around for another candidate to help in running for the same or another office later.

In 1932, Roosevelt won the Democratic nomination without entering any primaries, and he tapped Farley, then secretary of the New York State Democratic Party, to run his campaign as party national chairman. Farley recruited a very able "brain trust" to work on policy planning, but its members had no part whatever in devising the political strategy for electing the nominee. That task fell, as in the past, to proven party operatives in state organizations around the country, and they continued to do that work even after Farley split with Roosevelt in 1940 in disagreement over FDR's decision to seek a third term.

In 1933, all this began to change when a new political development was spawned in California that eventually would revolutionize the way campaigns were conceived and managed. The Pacific Gas and Electric Company was pushing a ballot initiative to repeal a new state law authorizing construction of a huge flood control and irrigation project in the Central Valley. Supporters of the law hired two public-relations specialists in Sacramento, Clem Whitaker and Leona Baxter, to defeat the initiative. On a very modest budget of $39,000, Whitaker and Baxter ran radio and newspaper ads that did the trick. The power company, impressed by their adversaries' work, put them on retainer; the groundbreaking political consulting firm of Whitaker and Baxter (later husband and wife) was born. The team in time gravitated from advancing or opposing ballot initiatives for large firms to handling candidates for public office. The era of the hired gun had arrived.

One of the first people they hired for their new business was a minor young Republican Party functionary named Stuart Spencer, who worked days as a playground recreation director and in the evenings as a volunteer with the California Young Republicans. In time he teamed up with a television salesman, Bill Roberts, also active at a low level in Republican politics, and they followed in the footsteps of Whitaker and Baxter. The small firm of Spencer-Roberts in time became the most celebrated in the growing field of paid political consulting. Eventually dozens and then hundreds of other fee-for-service political consulting firms began to spring up. It was a small step from providing political advice and strategy in support of, or opposition to, ballot questions to masterminding candidates' campaigns.

The Democrats lagged well behind the Republicans in contributing to the fraternity of the hired gun. It was not until the late 1950s that the first Democratic consultants emerged, including Joseph Napolitan of Springfield, Massachusetts, later a partner of John F. Kennedy's political adviser Lawrence F. O'Brien, and Matthew Reese of Washington, D.C., who got his start in politics in state government in West Virginia.

At first, the services provided by campaign consultants were mostly cerebral: mapping out strategy and performing elementary research on the opposition and the pertinent electorate. The income was adequate but certainly not astronomical—until the arrival of television and other technology that hugely increased the possibilities for mass communication to voters, and heightened the need to compete in the rapidly developing art of voter persuasion and manipulation. Candidates were now confronted with entirely new opportunities and imperatives in areas in which political operatives accustomed to working strictly within the structure and expertise of the political party were total strangers.

"In the 1960s," notes Bob Squier, one of the earliest Democratic specialists in political advertising on television, "you had these two technologies accidentally affecting each other—the mass production of the automobile, which took people out of the cities and therefore out from under the city political organizations, and television, where people could look at politicians and make up their minds for themselves. And once television became a way of making their decisions, it seemed inevitable that people who understood how television worked would then work with politicians to help them make their case. It's too complicated a medium to just stand there and bark at a camera and expect that will make people vote for you."

No longer were party tradition and loyalty the dependable glues holding voters to predictable patterns of political behavior. No longer could party beneficence, in the form of jobs or various forms of welfare assistance, dependably deliver voters at the polls. Most important, no longer could cities, states, or even the nation be organized adequately by doing party politics at the local level, neighborhood by neighborhood, as in the past. With the rise of radio, television, and other means of assaulting the sensitivities and allegiances of millions of American voters, politics swiftly shifted from retail to wholesale.

Candidates could reach and preach to massive audiences as never before. Voters could watch and listen to them in their own living rooms and decide for themselves. But that wasn't all. As Squier said, a whole new industry was born, created by those who recognized that a host of new professional political skills would be needed to make optimum use of the startling new medium—and that there was plenty of money to be made in doing so. In addition to commissions earned on placing television ads, media consultants usually received retainers from the campaigns they worked for, and some took a markup on production of the ads.

In 1969, some pioneer political consultants, notably a Republican, F. Clifton White, and a Democrat, Joe Napolitan, formed the American Association of Political Consultants, enlarged later by other pioneers such as the Democrat Matt Reese and Republicans Charles Black and Eddie Mahe. According to Black, ethical standards were generally observed, because "it was a tight, close-knit club," but in time "fly-by-nighters came in to work cheaper," and candidates hired them. Attempts were made to write a code of ethics for the young profession, but the field was growing too fast and it could not be enforced. Also, other members say, qualifications for membership in the association became so broad that people involved in almost any aspect of a campaign were able to join although they were not really consultants as measured by any serious yardstick. While a "sensible code of ethics" eventually was written, Napolitan says, "we had no enforcement power. What could we do? Kick somebody out? The people the most likely to do [offensive] things didn't join."

One reason Republican candidates led the way in hiring paid political consultants was that they were more accustomed to dealing with successful businessmen anyway, and because their style was more entrepreneurial. Democratic candidates were used to relying on old friends, often lawyers, to help them out. When it came to advertising, Republicans looked mostly to Madison Avenue while Democrats preferred not hucksters but storytellers, like the television documentary maker Charles Guggenheim. Money was another reason the Republicans got an earlier start; they had more of it. For all their protestations, the GOP remained the party of the well-off, and it was—and is today—easier in a general sense for Republican candidates to raise money than for Democratic aspirants; so they had more with which to buy the ever more expensive services of the pros.

At the same time, the growing number of primaries to be contested and the spiraling cost of television through which to reach mass voter audiences were like powerful magnets pulling in all manner of political professional operatives seeking influence, fame, and profit. The relatively few individuals who had earlier made their living running political campaigns (as opposed to people who signed on to help an old friend or political ally) had regarded themselves as all-purpose strategists who handled all aspects of a campaign, working in conjunction with the candidate and the party leaders who supported him. "We were basically generalists," says Spencer, one of the best of the early Republican consultants. He and his partner, he recalls, hired their own specialists if necessary, "and we were committed to our guy. If he was reasonable, we didn't care about the specifics [of policy positions]." The team at one time or another worked for Nelson Rockefeller and Ronald Reagan because, he says, "they were both reasonable people to us. We were party people. And the Democrats took basically the same position; we [consultants] never crossed party lines. We were concerned only about whether our candidate could win; is he articulate, can he get his story out, can he raise the money, is he appealing?"

Now, in the television era, new elements of campaigning were demanding more specialization and offering more opportunity for politically enterprising people to address themselves to new kinds of opportunities, not only at election time every four years but basically year-round. A permanent army of political mercenaries was emerging, and unlike Spencer some of them signed on with candidates regardless of party, provided the money and opportunity for success and celebrity were right. Morris himself was of this ilk, having toiled first for Clinton in his Arkansas campaigns, then for a Republican, Trent Lott, in his congressional races in Mississippi, then back to Clinton as a candidate for presidential reelection.

In an interview (held before a subsequent falling-out with Clinton), Morris steadfastly defended his attitude in a revealing monologue that expressed with rare candor the rationale of the political gun for hire. "I believe I was wrong in my career in that I took clients without regard to whether I thought they were good people or not," he began. "And some of the people I worked for, I believed then and I believe now, to be bad people, notably Jesse Helms. I plead guilty on that, and if I had it to do over, I wouldn't.

"On the other hand," he went on, "I do believe that I and most political consultants in the younger generation have tremendous loyalty to candidates, to individuals. I'm as close to Trent Lott or to Bill Clinton as any of the old lawyers ever were. I've worked with Trent for a decade, I've worked with Clinton for two decades . . . My career or that of the average consultant these days is defined by his loyalty to his candidate on a long-term basis, and I think it's incorrect to say we're not loyal to people.

"Now, most political consultants apart from myself are loyal to ideology or at least party. I'm not loyal to either of those, and I think I'm right, because I don't think that party stands for anything in this country anymore. I literally do not give a damn whether a person is a Democrat or a Republican. There's no difference. They have different ideas, but I don't believe that one party is better than the other. I think there are some things that Democrats are better at and some things that Republicans are better at. If I want to understand how to feed poor people, I want to work for a Democrat, and if I want to defend America, I want a Republican. I think there are good people and bad people in both parties and I don't believe that one party has an edge over the other.

"I'm like forty percent of the American voters, who are independent. To say that everybody in the process has to choose a side as a candidate, as a donor, as a consultant, is ludicrous. Why should we impose a discipline on the insiders that is not reflective of the discipline of the voters? Why should I not be able to make the choice that the plurality of the American people make, not to identify with either of the political parties?

"I don't personally buy into ideology, either. I strongly agree with the left on pro-choice. I strongly agree with the right on decreasing government regulation. I strongly agree with the left on gun control. I strongly agree with the right on mandatory sentences for criminals and the death penalty. Most Americans are not purely partisan. Whereas French politics is founded on ideas, American politics is founded on facts. The weakness of French politics is that in the face of the facts, they maintain their ideas. The strength of American politics is when confronted with a different set of facts, we change our ideas. I do not believe that ideology is a very important factor, or should be a very important factor, in American politics, because I think the American people are suspicious of ideologues of the right or of the left.

"That's why the center is so viable, and that's my idea of triangulation: take the best of each and merge them. That's not an act of political immorality, it's an act of political sagacity and a recognition of the notion of the Hegelian triangle—the thesis, the antithesis, and the synthesis—which Hegel posits and which Marx and I agree is how history moves forward."

Was consensus his guiding star and public-opinion polling his compass? Morris stoutly defended his heavy dependence on the latter. "All polling does is make this more scientific," he said. "It's like saying an EKG machine is a totally new situation from a stethoscope. The intent is still the same. You use the best you have and you go with it and you depend on it. But that doesn't mean the doctor is any less pivotal a force [because] he has a machine as opposed to a stethoscope."

The new breed exemplified—perhaps to the extreme—by Morris included experts in the use of television in political races; in the development of effective television advertising; in reaching out to the new mass audience for campaign contributions via direct-mail solicitation; in surveying public opinion for data by means of which one could gauge what messages were going down well with the voters and what were not. The concept of product sales, which is endemic to advertising—find out what the public wants and then sell it to them—began as never before to dominate all aspects of the election process. For the new kind of campaign, a manager schooled in the skills of old-fashioned electioneering and knowing his way around party politics was no longer enough. The era of the hired gun as salesman in the new universe of television and mass communication had arrived.

3 Television Raises the Stakes

Politicians seeking the White House have always tried to maximize their virtues and minimize or obscure their flaws. But until the advent of the hired gun and television, they resisted suggestions to alter their own positions, policies, or even looks if they thought doing so would distort who they really were; they depended heavily on their own well-developed instincts for meeting and connecting with voters.

When television vastly enlarged the number of voters who could be reached directly if not personally, one-to-one politicking no longer sufficed. Candidates became convinced they needed help when they wandered onto the unfamiliar turf of television-studio campaigning. They turned to the new cadre of political specialists who offered, at high prices, not only advice to the candidate about television but also advice on what the candidate ought to say to improve his chances of winning, where he ought to say it, and how. They produced polls that yielded answers to those questions, and they developed techniques to raise the money needed to produce the polls and air the message in costly television advertising.

Matt Reese, like Spencer and Roberts, pioneered in the consulting business as an old-time grassroots organizer. "When I started," he recalled shortly before his death in 1998, "my problem was not [competition from] another consultant. It was getting candidates to use a consultant at all." Napolitan, like Reese, was in his own description "a generalist, a strategist," and he remembers that it was once considered a luxury for a candidate to take a poll. In 1960, he recalls, the pollster Lou Harris "went door to door," long before polls by telephone with sophisticated sampling techniques took over.

The term "hired gun," Reese said, "doesn't offend me at all, because that's what I was. But I wouldn't work for everybody; I kept my integrity and my honor that way. The first Reese in America was a mercenary soldier. I guess I was a mercenary too, but I was never a whore. There were certain people I wouldn't work for." But when television converted consulting into a much more lucrative endeavor, the competition increased sharply and many consultants were not so discriminating. Reese soon found himself being squeezed out by the newly arrived specialists, especially in television. "I was not into film, that was my big mistake," he said. "I didn't do television. I didn't have the adequate skills. I had to have staff. It was too hard to make a living. I fashion myself as a generalist, but it had become very specialized. The guy who does the television has such a big part of the budget that it was very difficult for somebody like me to come in and superimpose the general consulting on top of that."

The television-oriented specialists struck gold, not only in selling their expertise but also in the commissions. "People honestly thought that television was the only answer," Reese recalled. The television specialists in their controlling position in the campaign not only produced lucrative commercials but also tapped into the costs for other aspects of it, from time buying to polling, printing, direct mail, targeting, and research. "They got fifteen percent of the buy," Reese said. "For every dollar I can get you to put into television, I keep fifteen cents of it . . . And once you've got the blessing of success, you have to rape a nun in order to kill that." Napolitan adds that in time much lower commission rates were often negotiated, especially in the expensive campaigns, and most of the money was made in time buying, "probably the least creative" of tasks.

Many specialists brought, along with their new skills, a new outlook toward candidates. Unlike the veterans, they saw the politicians more as vehicles for advancing their own political, ideological, or financial agendas than as people with whom they identified through personal friendship or common political heritage, belief, and commitment. The term "hired guns" was apt; they would hire themselves out to the candidate who could do the most for them or pay them the most. The benefit in some cases was in celebrity status as well as in money. "The publicity and media industry rewards people for the accomplishment of becoming well known," Napolitan says. On television talk shows and on the lucrative lecture circuit the most successful consultants, even sometimes just the most colorful or flamboyant, found themselves in as much demand as the candidates they worked for, and often as recognizable. "Somebody like James Carville becomes a rock star," says Bob Teeter, the Detroit pollster and chairman of the 1992 Bush presidential campaign. The old rule that a political operative was to be neither seen nor heard went out the window. Some, like Squier and the Republican media expert Roger Ailes, collared regular slots as political analyst-performers on network morning shows.

The emergence of the highly visible campaign consultant tended to produce "homogenized candidates," in the view of John Deardourff, a veteran consultant for moderate Republicans. Soon the politicians seemed less interesting to the press, being mere creatures of the political professionals who "handled" them, than the hired guns themselves. Nightly polls about public attitudes were fed to candidates like thought pills, which further eroded spontaneity on the campaign trail.

Ray Strother says that many candidates today are "consultant-driven," in the sense that they are dependent on the hired guns not simply to convey their message but also to create or at least shape it, and to coach them on how to implement it if they get elected. Once, Strother says, politicians "saw us as a necessary evil or a tool, but they didn't mix politics and legislation." But now Morris provided Clinton with his triangulation idea for dealing with the Republicans in Congress after the 1994 elections, and with balking Democrats there. And it is not unusual with the younger generation, Strother says, for a candidate or officeholder to get a group of consultants on a conference call and say, "Tell me what you want me to do" to cope with a particular political or legislative problem. The younger politicians, he says, seem to think that they "have to have consultants around all the time to keep them out of trouble."

As the campaign consulting business his become profitable, Deardourff says, "it's also become much more segmented." When he and his former partner, Doug Bailey, started their business in the mid-1960s, "there were only three, four, or five other firms, and there tended to be fewer people involved in campaigns. Now, there are many guys doing small pieces of each of these campaigns. Most of the major campaigns have half a dozen or more independent operators. One guy will do radio, one guy does television, another guy does direct mail, another guy does fund-raising, another guy does polling. Somebody else will be hired to do the phone banks, the get-out-the-vote operation, and somebody else to do opposition research.

"You've got all these people trying to make a living, and they have only a marginal commitment to the candidate. They take their work where they can get it. They may or may not have a strong belief in what the candidate says. Most of them are not asking the candidate to pass a litmus test before they go to work for him. And by and large they're anonymous. I'm sure there are people out there today who have never worked in a winning campaign and continue to go on year after year doing this thing they do. They don't even deserve to get blamed if the candidate doesn't win, they have such small, separate roles."

For twenty years, Deardourff recalls, he and his partner worked for the election and reelection of the same candidates. "We had an ongoing personal relationship with those people. They trusted us, and I don't see much of that going on today. I think a lot of times the candidates never meet half these people who are working for them.

"We got into the business because we wanted to help elect the kind of people we thought ought to be in public service, and we had a major role in those campaigns. We did the planning, consulting, the advertising. We wanted to be involved, and frequently we stayed involved with those candidates after they were elected." Deardourff worked for Nelson Rockefeller as part of his domestic-issues team and Bailey had once been Henry Kissinger's teaching assistant at Harvard. "We had a strong interest in the substance of the campaign and the platform of the candidate, and we had an interest in seeing that it got carried out once he got elected."

Now, however, what Deardourff sees is "a war on both sides among hired guns with only a marginal attachment to the political parties." And with all the campaign specialties that now abound, "it's amazing [that the] candidates are trained to believe that the hallmark of a good campaign is how many of these professional niche players you have. If you talk to somebody who's thinking about running for office or is in office and you ask how many paid consultants they have, it would be a dozen or more. They're people with individual responsibilities, they're not issue-oriented at all, and they see [the campaign] through a very narrow prism. And it doesn't make a whole lot of difference to their business whether their candidate wins or loses. You don't go to them because they had four winners last year."

Many of today's campaign consultants, Teeter says, are almost like defense lawyers who say that "even the worst crook deserves a lawyer and the best representation he can get," even if the client is "distasteful." John Sears, who ran Ronald Reagan's campaign in 1976 and in early 1980 but who is not a career political consultant, says that politics is now filled with a host of technicians who know the "mechanics" of what they do but "don't know much about politics." In the end, he says, "the tail is wagging the dog." And because it is easier for a candidate to go on the attack than to build a positive case, too many elections become for voters a matter of choosing "the lesser of two evils" and the winner finds himself in office without real public support.

Another veteran Republican consultant, Charles Black, says the younger type of political operative often seems to forget he's running somebody else's campaign. "You have an obligation, if a tactic is questionable from an ethical point of view, to give the candidate a chance to say no [to using that tactic]," he says. "There's almost nothing you can do in a campaign that the press won't know about. You can't let your candidate get blindsided" by an unethical move. Spencer adds that the younger, specialized political consultants are excessively focused on television. "Today, most consultants don't believe that organization makes a difference. I sit down with young politicians today and they don't even talk about organization." This attitude, he says, ignores the success of single-issue public groups like anti-abortion and gun lobbies, which help give voice to millions of voters at the grassroots level.

Deardourff notes that as the new technologies in campaign consulting developed, "the reason guys like us really got a toehold was that we were offering the kinds of services that the [political] parties were no longer able to offer. When political campaigns moved away from the parties, they left the candidates with a big void. They had to find somebody who knew how to use television, polling, all these things that party leaders didn't know.

"Anybody who runs for office now and expects to get help from the parties is almost forced to attend some workshops on how to do it. And one of the things they're told is: 'Before you do anything else, make sure you have a campaign manager, whether a professional manager or somebody you trust. Put somebody in charge to deal with all these other consultants.' But frequently that person doesn't have quite the stature or the leverage to exert a lot of influence on the highly visible media consultants." In Dole's campaign in 1996, he says, "people who thought they had charge of the campaign had endless problems with the media consultants."

Deardourff points out that the proliferation of state presidential primaries held only days or weeks apart is another factor leading to the greater demand for communications skills. Candidates now need more direct contact with many more voters than under the old system, when convention delegates were selected by state conventions and caucuses. "Four-fifths of all the states have some kind of direct primary. This changed not only the nature but the timing of the campaigns, and accelerated the need for more money. It's a whole lot cheaper to seek delegates in a state that doesn't have a primary."

More often than not, altruism has given way to the profit motive. When Strother got into the consulting business in the 1960s, he says, like Bailey and Deardourff "I got into it for the right reasons. I had this naive idea that we could save the world." He worked for candidates whose politics he supported and in whom he believed. But as the business became more "money-driven," and first dozens and then hundreds of newcomers entered the newly lucrative field, altruistic motives took a back seat to profit. "They didn't know anything about the past, they didn't know anything about communication, but they were good salesmen. I thought they didn't know enough about anything to hire them. It was weird. They would show me television I wouldn't put on the air. It was terrible." Yet he acknowledges that he himself was not immune to the pull of money. "It turned very lucrative for me too," he says. "Money was a great motivator. I think I made more money in the 1980s and 1970s than I do now."

The intensified competition led consultants to take on more and more campaigns simultaneously, at the expense of each political client. "What you get now," Strother says, "is that consultants feel they must do twenty-five or thirty campaigns. You only have seven days in a week. How can you be loyal to anybody? There's no loyalty to candidates, and more than that there's no loyalty to ideals." What motivates the newcomers, he says, is winning "so they can get a better job in the consulting business. It's all money-driven. That's what's happened to the business. You have these buccaneers out there."

One prominent consultant who is a throwback to earlier days is James Carville, who was the driving strategic force in Clinton's election in 1992. Now working mainly for foreign clients, Carville notes that from 1979 until 1992, "I would take one candidate at a time" and commit himself full-time. He labored in political campaigns for six years, sleeping on floors and working for subsistence pay, before he had his first statewide winner. Today, he says, "you have no idea how disheartening it is to me. People come up to me all the time and say, 'I want a job in a campaign.' The interns say, 'I want to manage a campaign. I want to do something *significant*. I want to be like you. I want to be on *Meet the Press*.'

"I want to say, 'Wait a minute, you want to be like me? I'll tell you what you do. You be thirty-six years old, practicing law in Baton Rouge, and you decide you want to be a political consultant. You beg on your hands and knees to get a job in Virginia for about two thousand dollars a month, and then go up there and lose an election by a percentage point. And then don't get a job for six or seven months. And then go work for Gary Hart's 1983–84 presidential campaign, and work there and be chronically six weeks late for your paycheck, and can't get your expenses back.

" 'Then go work for Lloyd Doggett in Texas, live in a garage, sleep on a floor, get 41.8 percent in the general election, and then have to come back home a freaking failure, okay, and get a part-time job in the mayor's office. And then after all of that, get a call from a guy who ran for governor of Pennsylvania three times and lost and is the only guy left who'll hire you, and go up there and work like an animal for nine, ten months, finally get a winner, go to Kentucky and live in a Holiday Inn for a year, and not a suite but a room, and get lucky there and then go up to New Jersey. And after you've done all of that, and you're a statewide winner, you're forty-two.' "

Many younger consultants, Carville notes, lacking this kind of experience in the political trenches, "screw up . . . they don't do what it takes to win. They just sit there. They're not going to cajole the candidate, they're not going to do that kind of stuff. I don't see a lot of guys who really get up early and stay late, and have relationships with their candidates." He deplores a trend toward "fragmentation" and "a blurring of roles" in campaigns, away from "defined duties and somebody in charge." Also, he criticizes the consultant business for failing to differentiate between its practitioners of integrity and those whose unethical practices demean it. "We used to know who the thieves were," he says. "I used to always be very proud of what I did. It was a kind of honorable thing. If my daughter wanted to do it, I'd [have been] glad. I'm not sure today how enthusiastic I'd be about my daughter doing something [in political consulting]."

The money to be made in the business inevitably affected motivation, though, even among those who got into it for the most altruistic reasons. David Doak, another veteran Democratic media consultant who came up in the Carville manner, agrees with the older generation, like Strother, that "there comes a time in your career when you cross the line from wanting to change the world to changing your bottom line. You have to make compromises to maintain a certain lifestyle. In 1980 [as a campaign manager] I made eight hundred dollars a month and slept on the floor. Those were the sacrifices you had to make to get into the business in those days. It was a hard business to get into." Doak soon realized that he would continue to be sleeping on floors unless he could find a way to make more money. And that way was to concentrate on media politics—media strategy, writing scripts for television and radio commercials, producing, editing, and directing them, buying airtime for them.

As with Strother and Carville before him, Doak's first work had been politics in the field. He and his former partners Robert Shrum, a speechwriter, and Patrick Caddell, a pollster, "were the first kids who came up in politics out of a strategic background, not an artistic background," he recalls, such as those who later came to consulting from advertising careers and who had never worked in grassroots political campaigns. "The younger generation came up working for guys like me," he says. After staying awhile without much hard political experience and also seeing that the real money was in television media consulting, he says, "they went out and hung up their own shingle."

These younger recruits, he says, "came to it as a business, we came to it as a cause. For a lot of these guys this is [just] a business, and that's a legitimate purpose. It's a business now for me, too. But I've always thought of myself as having a philosophy." At the same time, Doak acknowledges, "there are some people I've taken [as clients] I wouldn't have" if it hadn't been for the money. "It's hard to turn down [a candidate] who's going to make you three or four hundred thousand dollars."

Shrum argues that relatively placid times and a lack of political leadership have contributed to the lack of commitment. "There are a fair number of people in this business because they care about outcomes—and it's a way to make a decent living. And there are probably a fair number of people who are in it for careerist reasons. But we started doing this when the consequences seemed very large and very important, and you'd have to have been a very cold son of a bitch not to feel some personal stake in it. But politics has been increasingly relativized and the differences have shrunk. There's the end of the Cold War, the end of the first hopeful phase of the civil-rights movement, and Vietnam. We're in a period right now where the peaks of issues in politics are very low, and the valleys aren't very deep. We knew what Martin Luther King meant when he said, 'I've been to the mountaintop and I've seen the promised land.' Today I suppose someone would say, 'I've been to the hillside and I've seen an okay valley.' "

Simultaneously, money as a key motivation has created what Shrum calls "the Dick Morris-ization of the process," and he suggests "there may be a lot of little Dick Morrises running around inside people. The only test for him is: What works? And it ends with that . . . Morris as far as I can see has no beliefs."

Morris obviously disagrees, and insists that what he does is not basically unlike the services performed by his predecessors, with the significant difference of his use of public-opinion polling. "All it is," he told me, "is making scientific what used to be seat-of-the-pants judgment" on public attitudes and wants. "All it is, is a sophisticated weather device to tell you which way the wind is blowing." He compares his political strategy to "sailing a sailboat," tacking to one direction or another according to the prevailing wind and where you want to go.

The historian and political analyst Garry Wills, in *The New York Review of Books* after the 1996 election, wrote of Morris:

> *Too many have accepted Morris' promotion of himself as a donor, principally, of ideas and policy to Clinton. What he really gave him was a* mechanics, *skillfully tended, for turning cash into polls and polls into ads. Of course, Morris [in his book* Behind the Oval Office*] says nothing about his own financial stake in the structure he created to serve his interests while serving Clinton. But he does reveal, indirectly, a good deal about our system's present dependence on the triangle he belonged to, that of polling and television and money.*
>
> *He also shows us how Clinton's campaign was corrupted by the need to keep up the huge cash flow Morris demanded . . . Morris made it clear to Clin-*

tion that if he wanted a miraculous recovery from his calamitous condition in 1994, he would need polling and advertising on an unprecedented scale. The money raised from foreign sources was a measure of the desperate search for all possible income.

On the Republican side, the older generation, with the likes of Spencer, Bailey-Deardourff, Sears, Robert Goodman in Baltimore, and Roger Ailes, has been replaced, largely, by a second wave of consultants personified by Michael Murphy, who came out of the National Conservative Political Action Committee (NCPAC) that in the 1980s focused on negative attacks to defeat liberal Democrats. Such groups are permitted under the law to make unlimited expenditures in behalf of any candidate, provided they act independently of the candidate's formal campaign, ostensibly without any consultation or collusion.

In 1982, while still an undergraduate at Georgetown, Murphy recalls, he helped to turn out cheap television commercials for a freelance producer named Alex Castellanos, later his partner. "We'd go into a state, take a poll, then we'd go run, not always but generally, a negative campaign against the Democrat incumbent, to try to equalize things for the challenger. That was the big idea." Also, NCPAC would send him out to work in a primary "in some kind of pathetic congressional district," usually against the establishment Republican candidate and in behalf of "the more conservative or wackier candidate . . . I'd get down there on a cheap air fare, sleep on somebody's couch for two nights, and knock out three cheap television spots and get out of there for four thousand, nine hundred and ninety-nine dollars." NCPAC then, he said, was "like a little quasi-conservative Republican Party except we couldn't communicate with the candidate. We adhered to that pretty strictly. We didn't want to communicate with him because we had the arrogance of the outsiders. We could come and do our thing and get out."

Murphy and Castellanos set up their own firm, working for underdog Republicans in congressional primaries, fighting what Murphy calls "guerrilla wars," finally winning grudging respect from the party bureaucracy and eventually graduating into Senate races. And they specialized in negative campaigns for Republican congressmen struggling to be reelected. He failed with Senator Mack Mattingly of Georgia, who lost in 1986, he remembers, because "we ran a defensive campaign. We hurt [the Democratic candidate] Wyche Fowler, but we didn't finish the job at the end. We closed positive, which was a mistake. Fowler kind of came back from the dead on us."

As a team, he said, "we sold 'young, tough.' That was our shtick." After a brief stint for the Dole campaign in late 1987 and early 1988, Murphy and Castellanos were hired by Ailes for Bush's campaign to create a five-minute negative television spot against the Democratic nominee, Michael Dukakis of Massachusetts—"some Boston man-in-the-street stuff, you know, 'Why we hate our governor.' " Then Murphy and Castellanos parted amicably in 1989 and Murphy went on to run successful gubernatorial races in Michigan, Iowa, and elsewhere, finally moving up to the presidential level as chief strategist and media consultant for a Republican candidate, Lamar Alexander, in 1996.

Murphy has sophisticated equipment, in his office in a Virginia suburb of Washington, that can make highly complicated ads, complete with animation, and dispatch them to television outlets with a speed not possible even a few years ago. "It's made it very easy to do quick, interesting graphic spots, which are the staple of political television advertising," he says. With such equipment, he says, an ad maker can "turn around" an ad—pull an old one and replace it with a new one—almost too swiftly. One problem occurs when two campaigns get into a race and may turn ads around so fast "the voters can't keep up with them. The discipline to keep an ad on the air long enough to burn it in is one of the most important things in a campaign. We get seduced by our technology." The more significant seduction, however, is in the way voters are manipulated when public reaction to an opponent's charges can be tested and a television commercial responding to them can be created and placed on the air within hours.

The candidates who are the beneficiaries—or the prey—of the hired-gun phenomenon have mixed feelings about it. They recognize the imperative for having professionals in their campaigns, and the value of their ever-developing technologies for reaching and manipulating public opinion. But many openly express discomfort with the arrangement. Lamar Alexander, for instance, says on the positive side that "the wise candidate who is mature enough" to keep his consultants in perspective can take advantage of their ability to help him "retain his authenticity" in today's media politics, with its endless news cycles. But when consultants develop strategies and pollsters urge positions that may not be the candidate's own, and may not suit his personality and beliefs, then "it is more difficult to be real."

Consultants, Alexander says, "can completely overwhelm a candidate" and dominate his campaign. Facetiously, he predicts the day when a consultant announces his own presidential candidacy, backed by a pollster telling him what to say that will please the voters and a press secretary who tells him how to say it.

Bob Dole makes no secret of his skepticism about paid campaign professionals. "I guess they're a necessary evil," he says. "Some are your friends, but some are just in it because it's a campaign and they want to be in it. They get paid well and don't even show up the next day [after the election] to tell you goodbye. They're gone. They've moved on to the next body." In the old days, he recalls, "the local banker would be your finance director. It's an industry now. Back in my first race, I'm not even sure I had a campaign manager."

Bill Bradley, who complained on leaving the Senate that "politics is broken," began his campaign organization for the 2000 presidential race with reliance mostly on old friends and past campaign associates. He says of professional political consultants: "At some levels they're absolutely critical, because they bring real expertise to the process. I think what has to happen is, there has to be a mesh of the candidate and the consultant, not simply a client-type thing. The consultant has to feel that he, as much as the candidate, is on a journey of excitement and possibility, that it's a shared journey, and that the consultant is one critical player in a campaign [with] lots of critical players. In that sense it's a team." But, Bradley says, he doesn't know if that happens much in today's politics. Political consultants "are not going to be a key issue" for him, he says, "but I want to run a race in a way that will show other political consultants what the job could be. You want to bring some of the joy back into it, you want politics to sing again, you don't want it to be a business. You want it to be something people do because of commitment."

Political consultants "are more like sports agents" of the sort Bradley had when he first was a professional basketball player, but he adds, "I negotiated all my own contracts after the first contract, and that's the spirit of this campaign. You negotiate a contract with the American people directly, not through a sports agent."

As the new generation of consultants has moved into the field, focused more and more on television and with little experience in old grassroots politicking, presidential campaigning at the neighborhood level has become the stuff of old-timers' yarns, and fond memories. Dole nostalgically recalls "the old days when I used to go around western Kansas. Everybody came to the meetings. Even if a Democrat came to town, they'd come to that meeting. You'd have a chance to talk about the issues, you'd have cookies and coffee and people up on the stage doing dances. It was a big deal. Now it's all media. You don't go to those little places anymore. It would be impossible to meet everybody that way."

These small-town events are not completely a thing of the past, but they are much less frequent now, and usually serve only as part of the hired guns' calculated strategy to "humanize" the candidate in settings that make for positive television imagery, as presidential campaigning has moved from Main Street to Madison Avenue.

4 Main Street to Madison Avenue

For all the advances in presidential campaigning, the old basic approach of seeking votes on a retail basis has not been abandoned altogether in the face of the new technology—or at least not the appearance of it. On the surface, it has intensified as America has rushed from horse and buggy to train, automobile, and airplane, especially jet aircraft. Candidates are able to move from one Main Street to the next much faster and much more comfortably.

But these visits have become veneer rather than substance. The swiftest and surest means of transportation for a presidential candidate now is the instantaneous trip his image and words can make from television studio to American living room. But the cost of that trip is huge, as the market that the image and words can reach grows exponentially. Campaign managers, striving to make optimum use of whatever money they have, have learned that television advertising is the most cost-effective way to reach the most voters. Once they saw it that way, gone were the neighborhood storefront offices in every town of any size and in every section of the big cities, and gone were the volunteers licking stamps and envelopes there, having political discussions with neighbors who came by in search of buttons, bumper stickers, or a good argument.

James Carville laments, "It used to be you could walk in there, it had a smell, it had an energy, there was a vibrancy, there was something going on. I mean, people would get excited. Now it's all segmented. It's partly the money going into television. Everybody has decided this sort of thing doesn't matter anymore."

In place of the old neighborhood headquarters, today's presidential campaigns have remote, low-rent, walk-up offices in a few major cities, purposely inaccessible to average voters. Presidential elections have, effectively, moved from thousands of Main Streets across the land to Madison Avenue and other focal points of the giant television communications apparatus. While it might not be necessary anymore to have storefronts in every neighborhood, Carville says, "when you shut them all down, and you shut everything down, you just remove politics more and more from people. And that's what's happened. People have gotten less interested in it."

The American electorate has never been so accessible to candidates at such close range as television now makes possible. And with so much money to be spent reaching it, it has become all the more imperative that candidates and their strategists learn and understand the electorate's concerns, interests, wants, prejudices, and political leanings. As early as 1920, a major effort was made to poll the country in advance of the presidential election. The weekly *Literary Digest* mailed out eleven million postcards before and after the two party conventions in certain states to calculate the likely electoral outcome between Republican Warren G. Harding and Democrat James M. Cox. But Harding's victory was so one-sided it seemed preordained and no prediction was necessary. In 1924 the same publication polled voters and correctly predicted the victory of Republican Calvin Coolidge. Then it stumbled in 1936, projecting a large electoral college victory for Republican Alfred M. Landon over Franklin Roosevelt. The scattershot method of sending out postcards, the bulk of which went to the *Digest*'s mostly Republican readers, did not accurately reflect the composition of the voting population.

Soon more scientific public-opinion surveying emerged. In the same year of 1936, Dr. George Gallup's American Institute of Public Opinion and separate work by a pollster named Archibald Crossley correctly predicted Roosevelt as the winner, though not by the landslide he actually achieved. From this time on, political polling entered a new era of increasing refinement in measuring the voting universe and voter sentiments. Polls, however, had not yet become the information-gathering essentials to effective campaigning and strategy that they eventually would be.

By the time the national polls had established a reliable record for predicting the outcome of presidential races, campaign strategists were seeking much more information from them. They were looking to polls for information on what voters were thinking about the candidates, the country, and the world, and what there was to know about the voters themselves that would help the candidates appeal effectively to them. Poll taking moved from being an amusing measure of who's ahead and who's behind to being a critical campaign management tool to shape a candidate's message and, sometimes, even his persona. The same mechanism used to test the market for soap products was applied to politics, often with the same pollsters who were gauging the appeal of the one measuring the appeal of the other at the same time (called "piggybacking"). The information thus gained became raw material for campaign strategy and substance, particularly in television advertising.

In what may have been the first case of purchased television time by a presidential candidate, the Truman campaign in 1948 bought a segment on a local New Jersey channel to urge voters to go out and vote, to prove wrong all the poll predictions of Truman's imminent defeat. Four years later, the Eisenhower campaign, still under the direction of traditional politicians like Governor Thomas Dewey and his sidekick Herbert Brownell, hired the powerhouse advertising firm of Batten, Barton, Durstine & Osborn to handle its "account." BBD&O, as it was widely known, produced some short commercial spots primitive by later standards. The rival Adlai Stevenson campaign expressed horror at what one spokesman called "high-powered hucksters of Madison Avenue" taking over the Republican campaign. The Eisenhower campaign's hired guns, Stevenson charged, were trying to sell their candidate "in precisely the way they sell soup, ammoniated toothpaste, hair tonic, or bubble gum." He protested that the presidential campaign "isn't Ivory Soap versus Palmolive." Still, the Stevenson campaign had also hired some advertising men, though it didn't have the money to match Eisenhower's effort. (Stevenson himself was so uninformed about what a television adviser did that one night from his hotel room he phoned Bill Wilson, a young Chicago television producer who was doing that job, and asked him to come up and look at his set, which wasn't working!)

In 1960, both the Kennedy and Nixon campaigns used television advertising and polling, but they were still directed by personal and political intimates. According to Theodore C. Sorensen, in his book *Kennedy*, "no public relations agency or expert was employed [and] no nationally known political professionals were placed on the full-time payroll." Kennedy's younger brother

Robert and his longtime associates Lawrence O'Brien and Kenneth O'Donnell ran his campaign; a fellow Californian, Robert Finch, and former Eisenhower political adviser Leonard Hall ran Nixon's.

Kennedy, guided by polling data from Lou Harris, concentrated on nine large states as the key to his potential victory. Nixon, meanwhile, foolishly pledged to campaign in all fifty states and then spent valuable time, resources, and personal energy fulfilling the pledge. At the same time, he made a series of fifteen-minute nightly speeches on paid television and poured half a million dollars into an election-eve telethon, to no avail. Outfoxed by Kennedy in his management of time and resources, the defeated Nixon pondered the lesson, and looked ahead.

In 1964, after Kennedy's assassination, O'Brien and other Kennedy advisers loyally worked for the election of Lyndon Johnson, but they also reached out to the prominent New York advertising firm of the day—Doyle Dane Bernbach. Barry Goldwater, the Republican nominee, made a point of saying, according to his ideological soul mate and campaign adviser Karl Hess, "that he could not and would not have a chance to win the election or even want to run the race if it had to be run according to the advice of the so-called professional politicians." But even they could not have helped him escape the landslide defeat he suffered.

Nixon, the Republican nominee again in 1968, hired many people from the worlds of advertising and public relations for his campaign, which ran on two distinct tracks, one public, one private. The former served as a screen behind which the latter, more important one was played out. A public-relations expert, H. R. (Bob) Haldeman, a onetime J. Walter Thompson advertising agency executive in Los Angeles, had taken a hard, cold look at Nixon's failed 1960 run for the presidency and devised an unprecedentedly disciplined battle plan.

Meanwhile, Hubert Humphrey, inheriting the Democratic Party apparatus and nomination after the withdrawal of Lyndon Johnson, relied principally and successfully on party support for the presidential nomination against challenges from Eugene McCarthy and Robert Kennedy, both running in opposition to the party establishment.

Unlike 1960, when Nixon had raced through all fifty states in a physically exhausting stagger to defeat, Haldeman decided that with television as a tool, the era of that kind of extensive personal barnstorming was senseless, not to mention hazardous. The dismal relationship that Nixon had with reporters was well established by now. Haldeman and others in the 1968 Nixon entourage were determined that they would sharply limit their candidate's exposure to the press—and to spontaneous situations that might breed missteps—on the first, public track. While the energetic Humphrey continued to follow the old campaign formula, stumping from early morning to late night, Nixon eased his way through a leisurely daily schedule geared to the timetable of network television. Haldeman knew little about national politics and issues but a great deal about television and public relations. Understanding that the networks headquartered in New York were sensitive to any indication of unfairness, he fashioned a public schedule for Nixon that offered only a limited amount of television footage of his candidate, always doing his rested and scripted best.

Nixon would begin his public day with a carefully prepared speech before a staged pro-Nixon crowd, at an airport from which convenient flights were available to New York. He would deliver that one speech sometime before noon, giving the traveling television crews ample time to ship their product to their headquarters offices for processing and examination by the evening news editors. Then Nixon would return to his hotel room and remain out of public sight, safe from inquisitive reporters and the threatening spontaneity that had sunk more than one of his campaigns. Aides meanwhile would churn out position papers for the print press to chew on. Nixon would stay in his hotel suite for the rest of the day, or at least until an evening appearance at another staged event that could be used by the next morning's network news shows. If the networks wanted to use something from the Nixon campaign on the evening news, all they would have would be that one morning airport speech.

Meanwhile, Haldeman knew that Humphrey, running essentially a one-track public campaign guided by old political hands, would be putting in his usual frenetic campaign day of as many as a dozen events, some of which would show him in worse light than others. And he also knew that if Humphrey committed a gaffe, the network executives would be likely to choose it for the evening news, while they would have only the one well-honed event from Nixon, with the usual result that a "balanced" network report on the campaign day that would make Nixon look good—and Humphrey harried.

The Nixon second track, very private, led to television studios around the country. As described by Joe McGinniss in his revealing book *The Selling of the President 1968*, Nixon turned himself over to a team of image makers including Harry Treleaven, another J. Walter Thompson product; Frank Shakespeare, a CBS exile; Leonard Garment, a Nixon law partner; and Roger Ailes, soon to be known—unfairly, he always insisted—as the king of negative campaign advertising. Except for Garment, these men had had no previous attachment to Nixon. These men, with Nixon's full cooperation, crafted his real campaign of 1968, presenting their candidate in insulated situations that the traveling press corps, monitoring the first track, did not see. A centerpiece of the second track was a series of "town meetings" with Nixon answering questions from a private audience of selected Nixon supporters, taped for later showing on paid television by Nixon's own television crews. The questions and answers were spontaneous, but the chances of an unfriendly or damaging question from Nixon's own fans were minimal, and if any were asked, they could simply be edited out. We print and television reporters covering Nixon's campaign were barred from these sessions on the grounds that the spontaneity of the event would be hindered by our prying presence.

In the end, the two-track, insulated Nixon campaign orchestrated by the hired guns prevailed, but just barely—by seven-tenths of 1 percent over Humphrey in the popular vote.

In 1972, the same Nixon two-track strategy, with many of the same hired hands at work, easily succeeded against the Democratic nominee, Senator George McGovern, whose staff was composed mostly of people drawn to him by his opposition to the Vietnam War, including a young campaign manager from Colorado named Gary Hart. This time around, Nixon had the additional insulation of the White House, and he made the most of it. He left a frustrated McGovern trying unsuccessfully to arouse the voters about a somewhat confusing break-in that had occurred in June at the Democratic National Committee headquarters at the Watergate complex in Washington, by some men tied somehow to Nixon's reelection committee. The political significance of that caper was not appreciated until later—too late for the hapless McGovern.

In 1972, Senator Edmund Muskie of Maine had hoped the party apparatus would hand the nomination to him, but instead it went to McGovern, who bucked it with his aggressive anti-Vietnam campaign. And in 1976, former Governor Jimmy Carter of Georgia easily bested Senator Henry M. (Scoop)

Jackson of Washington, the party's closest thing to an establishment candidate.

By and large, Democrats who ran presidential campaigns during this period still were "one-horse jockeys"—individuals devoted to one candidate, either out of personal friendship and loyalty or commitment to the cause or causes that candidate represented. If their candidate failed to win the party nomination or lost the election (the Democrats won only once in six presidential elections through 1988), the one-horse jockeys would dismount and go back home to do what they had been doing in private or public life before the presidential race that year had begun. But they also were becoming obsolete.

The 1976 general election was masterminded by a mix of political amateurs and professionals. Jimmy Carter's campaign was administered almost entirely by his longtime and close political associates. Carter relied on a man who had been his chief political adviser when he was governor of Georgia, Hamilton Jordan; his old press secretary, Jody Powell; his old media consultant, Gerald Rafshoon; plus the young pollster from the 1972 McGovern campaign, Patrick Caddell. Together, they helped pull off one of the most surprising captures of a major-party nomination in history, and then the presidency itself. Meanwhile the campaign of Republican Gerald Ford, who had become president upon Nixon's resignation in disgrace in the Watergate scandal, was directed—and almost salvaged—by a team of old pols and astute hired guns. Ford, cutting himself loose from the discredited Nixon and most of the gang of political operatives who had helped win the White House for him twice and then helped him lose it in the Watergate mess, put his White House chief of staff, Richard Cheney, in overall charge. Cheney hired some of the most respected and ethical political consultants in Republican politics, including Bob Teeter, the party's premier pollster; Stuart Spencer, half of the old California team of Spencer and Roberts, as the campaign's troubleshooter; and the highly respected Washington-based team of Bailey and Deardourff.

Ford, bloodied in the primaries by a serious and debilitating challenge from Ronald Reagan, and with the albatross of his pardon of Nixon hanging around his neck, trailed Carter by as much as seventeen percentage points in major polls after the Democratic convention. But an astute campaign strategy and implementation by Cheney and the rest brought Ford to within an eyelash of victory in November. The Bailey-Deardourff team made the most of Ford's reputation as a well-meaning straight arrow whose ascendancy to the Oval Office had ended what he had called "our long national nightmare" of Watergate. In a preview of a strategy that later worked for Reagan, the Ford campaign struck an upbeat, optimistic theme, with a song called "Feelin' Good About America," that might have worked, except for a costly gaffe committed by Ford.

In a televised debate with Carter, Ford insisted that Poland and other countries in Eastern Europe were not under Soviet domination, and he would not be moved off that view. This mistake stopped cold a late-campaign surge of popularity generally attributed to Bailey-Deardourff television ads that focused on Ford as a breath of fresh air after the chill of the Watergate years. By the time Ford was persuaded to acknowledge that he had misspoken, it was too late; Carter won by 2.2 percent of the popular vote, with Ford only thirty votes short of an electoral-college majority.

By 1980, the revolution in political campaigning that had begun with the emergence of campaign strategists and operatives working on a fee-for-service basis continued to take hold, especially on the Republican side. The Carter campaign was run, as it had been in 1976, predominantly by the Georgians who had helped him win the presidency, but this time with an influx of some party pros with national campaign experience. The campaign of Ronald Reagan, by contrast, drew on a stable of Republican political technocrats from California and elsewhere that had been building over recent years, most of them paid consultants.

Carter was challenged for the Democratic nomination by Senator Edward M. Kennedy of Massachusetts, who relied heavily on old personal and political associates of the Kennedy family, led by his brother-in-law Steve Smith, for the nucleus of his campaign team. Doing so was in keeping with the traditional Democratic practice of building a campaign staff of men and women committed to one candidate for one specific race and engaged in national politics essentially because the candidate was, as Carter did with his team of loyal Georgians. In the Republican Party, with no incumbent seeking reelection, none of the seven presidential candidates could lay clear claim to the party establishment. Most of them hired political technocrats as campaign managers, principally consultants in the Washington area. Ronald Reagan had some of the best. John Sears, a veteran of the Nixon campaigns, who had also run Reagan's 1976 challenge to Ford, started the year as Reagan's campaign manager but was shunted aside in an internal struggle; left as the principal survivor was Michael Deaver, a master image shaper and protector going back to Reagan's California days.

As was the developing practice among the Republicans, when Reagan won the nomination many of the consultants who had worked for the losing candidates simply signed up to work for the winner. Republican political operatives as a general rule (though not Deaver, a Reagan loyalist) were more committed to the horse race, regardless of the horse, than were their Democratic counterparts.

For example, when Carter defeated Kennedy in 1980 after a brutal primary fight, most of the Kennedy people licked their wounds and went home rather than join Carter's team, which had resented their challenge to the party incumbent and did not welcome them. But when Reagan beat the rest of the Republican field in 1980, many of the losers stood ready to help the winner, and were asked to do so. George Bush was among the losers that year, but his campaign manager and longtime friend, James A. Baker III, though personally committed to Bush, joined Reagan's campaign as the key negotiator on arrangements for his debates with Carter. (Obvious exceptions were supporters of the Republican congressman John Anderson of Illinois, many of whom stayed with him when he ran as an independent in the general election.)

Reagan, the former movie actor, was an ideal candidate for a campaign run by political technocrats in the television era. He was a willing veteran at following professional direction; the consultants wrote the scripts for his television commercials, using sophisticated polling data on voters' concerns to hammer out his themes.

Although both parties now had a great number of professional consultants, usually from private firms that worked on contract to candidates, the Republicans were farther advanced than the Democrats in building and maintaining a permanent establishment of campaign operatives for hire. After the general election, it was becoming routine that key political operatives would be "warehoused" in well-paying jobs with the national or state parties or prominent Washington lobbying, political consulting, or law firms, on call for service in the next election.

In 1984, the Democratic nominee, Walter Mondale, rode party establishment support to the presidential nomination, but only after nearly losing to another anti-establishment candidate, Gary Hart. A traditionalist, Mondale took to television like a duck to sand, then lost badly to Reagan and his upbeat theme, "It's Morning in America," orchestrated by his team of hired consultants from Madison Avenue. The pièce de résistance in Reagan's advertising campaign was a commercial that reminded voters of the president's longtime reputation as a foe of Communism and suggested that the Democratic nominee was "soft" on the subject. It showed a huge grizzly bear coming up over a hill, as a voice said, "There's a bear in the woods. For some people, the bear is easy to see. Others don't see it at all. Some people say the bear is tame. Others say it is vicious and dangerous. Since no one can really be sure who's right, isn't it smart to be as strong as the bear?" As the bear lumbered along, a hunter with a rifle was seen watching him. There was no mention of Reagan except for the required reference to the ad's sponsor.

The old Democratic approach of the one-horse jockey was seen again in 1988, when Michael Dukakis chose as his campaign manager John Sasso, his longtime political strategist in Boston, and Paul Brountas, an old Harvard Law School classmate, as his campaign chairman. Both bowed out of the 1988 campaign after Dukakis was defeated, as did most of his other leading staffers. (One important exception was Paul Tully, a brilliant liberal loyalist who had labored for Ted Kennedy, Mondale, and Dukakis and went on to be political director of Bill Clinton's campaign in 1992, until he died of a heart attack in mid-campaign.) The Republican nominee, George Bush, by contrast tapped Lee Atwater, a veteran of the Reagan campaigns known for his Machiavellian approach to politics, as his campaign manager; Roger Ailes, whose political activism went back to Nixon's campaign in 1968, as his chief media consultant; and Bob Teeter as his pollster. Once again, after Bush had disposed of his primary opposition, paid consultants who had worked for the losers closed ranks behind the winner. Jim Baker, at this point Reagan's Secretary of the Treasury, supervised the Bush campaign.

That 1988 campaign marked the greatest triumph yet of negative television advertising concocted by hired guns. Dukakis, like Mondale, was uncomfortable with television and also unwilling to take the low road even when he was attacked. Brutal television advertisements masterminded by Atwater and Ailes assailed him mercilessly, and at the same time, Bush, who had been derided as a "wimp" as a result of the subservient manner of his vice presidency under Reagan, gave harsh stump speeches that implicitly challenged Dukakis' patriotism and toughness.

In 1992, Arkansas governor Bill Clinton's winning effort against President Bush was fashioned in large part by the fairly new national consulting team of James Carville and Paul Begala and other fee-for-services political specialists. In the previous year, after Carville and Begala had masterminded the upset victory of Senator Harris Wofford over U.S. Attorney General Richard Thornburgh in a special election in Pennsylvania, a bidding war had ensued for their services among the field of Democratic presidential aspirants, with Clinton winning out. So Carville and Begala, along with pollster Stanley Greenberg, media specialists Frank Greer and Mandy Grunwald, campaign manager David Wilhelm, political director Paul Tully, and close Clinton friends like Mickey Kantor and Eli Segal, ran Clinton's campaign. Of these, probably only Tully qualified as an old-line party functionary in the political lineage of Jim Farley.

Carville directed a much-ballyhooed "war room," first in the primary states and later in Little Rock, in which daily strategy was shaped and implemented, including a rapid-response operation that dealt swiftly with crises in the campaign, of which there were many. Learning well the lesson the Dukakis campaign taught—that charges unanswered were charges believed—Clinton's operation tried to extinguish every political brushfire that came along.

When allegations of womanizing and draft dodging were made against Clinton, the consultants gathered in Little Rock with the candidate and his wife, Hillary, to evaluate the resultant slide in Greenberg's polls. They decided that a frontal counterattack was in order, which Clinton would deliver personally in speeches in New Hampshire and on television, in paid commercials and network interview shows, including ABC's *Nightline.* Clinton weathered both storms and after a second-place finish in the New Hampshire primary, which his hired guns deftly burnished by having him call himself "the Comeback Kid," he went on to the nomination and election.

Bush, too, had his share of hired consultants, including Teeter, who stepped up as campaign chairman; Charles Black; Roger Ailes in a part-time capacity; and the party operative Mary Matalin. Later Jim Baker flew to the rescue from his lofty perch as Secretary of State. But President Bush, basking in public acclaim for his direction of the successful international military effort that had chased Iraqi dictator Saddam Hussein out of Kuwait in Operation Desert Storm, wanted to govern, not campaign for reelection. But his decision to break the pledge he had made in his 1988 speech accepting the Republican nomination, written for him by another paid consultant, Peggy Noonan—"Read my lips: no new taxes"—was causing deep resentment among conservatives in the party who had taken him at his word. The bloom of the Gulf War victory was withering fast.

Bush dragged his feet in getting his reelection campaign organized and ignored the advice of the consultants begging him to start laying out an agenda for a second term. By the time he was willing to listen to them, and to address the needs of his own campaign, he was in deep trouble. One of the most effective television commercials against him ran only fifteen seconds but was devastating. It opened with a close-up on Bush's mouth as he said, "Read my lips," followed by one word: "Remember?" Then it showed Bush saying, "You will be better off four years from now than you are today." As the voice-over intoned, "But it's four years later," the words on the screen said simply: "How ya doing?" This imagery effectively evoked facts already well known to the public—that President Bush's administration had raised taxes and the country was in a recession—in order to ridicule Bush and to make a point about his flip-flop.

Bush's reelection effort was further complicated by the on-again, off-again, on-again independent candidacy of the Texas billionaire Ross Perot. The president's paid consultants did the best they could to help, but an explosion of radio and television talk shows showcasing the candidates put the reluctant and often aloof Bush out on the firing line on his own. According to the then-retired NBC anchorman John Chancellor, writing in *Running for President: The Candidates and Their Images, 1900–1992*, Clinton appeared on the three network television news shows plus the *Larry King Live* and *Donahue* talk shows forty-seven times in 1992, to thirty-three for Perot and only sixteen for Bush.

Perot basically started this phenomenon with appearances on King's show, including his first announcement that he would seek the presidency if "volunteers" placed him on the ballot in all fifty states, which they eventually did with plenty of financial and organizational support from Perot himself. Perot insisted that he would have nothing to do with hired political consultants, deriding "sound bites, shell games, handlers, and media stuntmen who posture, create images, and . . . shoot off Roman candles but don't ever accomplish anything." But in the end he lured several to work for him with huge salaries, most notably Hamilton Jordan, who had run Jimmy Carter's two presidential campaigns, and Ed Rollins, who had run Reagan's second, as well as scores of races for lesser offices.

Perot skyrocketed in early polls, but as soon as press scrutiny turned on him, he began to slide, blaming his professional "handlers." He declined to follow their advice, flew off on his own for television appearances he set up himself, and refused to make the kind of arrangements for a traveling press corps that was commonplace with other candidates. He also refused to pay for professional polls that might clarify problems in his campaign, asking: "Why should I pay good money when I pick up a newspaper and read the polls there for free?" He never seemed to grasp the concept of using polls to assess his own political strengths and weaknesses, the better to shape an effective campaign.

When his hired managers told him, among other things, that he could not be nominated without running paid television ads that addressed the increasing questions asked about him and his business dealings, he balked again. "Why don't we just do it on Larry King?" he asked them. "I'll just get Larry to give me an hour. All you guys know how to do is come up with ideas on how to spend my money." Perot also nixed direct mail, Rollins said later, observing, "This is junk I get on my desk every day that I throw out. I'm not going to spend any money on junk mail." Rollins characterized Perot's attitude about the hired professionals like himself: "It was sort of like the volunteers were honorable and we were a bunch of whores because we took money."

When Rollins brought in Hal Riney, producer of the highly effective Reagan "It's Morning in America" ads in 1984, Perot in effect kicked him out. Rollins soon followed on his own, and Jordan told Perot he would be going, too. It was not the finest hour for the fraternity of hired guns.

Perot suddenly quit the race shortly afterward, professing to see that the Democratic Party had "revitalized itself," but clearly fleeing from all the press scrutiny of his background. He kept his organizing for ballot position going, however, and just as suddenly he jumped back in the race about a month before Election Day. He obviously did so to gain admittance to the televised presidential debates with Clinton and Bush while leaving little time for renewed press scrutiny to damage him again. In the end, Perot managed to garner 19 percent of the popular vote, the best showing by an independent candidate since Theodore Roosevelt's 27.4 percent on the Progressive ticket in 1912.

In 1996, the paid consultants found a much more receptive candidate for their advice in another multimillionaire, Malcolm S. (Steve) Forbes, Jr., son and heir of the *Forbes* magazine fortune. Totally inexperienced in politics, Forbes put himself and his millions at the disposal of a team of political professionals in his bold attempt to win—or, not inaccurately, to buy—the Republican presidential nomination.

Forbes's campaign was headed by William Dal Col, a former aide to Bush's Secretary of Housing and Urban Development, Jack Kemp. Up to $20 million of Forbes's fortune went into radio and television ads that first focused on his advocacy of a flat tax, dear to conservative hearts. These ads were astonishingly effective in boosting Forbes in the polls. Here was a candidate whose only real recommendation to the voters was his money and his willingness to spend it lavishly—with reckless effect on the overall presidential campaign. But when he started slipping, as the press and other candidates poked holes in his theory, his campaign's consultants switched to devastatingly negative television attacks. As internal polls indicated that not only front-runner Bob Dole but also second-string candidates like Lamar Alexander were eroding Forbes's own support, the ads targeted them as well. In the end, Forbes fell in the public-opinion polls, and he finally shut off the cash spigot.

Clinton's reelection campaign in 1996 was also dominated by a hired gun, as we have seen with Dick Morris. Several political consultants in both parties interviewed for this book made the argument, however, that the prime hired gun in Clinton's reelection campaign was really Clinton himself. "I have a theory," said Mike Murphy, "that Clinton is the first political consultant who's actually president. He does his own stuff. And I think he used Morris as a tool to get things done, rather than the other way around. I don't think Morris was the puppeteer and Clinton the puppet. Clinton is the first president we've had who is totally conversant with all the tactics and models that political consultants use, and could be a very successful political consultant himself. Anybody in our industry could have a totally technical discussion with the guy, and he'd know stuff that would absolutely mystify a Jimmy Carter or a George Bush or a Lyndon Johnson, a Reagan, or a Humphrey."

Clinton was consequently trusting of the tools, techniques, and tactics of the paid political consultant, and willing and eager to use them. "George Bush used to throw us out of the Oval Office," Murphy said. "He didn't want to make television commercials. Clinton's whole life has been in politics. He's a professional operative. He's the first of his generation who got into the Oval Office who knows what a gross rating point is." Squier agrees. "Does a fish think about water? Of course not," he says. "Does Clinton think about television? Of course not."

Although Clinton's Republican challenger in 1996, Bob Dole, was a throwback to the days before paid political consultants and by nature a politician who preferred to make his own decisions, he too fell into the hands of hired guns, as did the other challengers for the GOP nomination.

Dole was persuaded, against his longtime aversion to tax cuts as a means of budget balancing, to make tax cuts the centerpiece of his campaign. In doing so, he violated one of the central precepts of successful politics in earlier times: don't present yourself to the voters as someone you're not. He proved to be an unpersuasive salesman for tax cuts and was easily defeated. Circumstances made it equally easy for the new political technocrats in the Republican Party to blame him, and to look ahead to the next presidential election—and its new opportunities to build their own reputations and bank accounts.

For the 2000 election cycle, the deep pockets of Steve Forbes attracted some key consultants from other 1996 campaigns, such as Greg Mueller, once Buchanan's right-hand man. George W. Bush assembled an essentially Texan team, but other contenders signed up available consultants who had been battle-tested in 1996.

With fee-for-services political operatives now dominating American presidential politics, it naturally follows that money—the raising and spending of it by White House aspirants in both major parties, and the earning of it by their hired guns—is a problem that is mushrooming out of control, with dire consequences for public confidence in the credibility of the American electoral process.

5 SOUR MOTHER'S MILK

In a speech at a fund-raising dinner in Texas in 1995, Republican senator Phil Gramm summed up his theory for getting nominated and elected president: "The best friend you can have in politics," Gramm proclaimed unabashedly, "is ready money." For more than a year he had already been diligently courting that "best friend," holding fund-raising events of one sort or another almost nightly all around the United States. He estimated it would take $20 million to be a serious contender for the Republican nomination—a figure tossed out, others suspected, in an effort to scare off prospective competitors.

Yet there was valid reason to accept the truth that a small fortune would be required. Political strategists who appreciated the likely effect of the rush of presidential primaries and caucuses that came hard on the heels of the kickoff voting in Iowa and New Hampshire understood. A host of state parties in their wisdom had crowded their delegate-selecting processes into the weeks immediately following those first contests, thereby elevating their own states' importance—and the need for money to compete in them.

Even in earlier years, when there was a month or more between the Iowa caucuses and the New Hampshire primary, and some weeks after that before the next state voted for national convention delegates, money on hand or recourse to it had been a key determinant of a candidate's ability to survive. Either you had collected enough before the process started to sustain early setbacks at the polls or you managed to raise more by winning an early test or two. At the least, you had to exceed expectations you set for yourself or were set for you by reporters and commentators covering the campaign. If you neither had a nest egg nor could build one by virtue of your performance in the early competition, sooner or later you would have to drop out. The federal subsidy that went to qualifying candidates was not unlimited. The law stipulated that if a candidate failed to achieve 10 percent of the vote in two consecutive primaries, the subsidy was cut off until such time as the candidate did manage to get 10 percent in two in a row. As a practical matter, that seldom happened. So the legal provision also helped in the winnowing process, at least for candidates to whom the subsidy was political lifeblood.

Candidates are free to launch their quest for campaign funds anytime they wish for the next presidential election. But only money raised in the calendar year prior to the election year is eligible for matching funds, making January 1 of that prior year the practical starting point. This time frame all but guarantees that the presidential campaign will begin then, and it sets off the most industrious candidates on a search for contributions that will qualify for the "match." Big givers who are willing to "max out"—give the $1,000 limit to one candidate—have only the first $250 counted toward matching funds.

Gramm was relentless in pursuit of his $20 million goal. But despite tireless and impressive fund-raising, he proceeded to spend his "friends" faster than he could acquire them. By mid-1995, he and several of the other White House hopefuls had staffs of paid campaign consultants and experts in place, for none of them could afford to wait until the election year itself began, and they had to keep raising money as they spent it.

One who realized the difficulty of the ordeal was Jack Kemp, who had come out of an earlier presidential bid in 1988 saddled with a debt of more than $3 million and with memories of the endless fund-raising. For all his obvious political ambition, he decided not to put himself through it again in 1996. "The money is not only obscene," he said later, "but raising it is a terrible encumbrance."

Not, however, if you were rich yourself. The campaign finance reform legislation of 1974, in providing for the federal subsidy, attached the condition that recipient candidates agree to specified spending limits. But the Supreme Court in 1976 ruled that any limitations on a candidate's ability to spend his own money on his own campaign would violate his First Amendment protection of free speech, thereby opening the floodgates to rich Americans of political ambition. In 1995 and 1996, such a candidate was Steve Forbes. He invited himself into the competition with the explicit vow not to play by the rules that governed and limited the efforts of the other candidates.

Declaring he would eschew the federal campaign subsidy and pay for his campaign out of his own deep pockets, he freed himself of the federal campaign finance laws' limits and single-handedly raised the ante. He would, he said, spend "whatever it takes, but not one cent more." He quickly found out that it would take plenty. Not only could Forbes outspend the others; by raising the amount of radio and television advertising to unprecedented levels, he obliged them to bankrupt themselves to stay in the game. This strategy of attrition was akin to President Ronald Reagan's huge military buildup that sought to drive the Soviet Union to such levels of arms production that its economy would ultimately collapse, and the Soviet political empire with it.

It was not only the money; the whole tone and substance of the 1996 presidential campaign was polluted by the negativism of Forbes's advertising. While casting himself as a pious, selfless savior of the American public against the corruption and greed of Washington insiders, Forbes himself corrupted the very process by which Americans choose their president. According to Gramm, Forbes "ran almost the dirtiest campaign in the history of American campaigning. He distorted our records, and called his opposition trash—things I had never seen before. Presidential candidates are usually better than that." (If wealthy candidates are to be able to spend their own money without limit, Gramm argued, the law "ought to raise the contribution limits on other people." As it was, he noted, candidates like himself had to spend fifty cents to raise a dollar, doubling the impact of Forbes's open wallet.) "Nothing else about Steve Forbes made him a credible candidate except money," he said. And as for Dole, beyond having his own well-heeled campaign nearly bankrupted, he emerged from the primaries identified even more strongly than before as a Washington insider.

To be sure, Forbes was not the first wealthy man to seek to substitute his fortune for the customary credentials of public service as an entry ticket into a presidential campaign. Four years earlier, after all, Ross Perot had done much the same. But there was a big difference: Perot spent his millions in 1992, and again in 1996, trying to persuade a *national* audience, and his money did not have the pinpoint effect of Forbes's millions targeted at small states. Forbes demonstrated how a person who wants to try to buy the presidency can effectively distort the process, state by state. Forbes never had to meet the money-raising test to survive the early primaries. It might fairly be said that normal candidates who can't raise the money needed to continue are eliminated by the will of the voters who decline to support them. Gramm, for one, said, "The ability to raise money *is* a measure of support. If you can't do it, you're probably not able to do the job." But a self-financing candidate can make himself immune to this winnowing-out process by the voters. He can winnow himself *in* for as long as he is willing to spend his own money.

In not having to meet the fund-raising test imposed on the other candidates, says Bob Teeter, Forbes and Perot "hurt the other candidates and screwed up the process." In the end, he says, the press undercut their money advantage, serving as it is supposed to as a "legitimate filter" of the candidates' qualifications. The defeats of Forbes, Perot, and Gramm occurred because of their weaknesses as candidates and the weakness of Gramm's axiom that the best friend you can have in politics is ready money.

Still, Kent Cooper, former director of the Center for Responsive Politics, which studies the influence of money in politics, says the starting point of most presidential campaigns today is the estimate of a chief fund-raiser on what the campaign will cost and the prospects of raising it. The advice, he says, usually is "if you can't come up with this, there's no sense trying." Charles Lewis, chairman and executive director of the Center for Public Integrity, points out that in the last four presidential elections "every candidate who raised the most money the year before got the nomination. Money is the essential ingredient."

Dick Morris, self-proclaimed mastermind of Clinton's political resurrection in 1996, insists, however, that "the impact of money, and of mechanics and of technology in politics, is vastly overstated and overrated. I do not think they are nearly as important as everybody else seems to think they are. You need enough money, which is a rather precise amount, to make a message stick, for people to absorb it."

What is enough money? Morris calculates it this way: enough to run an ad on television seven times during a campaign and to have ten messages, for an approximate cost of $4 million. "People spend a lot more money than that, but they waste it. Instead of thirties [thirty-second commercials], they buy sixties, which cost twice as much. They spend more on filming it than they need to; they buy a lot of ads that are garbage and don't really say anything, just to fill up the space. They spend a lot on staff and field organization, on party-building activities, which have no impact on the election. I would say that of the $360 million that Bill Clinton spent on his reelection, about $140 million of it was well spent and the rest of it was basically wasted . . . We spent a total of $45 million on paid media prior to the Democratic convention . . . that $45 million basically got him reelected, because he was fine after that. I mean, the race was over by the convention."

The Clinton-Gore campaign, Morris says, also had to spend a huge amount for travel, "which you have to do when the guy's president and you need to pay for the Secret Service. But staff, organization, field people—they had five hundred full-time staffers working the New Hampshire primary and a similar number working the Iowa [caucus] for a year. And when it turned out there was no opposition, they didn't fire anyone, they just kept them on staff right through Election Day. The increased amount [of money] was what I wanted for media, [and] it's true that raising it got him into trouble. But that was the only important money. All the other stuff was just for this massive payroll."

Considering that Morris has no use for either political party or conventional organizers, and sees the kind of television advertising he makes plenty of money from as the real key to success, these anti-party, anti-organization views are not surprising. The conflict between spending for media and for field operations was at the core of Morris' dispute with Harold Ickes, the White House deputy chief of staff. Morris says, "The president resolved it by giving both of us everything we wanted and going out and raising extra money. But that was his failure to manage, not the system's requirement for money. Basically, most of the money that was spent that was so exorbitant was to buy a lot of patronage for a lot of political operations all over the country, so that everybody would be fat and happy and nobody would run against him."

Even Morris will admit that while money is obviously vital, alone it is no guarantee of success. Yet had President Clinton and his supporters been unable to raise the reported $32 million for so-called issue advocacy ads in 1995—ads that praised Clinton's policy positions without calling explicitly for his reelection—he might not have been able to resurrect his political fortunes after the Republican congressional takeover in 1994. Clinton himself, in a speech to major campaign contributors in 1996, acknowledged that this very costly television ad campaign was responsible for the revival of his public support in 1995.

The contributions were possible because of a huge loophole in the federal laws governing the financing of presidential campaigns. Limits are imposed on funds contributed directly to a candidate or to his campaign committee: this is "hard money," and only individuals may contribute it, not corporations or labor unions. But anybody or any organization may contribute unlimited amounts in unregulated funds for party-building activities such as voter registration and turnout and for advocacy of an issue position without referring to the election of any candidate; this is "soft money." In 1996 this soft-money loophole made a mockery of the contribution limits, because as a practical matter soft money found its way into the presidential campaign through the back door of state Democratic and Republican party committees.

On the Republican side, Dole's abundant campaign treasury of hard money enabled him to survive early setbacks—a narrower than expected victory in the Iowa caucuses and defeats at the hands of Patrick Buchanan in the New Hampshire primary and Forbes in Arizona and Delaware—and gain an early nomination. But Dole was hard pressed thereafter to finance what then amounted to a premature beginning to the general election campaign against the well-heeled Clinton, unchallenged in the Democratic primaries. At this point, Dole too had to depend on soft-money contributions to keep his campaign afloat; it was funneled in through state party committees ostensibly to be used for party building but in fact used for advocacy ads.

The same thing could happen in 2000 if Texas Governor Bush, by virtue of his huge advantage in fund-raising and party endorsements, were to clinch the Republican nomination early, while Vice President Al Gore and former Senator Bill Bradley of New Jersey depleted their campaign resources in fighting each other for the Democratic nomination. The Democratic survivor, like Dole in 1996, would be left hard-pressed to be competitive in the long period remaining until the national party conventions in August.

Adequate campaign funds have often been lifesavers in the past. They helped Clinton in 1992 survive his second-place finish in New Hampshire behind Paul Tsongas; George Bush in 1988 to continue after running third behind Dole and the television evangelist Pat Robertson in Iowa; Michael Dukakis in the same year to continue after losing to Richard Gephardt and

Paul Simon there and to Jesse Jackson in Michigan; Walter Mondale in 1984 to recover from early losses to Gary Hart in New Hampshire, Maine, Massachusetts, Rhode Island, Florida, and other states; and Ronald Reagan in 1980 to overcome Bush's upset of him in Iowa. In each case, the eventual party nominee entered the campaign year with plenty of money to get over the early bumps while developing solid public recognition and party establishment support. As another presidential candidate, Morris Udall (in 1976), liked to say in another context: "I've seen rich and I've seen poor, and rich is better."

Why do people give money to presidential candidates anyway? Some do it because they genuinely believe in the candidate they support and in the policies he espouses. Others give money because they are personal friends of the candidate. Still others, especially if they're well off, like to name-drop about how they have supported somebody running for president, and they enjoy rubbing elbows with the candidate at a fund-raising event. But probably the main reason is to gain access to the candidate and/or his advisers to advance the donor's self-interests of one sort or another. And access is what big contributors often get. "I'm going to talk to somebody with money way before I talk to somebody with ideas," says James Carville frankly. The exchange of words, along with the giving of money, often leads to favored treatment later concerning legislation that is of interest to the giver. An explicit arrangement of such a transaction would be an actionable bribe, but with a figurative wink and a nod rather than a handshake, it gets by as an old-fashioned quid pro quo.

Yet millions of dollars in the presidential campaigns are given by contributors who never meet the candidate they are supporting and never have a hope or chance of meeting him. Their contributions are achieved by high-powered direct-mail solicitations for relatively small amounts, encouraged by lengthy, often personalized letters that lay out in detail why the candidate needs help and what policies he advocates.

A prime pioneer in this direct-mail work was Richard Viguerie, a conservative activist who started a direct-mail operation in 1965 and soon had an office stocked with millions of names of proven and prospective givers who were committed ideologically to conservative causes and candidates. His work has been copied by a whole new generation of direct-mail operatives, in an impersonal relationship between the direct-mail impresario and the candidates he works for.

Such fund appeals can be highly emotional and in recent years very negative, tapping into strong voter dislikes. Thus, a letter indicating that a candidate is a strong foe of Senator Ted Kennedy of Massachusetts often generates a high yield of campaign money among conservative contributors. Similarly, liberal Democratic direct-mailers have their own favorite demons, such as Senator Jesse Helms of North Carolina, to attract campaign dollars. Either way, appealing to contributors who hope for access to the candidate or to people who care about certain issues or have an antipathy toward an identified political bogeyman, direct-mail solicitations are now a major, and sophisticated, mechanism for financing campaigns.

American politics has never been a perfect textbook example of unsullied democracy in action. Even the hallowed George Washington, in getting elected to the House of Burgesses in Virginia in 1757, was not above questionable spending. He parceled out money for his supporters to ply voters with rum, wine, beer, and cider. But the intention of Washington and the other Founding Fathers was to insulate the election of the president from corrupt practices and, indeed, any "party animosities" that might be divisive. That intention proved a pipe dream. As presidential elections evolved, they were less elite exercises decided by state legislatures, caucuses, and landowning voters and more and more expressions of a broader public will. The advent and proliferation of primaries and the extension of the voting franchise meant more casters of ballots and more money required to court them.

In 1867, Congress made its first attempt to regulate campaign fundraising in a naval appropriations bill that barred officers and government employees from soliciting campaign money from naval shipyard workers. In 1883, the prohibition was extended to all federal civil service workers, who until then had often been squeezed for money by the party in power as a condition of continued employment. Ready cash nevertheless remained an integral factor in determining the outcome of most elections. Mark Hanna, the first of the great campaign managers, is said to have proclaimed, "There are two things that are important in politics. The first is money and I can't remember what the second one is." When Hanna masterminded the election of William McKinley in 1896, nearly $7 million was raised and spent, an amount that snowed under the Democrat, William Jennings Bryan, who raised and spent only $650,000.

In the era of voting names off tombstones in such bastions of machine politics as Chicago and Jersey City, the essential ingredient was the greased palm. Politicians and their henchmen spread around what was variously called "street money" and "walking-around money" to citizens willing to cast votes, both legal and illegal, for whatever was the going rate. Franklin D. Roosevelt once joked that when he died he wanted to be buried in Chicago so he could keep on voting. And the politicians' plea to their constituents to "vote early and often" was frequently said only half in jest. The process of registering voters and then getting out the vote was routinely spurred directly by cash or indirectly by hiring drivers to take prospective voters to the polling place on Election Day. Modest attempts at reform and occasional convictions of political operatives for campaign finance violations did little to stem the practices.

In 1905, President Theodore Roosevelt recommended that all corporate contributions be banned and that public financing for all federal candidates be instituted. In 1907, the corporate ban was enacted but without adequate enforcement mechanisms. In 1925, campaign contribution limits and their disclosures were written into the Federal Corrupt Practices Act, which remained the basic regulatory tool for nearly fifty years.

Business interests dominated campaign giving, mostly to Republicans, until the mid-1930s, when labor began to weigh in on the side of the Democrats. In 1936, John L. Lewis, head of the United Mine Workers and the CIO, gave $250,000 to FDR. That division of loyalty has continued to the present day, but business givers still far exceed the unions in their generosity. In 1940, in the Hatch Act, federal employees were barred from contributing to federal candidates and a limit of $5,000 was placed on others, provisions that were extended to primary as well as general elections. But the rules didn't bar contributors from giving up to the limit to as many political committees as they chose. And in 1943, the bar on corporate contributions was extended to labor unions.

Rich people, the third major source, have generally favored the Republicans, but some fat cats have also given generously to the Democrats. Although corporations and unions are prohibited by federal law now from contributing directly to presidential candidates, they have given massive amounts of soft money to maintain their influence. Both factions, starting in the 1940s, established political action committees (PACs) through which they channeled the contributions of individual employees or union members and "bundled" the funds of groups of contributors to a single candidate to increase, theoretically at least, their political clout.

Political action committees in short order became both allies and rivals of the national parties. PACs developed into political power bases of their own, often giving to candidates regardless of party on the basis of the issues they supported, and by covering their bets, contributing to both parties and to candidates of both parties. Eventually the national parties found themselves on the outside looking in, while candidates looked to PACs for help and for guidance on issues, the way they had once depended on the national parties. Money, as California Democratic leader Jesse Unruh memorably put it, was indisputably by now "the mother's milk of politics."

Despite all this, most Americans never give a penny to presidential candidates. Although Theodore Roosevelt had considered public financing, it took the major political scandal of the Watergate break-in of 1972, in the midst of the reelection campaign of Richard Nixon and Spiro Agnew, to bring it about. "Ready money" in the hands of the Committee to Re-Elect the President (CREEP) unleashed a series of reckless and senseless political excesses, and Nixon's agents determinedly plotted to buy or steal a reelection that was already in the bag for him. There being no limit at that time on how much a candidate could raise or spend, a single Nixon supporter, a Chicago insurance executive named W. Clement Stone, poured an estimated $3 million into the campaign. The ready availability of money in turn led to the financing of various dirty tricks against the Democratic front-runner, Edmund Muskie, in the New Hampshire primary and later against the Democratic nominee, George McGovern, and the ultimate dirty trick—the break-in of the Democratic National Committee offices at the Watergate building complex in downtown Washington.

While the White House was busy covering up its involvement in the Watergate affair, lengthy congressional hearings brought public demands for immediate steps to clean up the corrupting influence of unharnessed money in the presidential election process. In 1974 and 1976, Congress enacted a series of amendments to a heretofore largely ineffective Fair Campaign Practices Act, aimed particularly at fat cats like Stone. The amendments produced major changes in how political parties chose their nominees and in how they financed and conducted their campaigns around the country and on television.

The new laws imposed a ceiling of $25,000 from any individual contributor to a presidential campaign and a limit of $1,000 to any candidate in a primary or general election campaign. They also specified that no political action committee could give more than $5,000 to any one candidate and placed strict reporting requirements and limits on candidates' fund-raising and spending. For the 1976 campaign, the ceiling was set at $10.9 million to run each candidate's preconvention campaign, plus nearly $2.2 million for fund-raising, and a per-state limit of two cents per voting-age person. (The ceilings grew with population growth in succeeding elections.)

In a further effort to reduce the influence of private contributions and as an inducement to candidates to accept the limits, the new laws also provided for a federal subsidy to qualified candidates, supported by a one-dollar taxpayer checkoff on income-tax returns. The subsidy was a dollar-for-dollar match of all funds raised by a candidate up to $250 from a single contributor; to qualify, a candidate merely had to raise $5,000 in contributions of $250 or less in twenty states—a simple task for any politician with a normal base in his own party. As we have seen, the law said that such contributions had to be raised no earlier than the calendar year before the election year. A candidate could choose, if he so desired, to avoid the spending limits by rejecting the federal matching money, but most candidates did not have the wherewithal to do so. In the first years of the law's application, only one—John Connally of Texas, running in 1980 for the Republican presidential nomination—tried. Connally raised and spent eight million dollars on his own and got one convention delegate for his trouble.

To administer the reformed campaign finance laws, Congress created a Federal Election Commission, consisting of two members appointed by the president and four by Congress. The Supreme Court soon declared the composition unconstitutional because the commission exerted executive powers but the executive branch was underrepresented. The problem was eventually rectified, but the FEC remained ineffectual and partisan; it never had enough funding to police violations in a timely fashion. Presidential candidates routinely risked commission reprimands and minor fines doled out years later, fudging on the laws or even breaking them outright in order to gain advantage during the campaign.

The most immediately important work of the FEC was to determine which candidates qualified for the federal subsidy and for how much, and to disburse the money quickly enough to keep the campaigns going during the presidential primary season. For the candidates accepting the subsidy and the limits thereby imposed, the money was critical.

The Supreme Court in 1976, in *Buckley* v. *Valeo*, also declared that while limits on contributions and spending could be imposed on candidates who accepted the public subsidy, no limits could be imposed on individual candidates' ability to spend their own money, on grounds that doing so would violate their freedom of speech protection under the First Amendment. Further, it ruled that individuals or groups making "independent expenditures" in behalf of a candidate—that is, outside his campaign structure and with no consultation or collusion with it—could not be limited, on the same free speech grounds. These rulings opened the door wide to allow rich men literally to buy their way into the presidential race, and to allow others to skirt the contribution limits. Along with the soft-money loophole, they in time all but destroyed the federal effort to limit presidential campaign spending.

In the 1976 campaign, the new money laws and the proliferation of primaries enabled a little-known former governor of Georgia to upset a field of more prominent Democrats and win nomination and election. With deft planning and positioning, Jimmy Carter surprised the party establishment by leading the other candidates in the kickoff Iowa caucuses and the New Hampshire primary. Then he managed to win at least one primary on every voting day thereafter, accumulating a delegate majority in advance of the national convention. In succeeding years, other presidential hopefuls in both parties followed Carter's strategy of seeking impressive showings in Iowa and New Hampshire as a means of generating money and publicity that could maintain their candidacies. But in the last four presidential elections, the candidates with the fattest campaign treasuries at the start of the election year were nominated: Reagan and Mondale in 1984, Bush and Dukakis in 1988, Bush and Clinton in 1992, Clinton and Dole in 1996.

For the first five presidential elections under the post-Watergate campaign finance reforms, the system worked well, according to Fred Wertheimer, longtime president of Common Cause, who now heads his own public-policy organization, Democracy 21. Although the public financing scheme at the heart of the post-Watergate reforms was widely criticized as an "incumbent protection act," Wertheimer noted that in those first five elections, the challenger won three times—Carter in 1976, Reagan in 1980, and Clinton in 1992.

The loophole Clinton so extensively exploited in 1996 was already apparent to Democratic campaign strategists in 1988, when a master fund-raiser, Robert Farmer, in behalf of the presidential candidacy of Michael Dukakis, got big contributors to send money to the various state parties, claiming it to be soft money ostensibly for party building. Under what came to be known as "the coordinated campaign," various kinds of campaign material were put out for the Democratic ticket, but the prime purpose was Dukakis' election. George Bush's campaign, after first complaining that the practice was illegal, soon followed suit. In 1992, the Clinton campaign seized on the subterfuge, raising more soft money through the Democratic National Committee from July to the end of the year, according to Wertheimer, than Bush's campaign managed through the Republican National Committee.

After the 1994 Republican takeover of Congress sent Clinton's prospects for reelection in 1996 reeling, Morris encouraged the president to use the national committee and state parties even more as conduits for what supposedly was "soft," party-building money. But, Wertheimer argues, it was really hard money that should have been regulated that was used to finance Clinton's massive television advertising campaign and resurrect his political fortunes. "The Clinton campaign ran two campaigns, one on the books and one off the books, and exercised the same control of both, with Clinton himself operating as the campaign manager," he says.

Morris wrote in his book that the early "paid media advertising" strategy was one he and Clinton had used successfully in Arkansas, touting the governor's legislative achievements and goals well in advance of his reelection campaigns. Lawyers at the Democratic National Committee told him, Morris wrote, that the law permitted unlimited expenditures by a political party for such "issue advocacy" ads. With that advice, he and Clinton in July 1995 were off and running. But Wertheimer says, "In my view, what the lawyers told him was wrong. What they were doing was flat-out illegal. Morris makes clear that this was a totally presidential campaign-run operation. If that's the case, then you can't call it political party soft money."

One indication that the Clinton campaign knew it was skirting the law is Morris' report in his book that heavy television advertising was targeted on twenty swing states that the campaign figured would be battlegrounds in 1996. At the same time, no ads were run in New York or Washington and only occasionally in Los Angeles because "these are the cities where journalists live and work. If the ads had run there, the press would have grasped the magnitude of what we were doing. But if these cities remained 'dark,' the national press would not make an issue of our ads," Wertheimer notes. "They made a big point of doing this under the radar screen. They were doing the time buys in local communities. They stayed off the networks and they stayed out of the East. It was a farce before that. Now they took it to a ridiculous level."

Until 1996, the system of public financing had effectively allowed a competitive process and reduced the influence of money on presidential decision making. "Then," says Wertheimer, "the soft money scam [broke] the system down." Sources like corporations and unions that were supposed to be prohibited from contributing to presidential campaigns simply sent their money to state parties, which turned around and wrote checks to the media consultants for the presidential campaigns—a blatant money-laundering scheme. By 1996, Clinton's campaign had made a shambles of the federal campaign finance laws, and the Dole campaign soon joined in. The Republicans were not in a position to launch the same kind of early television advertising campaign, however, because they did not have an early nominee. By the time Dole had the presidential nomination in hand, he was out of hard money, having had to spend it all beating off the sky's-the-limit challenge from Forbes. At this point, with months to go before his formal nomination that would bring a money transfusion from the FEC for the general election campaign, Dole's campaign also resorted to laundering soft-money contributions through the state parties to media consultants.

In 1992, according to Wertheimer, the Democratic and Republican parties combined raised roughly $72 million in soft money; in 1996, the figure shot up to $231 million, eclipsing by far the $24.6 million available through the federal campaign subsidy. In October 1996, a month before the presidential election, Common Cause, the self-styled citizens' lobby, urged Attorney General Janet Reno to appoint an independent counsel to investigate "an illegal scheme to circumvent the federal campaign finance laws" by each presidential campaign. It cited numerous published reports of how the two campaigns, and their principals, raised money in contravention of the agreement to abstain from such fund-raising as a condition of receiving the subsidies available to presidential candidates.

Common Cause noted that Clinton and Dole and their campaigns had solicited contributions and funneled them through the national party organizations to state parties for use at the state and local levels. Thus, it argued, the money was not in the category of unregulated or soft funds and in reality should have been treated as regulated hard money. In a second appeal to Reno in April 1997 after more information had become public, Common Cause again charged that both the Clinton and Dole campaigns had blatantly violated the law by raising money for the supposedly separate television ad campaigns, "with the political parties serving as mere conduits" for them. "The TV ad campaigns," it charged, "were prepared, directed, targeted and fully controlled by the Clinton and Dole presidential campaigns, not by the political parties." The complaint cited a book written by Bob Woodward before the campaign, *The Choice*, and the one written after it by Dick Morris, to show how President Clinton was intimately involved not only in the fund-raising but also in writing the television ads in close coordination with his media consultants. In treating the funds as unregulated soft money when they really were not, Common Cause argued, he had violated the ban on corporate and union contributions to a presidential candidate. Attorney General Reno took no action, however, other than to continue the Justice Department's investigation.

As already noted, the Supreme Court in 1976 ruled unconstitutional any limitation on what a group acting independently of the candidate's formal campaign could spend. What came to be known as independent expenditure committees could use as much money as they could get their hands on in behalf of whatever candidate or issue they chose, as long as they observed an appearance—if not always the reality—of acting strictly on their own. On the simplest level, if a candidate's campaign left a vital function unaddressed—such as television advertising on a certain issue in a particular state—an independent expenditure committee backing him could address the problem on its own. Later, after another court decision gave such committees a green light, they began intensive financing of television and radio ads concerning particular issues clearly associated with their favored candidates, but the cost of such ads did not have to be attributed to the candidate's campaign account regulated by the federal campaign finance laws.

Before he retired from the Senate, Bill Bradley of New Jersey argued that the Supreme Court in *Buckley* had held that "a rich man's wallet is no different than a poor man's soapbox," as an implementer of free speech. He proposed a constitutional amendment "simply to clarify that political money is not speech" and, hence, could be regulated by Congress and the states. There were those like Republican senator Mitch McConnell of Kentucky who fiercely and tenaciously insisted that any limits on candidates' contributions to their own campaigns are and should remain unconstitutional. But, Bradley told the Kennedy School of Government at Harvard in early 1996, his amendment "would protect rights by strengthening democracy. It would not limit the First Amendment, but would clarify that the right to buy an election is not a form of freedom of expression."

Shortly afterward, a group of constitutional scholars banded together to urge the Supreme Court to review and overturn the *Buckley* decision. But, they noted, lower courts were handing down rulings permitting even more unrestricted spending of money in campaigns for federal office. The Supreme Court itself upheld a decision in a Colorado case permitting political parties to spend whatever they chose in "independent" advertising for specific candidates if written and placed without coordination with the candidates' campaigns. The outlook for an early review of *Buckley* is not promising.

In 1996, a healthy economy and Dole's ineffective general-election campaign brought easy victory to President Clinton, in spite of continuing questions of personal misconduct raised about him. Even disclosures of outrageous excesses committed by Clinton and his campaign aides in dunning campaign contributions from wealthy donors, some of them foreigners, had little effect. But Clinton's rewarding donors with sleepovers in the Lincoln Bedroom of the White House and similar perquisites triggered two congressional investigations and public demands for real campaign finance reform on Capitol Hill. Yet in spite of a public pledge between Clinton and then House Speaker Newt Gingrich to cooperate in bringing such reform about, the two major parties remained far apart on achieving it.

Perhaps the most depressing aspect of this whole story was that public-opinion polls showed that Americans generally were not sufficiently aroused to hold their elected representatives accountable for failing to address reform. There isn't a greater public demand for it, Bill Bradley says, "because people don't yet see it as a barricade issue." That is, they don't see "the connection between campaign contributions and regulatory rulings, tax loopholes or subsidies" that lower taxes for those who give the money. "Once those things go in" to the tax code, he says, "that means somebody's got to make up the difference. The rest of us make it up by having to pay higher taxes." And when the issue is posed in those terms, voters begin to realize "that money is one of the reasons the thermostat of democracy is broken . . . They petition [their elected officials], they write letters, but the temperature doesn't go up when they push the thermostat because money short-circuits it."

Nor were our representatives interested in putting teeth into the Federal Election Commission. Congress repeatedly failed to provide the appropriations the commission needed to function effectively and promptly. FEC reports on campaign finance occasionally made for interesting reading but seldom amounted to more than belated slaps on the wrist.

For example, in May 1997, seven months after the 1996 presidential campaign, the FEC levied fines of $15,000 against Bill Clinton's campaign for violations committed in 1992! These chicken-feed fines were assessed because—of all things—the campaign had taken months to reimburse staff workers and volunteers for $64,799 in expenses, which because of the delay, the FEC ruled, constituted illegal loans. Talk about locking the barn door after the horse is stolen! And not much of a horse at that. Meanwhile, other abuses of the 1992 campaign went undetected or unfined. The FEC sent "admonishment letters" to the Clinton campaign and the investment banking firm of Goldman Sachs after finding reason to believe the firm had made at least $58,525 in illegal contributions to the campaign by deeply discounting rented office space and holding loans that were tardily repaid. This in a campaign that, according to the FEC, raised and spent about $102 million.

After the 1996 election, FEC auditors recommended to the commission that the Dole campaign be obliged to pay $17.7 million, and the Clinton campaign $7 million, for improperly assigning certain advertisement and other candidate expenses to their respective parties. But partisan commission members ruled that the ads themselves were proper. The Dole repayment was cut to $3.7 million and Clinton's to a mere $143,000.

As the presidential election of the year 2000 approached, money continued to be the great distorter of equity and fairness in American politics. Any candidate who hoped to have a chance needed more and more money and, notably, more and more help from the high-priced army of political technocrats. But even as the need for more campaign money rose, the increasing public disaffection from politics threatened to handicap the candidates who had the hardest time raising money. In early 1998 the staff of the Federal Election Commission alerted the commission to the fact that voluntary taxpayer contributions for the federal subsidies were approaching rock bottom. In earlier years, only about 28 percent of taxpayers checked off a box on their annual income-tax returns to authorize one dollar to be given to the fund. That percentage steadily fell until, in 1993, Congress agreed to raise the voluntary checkoff amount to three dollars, and the contribution rate fell to a dismal 13 percent.

After setting aside funds for the party conventions and the fall presidential campaigns, as the law required, the Treasury Department was projected to have only $25 million at the start of the year 2000 to disburse to those candidates who by then raised at least $5,000 in each of twenty states. If one presumed that there would be at least ten candidates in the two major parties (actually there were fourteen by mid-1999), that would mean only $2.5 million available to each. By early 1999, the Democratic chairman of the FEC, Scott Thomas, was estimating that the Treasury Department could give the candidate only 32 cents (later raised to 39 cents) of every dollar to which they were entitled in the early subsidy payouts of 2000. Phil Gramm, who said in 1995 that any serious candidate would need at least $20 million to have a chance at the nomination, actually raised $28.8 million and still lost. Clearly $2.5 million is a pittance. Even if a candidate raised the matching $2.5 million, he would have only $5 million heading into the most critical early phase of the campaign, where success would rise or fall on his showings in the first caucuses and primaries.

Meanwhile, the self-financing Forbes, and Governor Bush, who raised $37 million on his own in the first half of 1999, announced they would forego the federal subsidy for the primaries—which freed them to ignore the federal spending limits. This practice can overwhelm the other Republican candidates who accept the reduced federal subsidy, forcing them to ponder whether they too should reject it and take their chances on raising more money unburdened by the federal limits. Others, daunted, reconsidered whether to stay in the race at all. One, Representative John Kasich of Ohio, did quit early.

Thus, at a time when so much is being said and written about the corrupting influence of money in presidential politics, the program of public financing that was supposed to reduce that influence is in danger of going broke, and of being deserted by candidates it was designed to help. Kent

Cooper says that abandoning public financing gives candidates "a tremendous amount of flexibility" in not having to obey financing regulations, and they might not be deterred by fear of public retribution for adopting a sky's-the-limit policy. No notable public revulsion to self-financing was seen during Forbes's campaign in 1996, Cooper notes, and Forbes could say, "Mine is cleaner; nobody's bought me," as indeed he did, and said again in approaching the 2000 campaign.

Considering the low public esteem for politics, the chances seem slim that Congress might agree to raise the income-tax checkoff contribution again, perhaps to five dollars. Meanwhile, presidential candidates must continue to spend an inordinate amount of time raising money to qualify for the matching subsidy, even though it may not be fully available.

One reason for the inadequate pool of money is that during the administration of George Bush, while he contemplated a reelection race in 1992, the Treasury Department decided to stop including in the pool an estimate of available revenue in the election year itself. This took millions of dollars out of the calculation in 1992, as it did again in 1996. Including tax-return checkoff money expected to be collected from election-year returns would go a long way toward solving the shortfall for 2000.

Another obvious solution would be to change the priorities in allocating the funds. When the plan first was adopted, the two major parties insisted that public money for national conventions be set aside before any candidate allocations were made. This priority is ridiculous on two counts. First, the conventions no longer are decisive in selecting the presidential nominees, which is supposed to be their primary function. In any case, the parties on their own raise millions of dollars through souvenir programs and a host of other gimmicks; they are well able to finance the conventions themselves. Second, changes in the calendar for delegate-selecting primaries and caucuses, with three-fourths or more of them moved up to the first two or three months of the election year, have put enormous additional financial pressures on the presidential candidates. As Wertheimer says: "The time frames of fund-raising are out of whack with the time frames of the nominating process. Candidates need more money earlier. You can't get matching money until January 1 of the election year for a race that is going to be decided from January to March." The FEC bureaucrats, he says, "aren't saying you can't have the money.

They're saying you can't have it when you need it. It's ridiculous." FEC chairman Thomas acknowledges that the Treasury Department is adamant against changing the allocation priorities.

Another remedy, supported by many Republicans, including former FEC chair Joan Aikens, and by Thomas, would be to raise the limit on individual contributions to a presidential candidate from $1,000 to $5,000, enabling the candidates to raise more money in less time and with less effort. Inasmuch as the $1,000 limit has been in effect for more than thirty years, such an increase would do little more than keep pace with the rising cost of living. It can be, and often is, argued that no presidential candidate raising millions of dollars will be corrupted by a contribution of $5,000.

A first step in reform, for which there has been substantial congressional support from both parties, was the call to ban soft money altogether, as proposed by Republican senator John McCain of Arizona and Democratic senator Russell Feingold of Wisconsin. But this idea was caught up from the start in arguments for more sweeping legislation. In 1997, Senate Majority Leader Trent Lott successfully stalled the McCain-Feingold bill by putting forth a version of his own that included what the Republicans called a "paycheck protection" provision, which would require written permission of union members for their dues to be used to support political candidates. The Democrats accurately labeled the proposal a "poison pill" designed to arouse organized labor opposition and drive Democratic support away from campaign finance reform. McCain and Feingold had a majority of the Senate behind their bill but were short of the three-fifths or 60 votes needed to cut off the filibuster certain to be brought by anti-reform Republicans led by Senator Mitch McConnell of Kentucky.

In 1998, when the McCain-Feingold bill got to the Senate floor again, Lott again attached his poison pill and again the legislation was blocked. Nevertheless, supporters in the House, with bipartisan leadership from Republican Christopher Shays of Connecticut and Democrat Martin Meehan of Massachusetts, pressed ahead with a very similar version. In the summer, they outmaneuvered delaying tactics used by Speaker Gingrich and won House approval, giving hope to reform advocates. But McCain and Feingold could not overcome Republican obstruction to their bill in the Senate. The advocates vowed to continue their fight for campaign finance reform, which now had majority support in both the House and Senate, but not enough to break the Republican roadblock via filibuster in the Senate.

Again in 1999, the House Democrats and McCain resumed their efforts to enact the same bill, but they encountered more Republican stalling tactics, leaving its fate in doubt.

The basis of the GOP opposition is obvious. Republicans, because of the greater wealth of their supporters and their more advanced and diligent techniques for tapping it, regularly raise considerably more money than the Democrats. Sponsors of reform may have to await Democratic recapture of the Senate to achieve their objective. Meanwhile, the "mother's milk of politics" continues to flow in defiance of laws riddled with loopholes that are sought out and exploited by the armies of hired guns in both parties.

6 ANYTHING GOES

Saying negative things about an opponent is a practice as old as politics itself. Thomas Jefferson was denounced by a Federalist foe as "a howling atheist." The bitterness between Alexander Hamilton and Aaron Burr led to a pistol duel that cost Hamilton his life. John Quincy Adams was accused (apparently correctly) of swapping the job of Secretary of State for the support of the presidential contender Henry Clay, leading Andrew Jackson, the loser, to dub Clay "the Judas of the West."

In the election of 1840, supporters of William Henry Harrison, hero of the battle of Tippecanoe, boosted him as a backwoods stalwart while rapping Martin Van Buren as a city dandy; the campaign song went: "Old Tip he wears a homespun suit, he has no ruffled shirt-wirt-wirt; But Mat he has the golden plate, and he's a little squirt-wirt-wirt"—followed by a spray of tobacco juice from the singer. In 1848, Daniel Webster called Zachary Taylor "an illiterate frontier colonel," and in 1892 Grover Cleveland was hounded with a taunt about his fathering of an illegitimate son: "Ma! Ma! Where's My Pa? Gone to the White House, Ha! Ha! Ha!" In the 1912 Republican primaries, Theodore Roosevelt and William Howard Taft traded such epithets as "demagogue," "fathead," and "apostate."

In 1916, the Democrats ran a newspaper ad in support of Woodrow Wilson and his slogan of "He Kept Us Out of War" against Charles Evans Hughes and Hughes's supporter Teddy Roosevelt: "You are working, not fighting! Alive and happy, not cannon fodder! Wilson and peace with honor? Or Hughes with Roosevelt and war?" And in 1948, Thomas E. Dewey, the stiff and proper Republican challenger to Harry Truman, was demeaned by Roosevelt's daughter, Alice Longworth, as "the little man on the wedding cake."

In 1952, the Republican vice presidential nominee, Richard Nixon, railed at the Democratic presidential nominee, Adlai Stevenson, for being inheritor of a Truman legacy of "Communism, Korea, and corruption," only to be thrown on the defensive himself when it was revealed that he benefited from what the Democrats called a "secret slush fund" from California supporters. Nixon blamed the furor on "the Communists and the crooks in government" out to smear him. In 1956, Stevenson, the repeat Democratic presidential nominee, renowned for his courtesy and decorum but stymied once again in opposing the aging national hero Dwight D. Eisenhower, hinted at the president's mortality and leveled his sights on his vice president. In a televised election-eve speech, he intoned: "I must say bluntly that every piece of scientific evidence we have, every lesson on history and experience, indicates that a Republican victory tomorrow would mean that Richard Nixon would probably be president of this country within the next four years. I say frankly as a citizen more than a candidate that I recoil at the prospect of Mr. Nixon as custodian of this nation's future, as guardian of the hydrogen bomb, as representative of America in the world, as commander-in-chief of the United States armed forces."

None of these remarks, however, compared to the vitriol that came with the advent of heavy television advertising in behalf of presidential candidates in the 1960s. The unprecedented opportunity to reach mass audiences of voters in their own living rooms brought forth a new concentration on what the emerging corps of professional consultants called "paid media"—and a gradually developing focus on negative attacks.

At first, however, this approach was relatively prudent. Standard strategy called for a candidate to establish his own positive qualifications before venturing to say anything negative about his opponent. The idea was that unless voters first had a reason to respect a candidate for his own strengths, he could not persuasively convince them of his opponent's weaknesses. And besides, it was considered foolhardy even to mention a little-known opponent's name and thus give him more identification with the voters. Furthermore, if negative attacks were deemed necessary at all, it was thought they should be reserved for the end of the campaign, when desperate measures were called for to snatch victory from defeat—and when it would be too late for the attacked candidate to defend himself.

Negative ads were quite mild compared to today's products. "We didn't talk about people's genitals and their bedrooms," Matt Reese recalled. At first such ads were used sparingly and with supreme caution, if not timidity. In the 1964 presidential campaign, the famous "daisy commercial" was pulled after only one airing. It showed a little girl picking a daisy as a voice was heard counting down from ten to zero. Then a mushroom cloud replaced the girl as President Lyndon Johnson's voice intoned: "These are the stakes: to make a world in which all of God's children can live, or go into the dark. We must either love each other or we must die." There was no mention of LBJ's Republican opponent, Barry Goldwater, but the clear intention was to suggest Goldwater's reputation as a trigger-happy gunslinger impervious to the perils of nuclear war. It was taken off the air because there was an immediate outcry from Republicans, but the ad—created by a New Yorker named Tony Schwartz—is remembered to this day as the prototype of the negative commercial.

Two other television ads for Johnson in that campaign, made by Doyle Dane Bernbach, were more explicit. One, also used only once, showed a little girl licking an ice-cream cone while a woman's voice told of the dangers of nuclear fallout and mentioned Goldwater's opposition to President Kennedy's earlier ban on atmospheric nuclear tests. The other showed two hands tearing up a Social Security card—a reminder of Goldwater's earlier musings about making the old-age retirement program voluntary.

In 1968, Hubert Humphrey's campaign, playing on Republican vice presidential nominee Spiro Agnew's lack of experience and his well-earned reputation as a hatchet man, ran an ad in which one heard first the sound of a thumping heart and then a voice intoning: "Imagine Spiro T. Agnew a heartbeat away from the presidency." Another was a television ad with a long soundtrack of laughter followed by a simple question on the screen: "Agnew for President?" But according to Lawrence O'Brien, then Humphrey's campaign manager, "we canceled it after getting protests from our own people that it was too tough and might backfire." The Humphrey campaign also considered running television commercials using film from Nixon's maudlin "Checkers" speech of 1952 and his "last press conference" in 1962 after being defeated for governor in California, in which he proclaimed to the press, "You won't have Nixon to kick around anymore." But in the end, according to Joe Napolitan, a media consultant for the Humphrey campaign, it was decided to do neither for fear they might draw sympathy for Nixon and resentment of Humphrey.

By the 1980s, all such caution was disappearing. Basic axioms in the old handbook such as attacking an opponent only late in a campaign and out of desperation had come to be considered naive and even laughable. "Going negative" today is more often than not used at the very start of a campaign, to throw an opponent on the defensive and keep him there. It's euphemistically referred to as "defining" one's opponent before he has a chance to define himself.

This axiom was most forcefully demonstrated by George Bush's campaign in 1988 against Massachusetts governor Michael Dukakis, the most negative presidential campaign of the television era, at least up to that time. Dukakis, who was ahead in the polls after the Democratic convention that had nominated him, imprudently went back home to Massachusetts to attend to state business and rest before starting the fall campaign. During the resultant political vacuum, Bush's hired guns rushed to define Dukakis in their own terms. First, they attacked his having vetoed a state law that would have required public-school teachers to lead the Pledge of Allegiance to the flag in their classrooms. Dukakis had acted on the basis of a state supreme court advisory that such a law would unconstitutionally abridge freedom of speech. But in short order, Bush was flag-waving with gusto, visiting a flag factory in New Jersey at one point to demonstrate his own patriotism—and implying that Dukakis didn't respect the Stars and Stripes.

Second, the Bush strategists seized on an event that had come to light during the Democratic primaries—from Democratic challenger Al Gore, in fact. A convicted murderer named Willie Horton, released under a Massachusetts prison furlough program during Dukakis' tenure, had fled to Maryland and committed rape there. The furlough program was used in many states, including California while Ronald Reagan was governor. But Lee Atwater, Bush's campaign manager, pounced on the story as a way to suggest that Dukakis was soft on serious criminals and insensitive toward their victims. In a speech to the Texas Republican convention, Bush castigated his rival for permitting "unsupervised weekend furloughs to first-degree murderers," a claim that was soon sharpened to letting "murderers out on vacation to terrorize innocent people . . . even after one of them criminally, brutally raped a woman and stabbed her fiancé." Soon the Bush campaign aired an ad known as "the Revolving Door," produced under the aegis of Roger Ailes, a consultant first prominent for coaching Nixon in his carefully staged televised "town meetings" in 1968. The ad showed a prison guard and a long line of convicts walking through a steel revolving gate, while a narrator said, "Governor Michael Dukakis vetoed mandatory sentences for drug dealers. He vetoed the death penalty. His revolving-door prison policy gave weekend furloughs to first-degree murderers not eligible for parole. While out, many committed other crimes like kidnapping and rape, and many are still at large. Now Michael Dukakis says he wants to do for America what he has done for Massachusetts. America can't afford that risk."

Democrats and many editorialists around the country charged that the ad was racist, since Horton was black, to which Ailes replied that Horton had not been shown in it. But some supporting Republican groups were not so subtle. The state party committee in Illinois circulated a flier that told voters: "All the murderers and rapists and drug pushers and child molesters in Massachusetts vote for Michael Dukakis. We in Illinois can vote against him." In Maryland, a Republican fund-raising letter included photographs of Dukakis and Horton and asked: "Is this your pro-family team for 1988?" The College Republican National Committee printed and distributed yellow "Get Out of Jail Free" cards in the style of the ones used in the Monopoly board game that recited the Willie Horton story, ending: "In the last several years, Mike Dukakis has furloughed more than one murderer a day. Mike Dukakis is the killer's best friend, and the decent, honest citizens' worst enemy." Also, an independent group calling itself the National Security Political Action Committee ran a television spot with a picture of Horton.

After the election, Ailes made a modest career of dressing down news organizations that said he was the creator of what now was often called "the Willie Horton ad." He continued to point out that no ad he produced either pictured or mentioned Horton, but the Horton story had clearly been the inspiration, and Ailes's crocodile tears were as artful as his product.

To all the hammering, Dukakis at first merely turned the other cheek, convinced that voters would not be swayed by the negativism of the attack, and he refused to respond in kind. The attacks went largely unanswered, as Dukakis ignored the basic political axiom in the television era that an attack unanswered is an attack believed. His lead in the polls quickly vanished. Finally he demanded, futilely, that Bush do something about the attack ads. "When you throw garbage in the street," he said at one point, "you've got the responsibility to go out there and clean it up." Bush and his advisers ignored him.

The use of ridicule and fear is old hat in politics, but the new visual dimension in television offered opportunities that no one could pass up, especially professional manipulators of public opinion. Bob Teeter suggests that campaign consultants who think and operate "like star defense lawyers" contribute greatly to negative campaigns. Like lawyers, he says, they operate on the premise that their job "is to do whatever it takes for their client to win," and they do it.

Two years before the Bush-Dukakis campaign, actually, the old axiom that negative attacks should be reserved for late in a campaign had already been discarded, in favor of "defining" an opponent early. In 1986 in California, a young moderate Republican congressman named Ed Zschau won a tough primary fight for the right to challenge veteran Democratic senator Alan Cranston. For the last five weeks of the primary period, Cranston's media strategists—then the consultant team of David Doak and Bob Shrum—had run positive ads about him. But on the very next morning after the primaries, Cranston's campaign began running television ads attacking Zschau, to the shock of many in the political community who were aware that this tactic ran counter to the conventional wisdom. Doak, recalling that campaign later, explained why that unorthodox step was taken. Cranston had been state controller for ten years and in the U.S. Senate for eighteen, and "everyone had an opinion of him. So we thought while we might marginally move the voters a little here and a little there, that they'd had a lifetime, really, to judge Alan. This was really more of a decision about who his opponent was. And if there were enough people who disliked Alan, and Zschau was able to establish himself as a young, moderate, farsighted Republican from the Silicon Valley, thoughtful and everything, that he'd probably beat Alan. So we thought we had one chance, which was to define Zschau before Zschau defined himself."

Doak recalled that "we had a huge debate about it that raged for two or three weeks, and we knew it was risky. Somebody said to me, 'You realize, we have to disqualify this guy if we adopt this strategy.' There was some fear that you could run this negative and be left holding the bag at the end [if you hadn't] disqualified him. Alan in a sense was a safe choice [for voters]. Everybody didn't like him but he was acceptable. The only question was, was there someone they liked better? That campaign really changed the strategic landscape and it certainly opened the door for earlier negative advertising.

"The ads weren't really mean-spirited. We attacked him mostly [for] flip-flopping, [for] changing positions. Zschau was a moderate-to-liberal Republican, a Silicon Valley type, who to win the Republican primary against a right-winger, changed some of his positions and became more conservative."

It turned out that California voters may have started out liking Ed Zschau better than they liked Alan Cranston, but after the negative ads worked their magic, they liked Zschau less, and Cranston was reelected to a fourth Senate term.

Mike Murphy says that the idea to "mug them coming out of the primary when they're vulnerable" was current with other people in other places. It caught on quickly, he says, and now "it's very much standard practice to jump people out of primaries. We tend to look at these things as two glasses of water. You want to fill your own glass with a liquid of your choice, and you want to fill their glass with mud." Or, as Bob Squier prefers to put it: "If you know of something you believe disqualifies your opponent, it's your democratic obligation to bring it to the voters."

In those days, ad makers used what was known as the "weather-vane ad," which showed a picture of a candidate spinning from one position to another, and variations of it. This technique eventually developed, with new cinematic technology, into the use of "morph ads," in which the opposition candidate would be seen "metamorphosing" into someone else, either his opponent or some other unpopular politician on a given issue or a series of them.

Among the first to use this technique in a statewide race was Murphy as media consultant and strategist for Republican Senate candidate Spencer Abraham of Michigan in 1994. The opponent, Democratic representative Bob Carr, wanted to succeed retiring Democratic senator Don Riegle, who was under fire in the savings-and-loan scandal of that time. Murphy's ads had Carr "morphing" into Riegle as a narrator recited positions they shared. Murphy hired a freelance crew to go to the Democratic state convention and film Carr and Riegle standing together. The purpose of the ad, Murphy explained later, was to suggest that the more moderate Carr "was just like Riegle. We had him and Riegle standing next to each other and we had them morphing back and forth. And our negative slogan was: 'Carr is everything that's wrong with Washington.' It was '94, a great year to run against D.C."

Although Murphy has a reputation as a master of negative campaign ads, he insists he uses them only when appropriate. "I think a lot of people are awfully quick to pull the trigger, to run a negative zero-sum campaign," he says. "Unfortunately and tragically, the voters tend to reward negative campaigns. The voters love 'em. They say they don't, but they reward them."

In place of the old axiom for a campaign manager to establish your own candidate positively before saying anything negative against your opponent, Murphy says, "The rule now is in most cases make sure you do a good preemptive job. Voters have become so cynical that they believe negative information more than positive information. So politicians aren't shy. We give 'em what they want. That's the nature of the business, unfortunately. There used to be more strategic elegance in campaigns. Now it's often becoming just megatonnage of ads. How much money you have, and go very negative."

At the same time, Murphy says, the news media's fact checking of ads is weak and the general belief is that no ads tell the truth. There is, he says, a general "dumbing down" of political coverage, which also encourages more negative advertising to reach an increasingly "dumber" public. "So now instead of an elegant strategy, what you really need is five thousand gross rating points of negative commercials in the last five weeks," he says. "Most people I know who are at the top of this business are spending a lot of time trying to get out of it. We're all doing more corporate work, because the campaigns are less and less fun . . . It's just a cheapening of the political dialogue."

Murphy notes that "the good government crowd would point and say, 'You consultants have made it worse.' Well, I don't know if that's true. Voters tend to reward what they want. They vote for what they want and sometimes they get it."

The new technology that makes it possible to "turn around" an ad quickly—that is, take one off the air and replace it with a new one—is an important facilitator of negative campaigning, Squier says. Because an unanswered assertion is an assertion agreed to, it is vital to respond swiftly to any charge. Once, "it was like World War I. We'd do our polls, they'd do their polls. We'd make twelve spots, they'd make twelve spots. We'd fire them off against each other for about three weeks, then we'd stay up all night on election night and see who'd won. It was trench warfare." Now, when a time buyer alerts campaign headquarters that the opposition has put a new ad on the air at noon, the ad can be transmitted by computer and analyzed, a response prepared and screened by the candidate wherever he is, then transmitted by satellite to replace the old ad in time for nighttime airing.

Doak says the Watergate scandal created a public climate conducive to negative advertising. "Prior to Watergate," he says, "people always presumed the best about their leaders. Watergate was the pivotal event that made negative campaigning work. After Watergate, the presumption switched. The bloom was off the rose and people were more cynical and willing to believe the worst about their leaders." But John Deardourff, who along with his partner Doug Bailey comprised one of the most respected Republican consulting teams in the 1970s, worked mostly for moderate Republicans. He argues that the public distrust in politicians goes back to the time of the Vietnam War and the chaotic presidential election of 1968. "The disillusionment and cynicism were established then," he says, "and feeding on that [was] the whole phenomenon of Reagan and his clearly anti-government message—that government was too big, too wasteful, and so forth. It fanned the flames and left people running for office with very little to say that was positive and pro-government."

Negative campaigning and negative advertising found fertile ground in this political environment, Deardourff says, and it was impossible to buck them. He recalls the effort in Pennsylvania in 1986 when Republican gubernatorial candidate William Scranton, son of the former governor and 1964 presidential candidate, declared less than three weeks before his contest against Democratic nominee Bob Casey that he was pulling all his negative ads off the air. Obviously he hoped revulsion against negative advertising would accrue to his benefit. He had not gotten into the race to attack Casey, and he jumped 6 or 7 percent in the polls when he said so.

Unknown to Scranton, however, the state Republican Party began sending out direct-mail letters that attacked Casey, leading *his* consultant, James Carville, to call Scranton a hypocrite. "It blew the whole thing for us," Deardourff says. Casey's campaign piled on with ads against Scranton that claimed he had used drugs in his college days. "In a way," Deardourff recalls, "it launched Carville on the idea that this negative stuff worked. It continues to work. I don't see any subsiding." He suggests now that to achieve what Scranton wanted in that race, "it will almost take somebody at the national level" to swear off negative advertising, and make sure he is not blindsided as Scranton was.

Dick Morris, the deposed Clinton strategist, agrees that public disillusionment and cynicism bred negative campaigning but says its effectiveness is often overstated. Listen to the thought process of the ultimate hired gun as he explains how, he believes, Clinton's campaign in 1996 turned Dole's negative attacks against him:

"When a politician throws a negative and can't back it up, can't prove it, or it turns out it's distorted or inaccurate, he destroys his own campaign. He not only loses the issue, he loses his credibility. In the '96 race, after we made our positive points, our comparative points about Medicare, budget, and all that, our strategy, as soon as the Republicans came on the air, was a deliberate defensive strategy. The way I phrased it at the time was: We have told these people that we're not liberals, that we're moderates, and we've told these people we're New Democrats. Now we need to take all of Dole's attacks and rebut them, so that in the crucible of controversy, we are right about characterizing ourselves, and nobody can prove that we're not. We have to sit back and let Dole have the initiative for three months; let him attack us with everything he has, and defeat each attack and counterpunch over credibility."

Dole's campaign began with criticism of Clinton for his statements that he would balance the budget in between five and ten years, so the Clinton strategists, Morris says, "replied with ads that talked about how we had brought the deficit down steadily and wanted to balance the budget." When Dole then attacked Clinton for his immigration policy and for the national drug problem, Clinton ads countered by discussing strengthened border guard forces and reduced crime and drug rates.

This strategy, Morris says, was the same as the much-ballyhooed "rapid response" tactic of another Clinton political mastermind, Carville, in the 1992 campaign, except "the rapid response plays to a very small inside community focusing on that news flow." His own effort in 1996, Morris says, was "national paid media that everybody in the country [was] seeing."

Morris acknowledges that "sometimes the negative works [against you] because you are caught with your hand in the cookie jar, but most of the time the negatives are not that effective . . . They work, but they make you incredibly vulnerable." For this reason, "the process becomes self-policing. Inaccurate negative ads increasingly blow up on the person throwing them. And the idea that the truth is too complicated to get it out in a response is just wrong. If you're good at this thing, you can say anything in thirty seconds."

The time when the vulnerability of negative ads to rebuttal outweighs their effectiveness clearly has not come, however, for most consultants. Doak says that he explains to candidates who are reluctant to use negative advertising, "Imagine you're interviewing somebody for a job. You have ten references and the first nine say he's honorable, but the tenth says he's dishonest. You may not believe it, but you say to yourself, 'Why take the risk?' That's what voters do." The operating principle behind negative ads is that if you can raise one doubt, you can erase all the positive information the voters have. This concept, Doak says, "has become the framework by which people who have less resources are able to win. In a sense it's one of the good things about negative—it's an equalizer. Because if we just had a positive campaign rule, then only the rich people would win. Now, there's a lot wrong about negative that I don't like; that's one of the good things I do like."

Younger people in the business, Doak says, are probably more inclined to use negative advertising because "they probably can't remember the day when you didn't do any of it or did very little of it. It has become sort of a sport—almost a blood-sport feeling—among some of the younger folks." He sees this as the most significant difference between his and younger generations. "I don't say I'm any better than anybody else, but I think we see the purpose differently. It's a business for me too, but I've always thought of myself as having a philosophy." Still, he acknowledges, he isn't indifferent to the opportunity to work for a free-spending candidate. But he adds: "I only have one rule in this business. I don't go to jail for anybody."

Bob Shrum argues that "consultants are only instruments" candidates use to get done whatever it takes to win. He says many of the younger consultants resort early to negative advertising because "it's easier. It's harder to do positive ads. But negatives don't work as well without a positive foundation."

Ray Strother agrees. "People who got [into the media consulting business] without the talent and skill looked around and tried to understand how people won elections or lost elections. Negative advertising looked like an easy vehicle to do it with. I think it's just a knee-jerk thing." Today, he says, "people are basing all their decisions on television. The idea is, somebody's going to tell the voters who this guy is. Do you want it on your terms or his? I'm going to define my opponent before he defines himself. The defining of your opponent is as important as your definition of your own candidate. There's always a yin and yang to it. If you run too much, your own negatives go up. But if a candidate insulates himself well, and people have a good impression of him, it rolls off him."

The key to Clinton's victory in 1992, Strother says, was the positive advertisements his campaign ran during the New Hampshire primary, when he was being bombarded with the accusations of Gennifer Flowers and questions about his draft record. In those ads, he notes, Clinton introduced a specific plan for economic recovery, which was popular with voters at a time of lingering recession. They allowed Clinton, finishing second to Paul Tsongas, to present himself successfully as a self-styled "comeback kid."

On the other hand, Shrum observes, Steve Forbes in 1996 began with "a hopeful message" but made the mistake of having negative advertising specialists do his ads. Forbes, Shrum says, "was the perfect candidate to run positive ads. He had something to say—a big idea." Under those circumstances, he says, going negative "is totally wrong and basically will be punished in time by voters throwing out the irrelevant. Voters are getting much, much better at sorting out."

When allegations of illegality are made about candidates, such as the Whitewater and other accusations against Clinton in 1996, Shrum says his response is: " 'Take it to the DA. Don't bother me with it.' And I think that is also the public's reaction: 'If something is wrong, let the authorities take care of it. I can't sort it out.' " New tricks surface with every campaign. In the 1996 Republican primary in New Hampshire, Pat Buchanan's campaign accused Dole of using "push polls," a device to spread rumor and lies about an opponent by pretending to conduct legitimate voter surveys. Callers identifying themselves as representing "National Research" in Houston asked voters whether they would still vote for Buchanan if they knew that the candidate was anti-women and favored "arming the armies of Taiwan, South Korea, and Japan with nuclear weapons." The Dole people denied having anything to do with the callers.

There were other reports of this device being used in other campaigns. Twenty Republican and fourteen Democratic pollsters signed a protest letter to the American Association of Political Consultants complaining that "the rapid rise in the use of 'push-polling' as a campaign tactic has led to significant confusion between advocacy calling and legitimate survey research."

They asked the association to publicize the unethical aspects of the technique—the infrequent identification of the sponsor of the polls, usually thirty-second or sixty-second quickies, the "negative persuasion phone calls that should not be referred to as 'polling' in any form." The spotlight on the practice quelled it for a time, but there was no certainty that it might not be used again in the 2000 campaign.

As for negative campaigning, it began early for the 2000 cycle. In advance of a Republican straw poll in Iowa in August 1999, an underfunded Lamar Alexander ran a television ad in which a "television reporter" announced: "This just in—the Iowa caucuses have been cancelled. An auction is under way on the White House lawn," with Alexander adding that the presidency is "too important to be bought or inherited"—an unsubtle dig at Bush, the well-heeled son of a former president, and Forbes. More of the same was certain to follow from other candidates.

Doak says, however, that technological advances may be diminishing the ability of hired guns to deliver negative messages, simply because the old captive audiences of television are less captive now. In earlier days, he says, "the beauty of television was, especially before you had remote controls, [voters] watched that commercial and they sat there." Now, with remotes available with all television sets, and with more and more channels, voters can easily escape the political ads if they choose.

Deardourff offers one of the most significant criticisms of negative campaigning. Not only does it depress voter turnout on Election Day, he says, but "it makes it more difficult [for a winner] to govern. It leaves people with a diminished view of everybody in politics. It leaves the [politicians] crippled, so badly beaten up that it's difficult to get a toehold [in office] and be believable."

Campaign managers and consultants will tell you they deplore using negative tactics and television advertising but they are obliged to do so because "it works," and there is ample evidence of the truth of the contention. Even Stuart Spencer, a pioneer consultant, says, "My biggest problem is, goddamnit, it works, and I can't hold it against consultants if it works." Whether one credits this effectiveness to the hired guns or not, it is clear that the much more aggressive "anything goes" attitude in presidential politics has paralleled their emergence. Wertheimer identifies the use of thirty-second attack ads, replacing positive ads as long as five minutes, as a key culprit. "It has changed the language and tone of the debate," he says. He proposes some kind of incentive to return to the longer ads and perhaps to provide free television time to candidates who appear live on their own commercials and take responsibility for them.

The very language used to describe presidential campaigns has become more inflammatory. In earlier years, it was commonplace to speak of presidential campaigns, and politics in general, in terms of sporting events. There were winners and losers, campaign managers and teams. The "horse race" was "handicapped" by public-opinion pollsters and the news media; in the debates you were in a contestant's "corner" as you mapped strategy for a "knockout" of your foe or at least "a draw." You sought a "level playing field," and when a number of presidential primaries were to be held on a single day, that day was called "Super Bowl Tuesday" (later shortened to "Super Tuesday"). The language of politics was the language of sports.

But as tactics have become more pointed, harsher, more ruthless and deceptive, the language of politics has become the language of war. Candidates who venture early into the first presidential primaries and caucuses are compared to guerrillas infiltrating the grass roots, often sending young political operatives into the countryside to "live off the land"—sleeping on the living-room sofas of local supporters and grubbing meals from them. They engage in money wars of attrition, trying to drive opponents from the battlefield by raising the cost of competing and outspending them on television. Doak explains: "You don't win by talking about a little bit of everything. You win races by massing your forces at the point of attack. That's one of the classic Clausewitz principles."

The field generals and combat commanders of American politics are increasingly Hessians—political soldiers for hire who wage political battle in whatever cause pays their way, and who are willing to use whatever weapons are required to achieve victory. At a postelection seminar on the 1996 presidential campaign at Harvard's Institute of Politics, Tony Fabrizio, a campaign pollster and strategist for Senator Dole when he ran for the presidency, talked of having researched the background of retired General Colin Powell at the time when Powell was said to be considering a candidacy for the Republican presidential nomination. A questioner, referring to the harshly negative campaign that Steve Forbes had waged against Dole, asked Fabrizio whether "you were prepared to do to Powell what you say Forbes was doing to you."

Fabrizio unhesitatingly replied: "Exactly what we did to Forbes [in return] and [Lamar] Alexander . . . Absolutely. All is fair in love and war."

This attitude was by no means new. Twelve years earlier, in 1984, when Ronald Reagan's reelection campaign manager, Lee Atwater, submitted a long strategy paper to his candidate, he prefaced it with two quotations, not from some eminent political leaders of the past but from two of the great warlords of history, Sun Tzu and Napoleon Bonaparte. From Sun Tzu's *The Art of War*: "The military arts are like unto water; for water in its natural course runs away from high places and hastens downwards. So in war, then, to avoid what is strong is to strike what is weak. Water shapes its course according to the ground over which it flows; the soldier works out his victory in relation to the foe whom he is facing." In other words, seek your opponent's greatest vulnerability, and when you have found it, exploit it any way you can. And from Napoleon: "The whole art of war consists in a well-reasoned and extremely circumspect defensive, followed by rapid and audacious attack." In the same 1984 campaign, the late Paul Tully, an intensely loyal Democratic partisan who was a key adviser to the Democratic presidential nominee, Walter Mondale, observed at the time the "anything goes" mind-set of the hired guns in that campaign: "The mentality around here was, 'Crush people. Crush campaigns. Crush candidates. Crush 'em.' "

This equating of politics with war was at the core of the thinking that led to the Watergate break-in in 1972, when Richard Nixon's campaign was determined not only to defeat his weak opponent, Democrat George McGovern, but to annihilate him politically. And that same mentality appeared to be at work in the relentless excesses in fund-raising and spending in Bill Clinton's 1996 reelection campaign against his demonstrably weak challenger, Bob Dole. In the next presidential campaign, especially with all the money involved, once again it will be "anything goes," to the detriment of public confidence in politics and in its practitioners at the highest level.

7 The 800-Pound Gorilla

With money more than ever the driving force in presidential politics, its prime consumer is television. Presidential campaign budgets are heavily weighted to spending for television advertising, and the campaigns themselves are orchestrated to draw maximum television coverage.

The fund-raising excesses of the Clinton-Gore campaign in 1995–96, as already noted, were dictated by the White House's belief that only a saturation television advertising effort could resurrect the political fortunes of the incumbent president after the 1994 Republican takeover of Congress. Television offered a unique opportunity to Clinton-Gore strategists like Dick Morris to smother the public consciousness with messages about a reformed Bill Clinton cured of the perceived liberal excesses of his first term. The Clinton team seized that opportunity just as the Gingrich revolution was destroying itself with such foolhardy policies as allowing the shutdown of all but the most essential federal government activities at the end of 1995.

In the 1996 campaign, Democratic and Republican candidates all tailored their bids for the White House to the demands and preferences of television, and the national political parties shaped and shrank the schedules of their conventions to accommodate the dominant television networks. And, as had been the case ever since television arrived in presidential campaigning in 1952, the rest of the news media was largely shunted aside, as politicians rushed to court the cameras, and the men and women who wielded them and offered commentary on the pictures.

In 1952, both party conventions were heavily covered by television news teams, including credentials committee hearings at the Republican event. This visual coverage showed Americans the strongarm tactics being used by the conservative forces backing Senator Robert A. Taft of Ohio, to the advantage of the Eastern Establishment camp of Dwight D. Eisenhower. Millions of voters around the country were engrossed by the proceedings in both parties, and they had front-row seats in their own living rooms to watch as the presidential campaign unfolded. The coverage techniques were primitive, as were the first political television commercials. But presidential campaigns, it was clear, would never be the same again.

The power of television as a political force was demonstrated particularly in the controversy surrounding Eisenhower's running mate, the junior senator from California, who was found to have been the recipient of a "secret fund" from business interests that helped him pay for his travel as a senator. The uproar from Democrats, and some Republicans who wanted Nixon off the ticket, produced Nixon's famous television speech in which he defended himself and his acceptance of a little dog named Checkers given to one of his daughters. Nixon deftly asked viewers to let the Republican National Committee know whether they thought he should quit the ticket or stay on, and the positive reaction overwhelmed opposition within Eisenhower's camp. The presidential candidate summoned Nixon and embraced him in a scene of high drama that made optimum political use of the powerful new communications vehicle, and removed any last barrier to an Eisenhower-Nixon landslide.

In 1956, television also contributed to the political rise of Senator John F. Kennedy, when cameras captured the exciting drama of the selection of a running mate for Adlai Stevenson. The Democratic presidential nominee had thrown the choice to the convention, and the choice came down to Estes Kefauver or Kennedy. Kefauver narrowly won, but the television exposure for the photogenic and charismatic Kennedy helped ignite interest in him as a presidential candidate four years later.

Television increasingly dominated other aspects of presidential politics. In 1960, the first televised debates between Kennedy and Nixon drove up voter interest and were probably the key factor in Kennedy's narrow election victory. "It was the first time," says Hal Bruno, retired political director of ABC News, "that the candidate who could handle television beat the candidate who couldn't. And today that has become the standard. If candidates can't master the art and techniques of television, they're not going to be successful in modern American politics, with possibly a few exceptions. People will say, 'Well, that's unfair,' but it's the way it is, just as in the 1930s and 1940s FDR showed how radio could be used. Television has just overwhelmed politics, and politics has changed in order to take advantage of television, to make use of this medium that enables you instantly to reach millions of people."

In succeeding presidential elections, television cameras captured dramatic developments during the primaries, at the conventions, in the new genres of political advertisement, and in a range of developments that affected voter attitudes at home and abroad. On November 22, 1963, it brought the shocking scenes of Kennedy's assassination in Dallas into America's living rooms, along with the great public national mourning that followed. Voters saw Vice President Lyndon Johnson being sworn in as president, leaving the vice presidency vacant for the fifteenth time in the history of the Republic. (Congress decided something had to be done. It enacted the Twenty-fifth Amendment, which provided in the event of a vacancy in the vice presidency that the president nominate a replacement, subject to confirmation by a majority vote of both houses of Congress.)

In 1964, the television cameras conveyed the raucous scene at the Republican convention in San Francisco when the nominee, Barry Goldwater, declared that "extremism in the pursuit of liberty is no vice," a comment that helped seal his defeat at Johnson's hands.

In 1968, television brought into American homes the dramatic embarrassment that Senator Eugene McCarthy inflicted on Johnson in the New Hampshire primary; Johnson's surprising announcement that he would not seek reelection; the assassinations of Martin Luther King, Jr., and six weeks later, Robert Kennedy, and all the national traumas in their wake. Nightly visions of the war in Vietnam and the protests against it at home were soon followed by scenes of the police riot against anti-war demonstrators in Chicago during the Democratic National Convention.

For more than five years by then, television had pounded the Vietnam War into the sensibilities of Americans. So powerful had the medium become that it was the declaration of the war's futility, not by a politician, general, or cabinet member but by the network anchorman Walter Cronkite after a visit there in 1968, that was widely credited with effectively crystallizing public discontent over American participation in the Indochina war.

Richard Nixon's presidential campaign of 1968 was the first to appreciate fully what television had done to American politics and, as noted earlier, to tailor the candidate's schedule to the camera. The whole focus of Nixon's campaign day was his carefully scripted morning or midday speech, or some other event that looked good on television taking place at an airport rally in a city with ready airline connections to New York, so that footage could be swiftly and reliably transported to network headquarters. And then, from 1972 to 1974, from the break-in at Democratic National Committee headquarters in Watergate to the resignation of the disgraced Richard Nixon, television dominated the political agenda of Americans. The televised Senate Select Committee hearings concerning the break-in and the subsequent White House cover-up of its involvement, and the House Judiciary Committee hearings considering Nixon's impeachment, brought the seamiest side of presidential politics to the American people.

But it was television's impact on the political process itself that was most significant and in some ways most destructive. In television's first years, it had been a relatively unobtrusive observer, recording events as they unfolded on the campaign trail, in the state primaries and caucuses, at the national conventions, and in the fall campaigns. But as candidates and their paid consultants came to appreciate the political value of extensive television coverage and shaped their campaign strategies and events to draw it, the "visuals" of what a candidate did, and where and how he did it, often became more important than what he said. The "photo opportunity" became commonplace and the press conference a relative rarity.

"The traits that the old-style orators and politicians used to value no longer work on television and therefore no longer work in a national campaign," Sam Donaldson of ABC News says. "When I started, you guys in print controlled the main communications flow and the politicians played to you and your deadlines. I remember going to these big Goldwater speeches at large auditoriums past the evening news deadlines but in time for the late editions of all the morning papers. That doesn't happen anymore. All the [campaign] deadlines are skewed toward television's purposes. But it's not just that. It is that the values that work on television were not ones you had to have when you did it in a retail fashion."

In pretelevision days, Squier says, "there was basically one channel of communication, other than getting hold of a pair of ears live in a speech or a debate, and that was through newspapers. So it had to go out of the candidate's mouth, into your ears, through your pen, onto a notepad, and then you would figure out how to interpret that for a newspaper story. Radio, and then television, blew up that system forever, so you begin to have the sound bite on radio and then the sound bite on television, and then the picture on television. And you began to have a much richer experience in terms of the senses. It may also be a debased experience in terms of the issues, but you also want to know what sort of person this is—it's always a great question mark. That's very difficult to do by just reading his speeches. You may have just determined what kind of person his speechwriter is."

Candidates, Hal Bruno agrees, see the great advantage of going to the voters unfiltered by the writing press. "They are not fools," he says. "Successful candidates have learned how to deal with television. Conventions are staged for television. We criticize the parties for doing it, but we would criticize them for being stupid if they didn't. Any party [in the television era] that has had a raucous convention has ended up losing the election."

That certainly was true of the Republican convention in 1964 at the Cow Palace outside San Francisco, which nominated Barry Goldwater in a tumultuous embrace of "extremism in the defense of liberty" and menacingly hostile shouts and gestures toward the press gallery. And it was even more true of the Democratic convention in 1968 in Chicago's International Amphitheater that dejectedly chose Hubert Humphrey as police pummeled and tear-gassed demonstrators in downtown streets and parks.

As television achieved dominance in presidential campaigns, print reporters—"the pencil press," in the dismissive phrase of many hired guns—found themselves reduced to being spear carriers in the extravaganzas staged to lure the film, later the video, camera's blinking eye. Candidates learned to time events for the convenience and schedules of the camera-toting network grunts, even waiting for them to show up when they were late and demolishing their own schedules in the process. Print reporters, whose deadlines had no flexibility, had to wait around for the action to start.

Candidates who had already conducted a spontaneous, newsworthy event or made an important spontaneous remark sometimes even repeated the event or remark for cameramen who turned up later. When a cameraman ran out of film in the middle of a news conference, the candidate might obligingly halt in mid-sentence and wait for him to reload. No such courtesy ever accompanied the breaking of a point on the yellow No. 2 equipment manned by "the pencil press."

Terence Smith, who became a CBS correspondent in 1985 and later a media reporter for PBS' *NewsHour* after twenty years as a reporter for *The New York Times*, immediately noted the difference. A candidate would return his call requesting an interview more quickly, he says: "In his eye, it is very important for him to make his forceful, bold, and statesmanlike statement on the evening news in his own voice, in his own image. More important than if you get it down on your pad and send it out to your readers. That is [their] perception. That's why you get your phone calls answered more rapidly and you get, generally speaking, greater access." Television correspondents "knew you were being used, but that's a two-way street. You hoped that in exchange for the use of your airwaves to pull more of the story from officials at the White House . . . So your first imperative was to be there for the pseudo-event. Your second imperative was to try to carry it further by your reporting."

The priorities in television and print are reversed, says this veteran of both disciplines. "In print, what you need to know is the substance—what was said, but you don't have to be there. In television you have to be there. If ninety percent of success is showing up, in television it's a hundred percent. Your camera has to be focused on the event. For television, much of your time in the White House and in the campaign is covering the mechanics—the movement of the president from A to B to C, and these kinds of empty pseudo-events, be they in the Rose Garden or on the tarmac on a campaign stop. But you need to be there and cover it and pay attention to it."

By the time Ronald Reagan became president, Smith says, image was everything in the minds and hands of his campaign strategists. The Reagan strategists "would meet in the morning and talk not necessarily about the message of the day, but the image they wanted to get across. And every effort would be bent to make sure that that image was available to the networks in enough time to make the evening news, Eastern Standard Time . . . That's what Jim Baker and Ed Meese and Mike Deaver worried about first thing in the morning, and when they took stock at the end of the day. Ever since Mike Deaver, campaigns devote a lot of time and energy toward structuring those photo ops and that image."

Lesley Stahl, who covered the White House for CBS News during the Reagan years, recalls doing a very critical assessment of the president during his

1984 reelection campaign. The camera showed a smiling Reagan visiting a nursing home and other facilities while Stahl commented that he had cut their funds in the federal budget. Right after she watched the segment being aired, she says, her phone rang. It was a White House official, who said to her, "Way to go! Fabulous! We owe you. You're our favorite." Startled, she asked her caller whether he had heard her commentary that accompanied the pictures. "Nobody heard what you said," she says he told her. "You guys in television have never figured it out. When the pictures are powerful and emotional, they will drive you out every time."

There no doubt was, and continues to be, a certain amount of resentment among newspaper reporters about the primacy of, and special privileges extended to, network television reporters and cameramen. Also, the constant presence of television cameras and tape recorders on the campaign trail inhibits the candidates' willingness to talk candidly with reporters. They often dare not speak frankly out of fear that their remarks will be recorded and broadcast, even if there has been a prior agreement that this will not happen. During one trip in the 1972 presidential campaign, the Democratic nominee, George McGovern, came back to my plane seat for a private chat about his efforts to shed his embattled running mate, Senator Tom Eagleton of Missouri. In the midst of our muffled conversation, McGovern suddenly noticed a sound technician's boom microphone dangling over our heads. End of conversation. This scene was often repeated in subsequent campaigns, and thereafter candidates seldom venture into the press sections of their planes.

Television encourages communication by sound bite—the conveying of ideas in the fewest words possible, which satisfies television's demands for brevity, often at the expense of clarity and qualification. Younger politicians have mastered the art of the sound bite, along with political analysts whose glibness, if not their knowledge or accuracy, put them in demand on weekend television talk and interview shows. All these further diminish the currency of intelligent and informed political discussion.

Yet it cannot be disputed that the political technocracy views television as so critical to success in elections that it has revolutionized both the presentation of candidates to the voters and the political priorities. Accommodation to television was most blatantly illustrated in the severely whittled-down party conventions in 1996. The accommodation was perhaps overdone: for its trouble, it received a conspicuous thumb to the nose from ABC News *Nightline* host Ted Koppel, who deemed the Republican convention in San Diego unworthy of his time, packed up, and went home. Fortunately for Koppel, no major news broke after his departure. (Other ABC correspondents and crews did remain in San Diego, however.)

In the early days, the new medium drew heavily on men (and very few women) who had been trained in print journalism and covered campaigns much as they always had. When former *New York Times* political reporter James Hagerty, after his stint as White House press secretary to Dwight D. Eisenhower, took charge of ABC News, he hired many of his old colleagues. Their qualifications were their reportorial skills; they didn't have to be handsome or golden-throated.

One old story, perhaps apocryphal, had it that after William Lawrence, another esteemed *Times* political reporter of gruff appearance and voice, was hired by Hagerty, a phone call came one day to the ABC newsroom. "Is Bill Lawrence there?" asked the gravel-voiced caller. He was told no. "Well, tell him his voice coach called," the caller growled. It was not uncommon in those days that refugees from newspaper work did have to undergo such training. But in time the special demands of television, which included an attractive appearance and silver lungs to go with it, drew career aspirants with those qualifications built in, and they learned how to wed their reportage and commentary to pictures.

"The people in television now are, with just a very few exceptions, absolutely oriented to television," Donaldson says. "The great names we all can recall, every one of them, came from print—Cronkite, Howard K. Smith—they were wire-service people, they were print people, and their preoccupation was the substance of their reports, the writing, the research, and all that. But who were the people who came to the fore? They were people who by hook or by crook also had a theatrical side. Edward R. Murrow is out of Hollywood typecasting. He's handsome, his voice was one of the great voices. Cronkite, in his own way, is a guy you would love to reinvent if you were a network executive now. But today, it's almost one hundred percent oriented toward appearance."

Some of the outstanding television reporters were once, Donaldson says, "right below the anchor level, the mainstay reporters," but did not have the looks or flair of their younger successors. "I don't think at the entry level they'd be able to get a job today . . . If two guys are applying for the same job, and one of them has all these television attributes and also knows the craft, and the other one just knows the craft, it's not close. In the old days, if it was the handsome guy and just the regular-looking guy, it would be a close call."

For all the focus on appearance and style, Donaldson says the younger crop of television reporters he encounters have gone through the mill of journalistic discipline, but it is a different mill. At smaller television stations, "they do learn that you need to be accurate, and they do learn what the laws of libel and slander entail, also the sense of how you write a news story, who you should call, and how to check it." But then, he laments, regarding the Internet's prime gossipmonger, "a Matt Drudge appears on the scene."

"In the old days," Donaldson says, "the story came first and the substance came first. More and more, it is not the substance, it's who's giving it. If you heard on television: 'Tonight, Barbara Walters interviews a stone, a rock,' you'd say, 'God, we gotta watch that.' I have had in my mind for thirty years now the image of Mike Wallace chasing a cheap crook. We cannot remember a single crook he caught, but we see Mike."

Concerning himself, Donaldson has no illusions about how the entertainment quotient in television news, little present in print journalism, will affect how he is remembered. "On the air, I've always tried to be solid," he says, "but if I have any legacy at all, it's 'He yelled at the president.' Yeah, behind the rope line a few yards away, I often did yell—still do. But the question was serious, trying to get a serious answer on a serious subject." Similarly, Donaldson notes, even a television reporter and commentator who was highly respected for his work, the late John Chancellor of NBC News, will probably be remembered just as much for the humorous way he handled his arrest and forced exit—"somewhere in custody"—from the floor of the Republican National Convention in San Francisco in 1964.

"You can say that really demonstrated the mood of that convention, that really capsulized it. Yet, on the other hand, it had nothing to do with the work of the convention. It was a little piece of trivia, but it was the one thing they remember about Jack. He didn't come in as this airhead, but despite his efforts to have his legacy be good, solid reporting in the old tradition, it's the one thing he does that is in this new tradition that he gets remembered for."

Terence Smith was a product of the old television policy of seeking out skilled print journalists. "Today, there's a much greater emphasis on broadcasting skills," he says, "so a good junior anchorman out of a smaller affiliate can get a network job based on his or her ability as a broadcaster." There is inexperience in political reporting, Smith notes, but then the networks hire politicians and political aides like George Stephanopoulos and David Gergen to fill the gap. "You can't expect the latest acquisition from the Atlanta affiliate to have access in the inner circles of the administration."

Television as a cost-effective means of reaching enormous audiences in a presidential campaign has also had a huge effect on campaign budgeting priorities. Candidates spend so much money on television commercials that other, more traditional means of voter contact and persuasion have been all but dried up. The practical effect has been that while the presidential campaign has come into America's living rooms, it has almost entirely disappeared from America's Main Streets. Presidential campaigns can no longer afford to establish the neighborhood campaign offices that were once the focus of community political activity in towns all across the country. Many practices of old-time grassroots campaigning—from distribution of campaign buttons, bumper stickers, and lawn signs to door-to-door canvassing—have been reduced or totally abandoned, along with the storefronts from which they originated and that were magnets for neighborhood political dialogue.

It is, to be sure, surrendering to nostalgia to hope that a return to politics as practiced in the pretelevision days might still be possible. For all its shortcomings, television brings more people into greater touch with presidential candidates than ever before. Still, the television networks often seem to treat presidential campaigns as bothersome intrusions into their pursuit of profit through commercial sponsorship of entertainment programs. They are reluctant to yield prime time to politicians on any regular basis and contemptuously turn their backs on proposals that they give specified amounts of free time to presidential nominees in return for what is, after all, their free use of the taxpayers' airwaves. They take shelter behind the First Amendment, which prohibits Congress from "abridging the freedom of speech, or of the press," arguing that such free television time would impose an unconscionable burden on them.

In 1996, a public-interest group called the Free TV for Straight Talk Coalition, headed by Walter Cronkite and Paul Taylor, a former *Washington Post* political reporter, called on the networks to give two or three minutes each to Clinton and Dole, to appear on alternate nights in September and October, in what was hoped would turn out to be a running debate. They called for a "roadblock" across the networks—all presenting the commentaries simultaneously. But the networks declined, offering variations of the proposed formula instead. CNN, PBS, NPR, and the United Press Network did accept without the roadblock provision, and Clinton and Dole did appear alternately on most nights between October 17 and November 1. But the results were spotty. The general level of discourse was more positive than in television and radio commercials and more issue-oriented than many press accounts of their campaigns, but the hoped-for running debate did not develop, and the size of the audiences did not approach those for the formal debates or television advertising. (A survey by the Annenberg School for Communication found that only 22.3 percent of registered voters said they had seen at least one free-time segment, compared to 71.8 percent who had watched or listened to all or part of a debate and 83.5 percent who recalled seeing or hearing a Clinton or Dole ad.) Nevertheless, it was a start in the direction of extending and improving the quality of the campaign dialogue, and the effort continues.

Meanwhile, the networks have abandoned their earlier practice of keeping veteran correspondents and television technical crews on the road with the major candidates. Instead, they send young "off-air" neophytes with the title "producer" to follow the candidates as the networks' "eyes and ears" on the campaign trail, with veteran reporters and crew available to be sent out if a young producer encounters something worthy of fuller coverage. Bruno defends this practice as making optimum use of talent and providing excellent training for young reporters who later "blossom into correspondents and producers." The networks did save money, he says, but "journalistically it made sense." Keeping high-priced reporters and crews on the road constantly was "absolute madness," he says. As for missing unpredictable news events with major "visual" significance—such as Muskie "crying" in the snow in New Hampshire in 1972, or the assassination attempt on George Wallace that same year—"you can always recoup on pictures," he says, getting them from affiliated local stations.

Terence Smith says the policy of replacing network television veterans with "the kids on the bus" has occurred because the news-show producers' demand for a daily story has sharply diminished. Once they would routinely pencil in a campaign story, but now "they no longer do a nightly piece. They have acknowledged to themselves that they're in the packaging business rather than the newsgathering business. Half the events are pooled [by one cameraman sharing his videotape with all the others]. Pool cameras are taking in the material and feeding it simultaneously to all networks. These young kids, who are energetic and tireless and willing to go nonstop for the length of the campaign, get the basic flow of information that's handed to them, but as a rule they don't have the contacts to get anything beyond that."

For example, Smith says, in the last two months of the 1996 Clinton-Dole campaign, there was very little live coverage on the networks of what the candidates were doing or saying. "They reduced it to what they call 'a tell,' when Dan or Peter or Tom tells you the news of the day. For that, that young kid on the bus can provide them all they need. It's strictly economy of scale and the changing nature of the beast. And the beast wants a different diet now." Academic studies, he says, have shown that people like to watch "human-interest stories, news-you-can-use stories, health segments. It is remarkable to me that there is any disease left in this world, given that we have a breakthrough every night on the evening news. Cancer has been cured innumerable times. Of course, at the end of the report you learn that it's only true in mice, and it will be another fifty years before we know whether it's any good for people."

Perhaps this encourages cynicism about the public interest and appetite for news about the political process, Smith acknowledges, "with the emphasis on the word 'process.' The worst of it is that it becomes a self-fulfilling prophecy. If you don't cover [an event] because you think the public doesn't think it's important, it follows that the public doesn't think it's important because you didn't cover it."

Yet television does have a notable effect on the coverage of presidential campaigns in quite another way: it has been largely responsible for the spread of celebrity journalism, making stars of familiar faces in television journalism, luring print reporters into television, and bringing celebrities in other fields, notably politics, into television journalism. The pull for all three is the same—fame and fortune. Success is now widely equated with appearing on television and earning television's handsome salaries. After the 1996 election, for example, Clinton White House aide George Stephanopoulos became an ABC News television commentator and Tony Blankley, press secretary to House Speaker Newt Gingrich, took similar jobs with the CNN television network and *George* magazine.

There was a time when fame and fortune for a political reporter lay in book writing. The late Allen Drury of *The New York Times* achieved both with his Washington novel *Advise and Consent*—so much so that he eventually turned to fiction writing full-time. The late Theodore H. White, for years a correspondent for *Time*, became a huge celebrity after the 1960 presidential campaign with his inside account of John Kennedy's victory over Richard Nixon, *The Making of the President 1960*.

Book authorship brought with it special access to the candidates. One story, possibly apocryphal, has it that one night during the 1960 campaign an enterprising newspaper reporter gained access to the hotel floor on which Kennedy was staying and knocked on his door, hoping for an interview. The door opened and there was White, who reportedly said, "Sorry, no press," and closed the door.

In some recent campaigns, *Newsweek* has managed to gain special access to presidential candidates for reporters who have been assigned exclusively to gather material for a postelection book, the condition being that nothing learned in the inner sanctum is to be reported until after the election. This procedure raises serious questions about the reporter's and the newsmagazine's journalistic commitment to reporting what they know when they know it. And it poses a potential dilemma: what if the reporter learns something that, if reported then and there, could severely damage or even destroy the candidacy? Yet in fact the arrangement has seldom produced any subsequent earthshaking news or insight.

But the more common way to gain access—and celebrity—is television. Because journalism in the visual medium is only part serious newsgathering and part entertainment, quick-witted and quick-tongued print reporters who cover national politics, the politicians themselves, and high-profile paid consultants are all in demand on television shows. In the process, politics is increasingly perceived as a game, carried to the ultimate extreme in such weekend shoutathons as the noisy circus hosted by John McLaughlin, the former priest who was Nixon's staff apologist during the Watergate cover-up. He has brought the televised political talk format to a newly obnoxious level and, sadly, has inspired several copycats.

Print reporters trained in being precise and fair doff their newsroom hats and put on buffoon's headgear before the cameras, saying the first thing that pops into their heads. Small wonder that the serious craft of journalism has in many quarters become no more credible than the used-car sales business.

Lumping trained journalists together with political escapees who obviously have partisan axes to grind undermines their credibility. "Journalism should be practiced by journalists," says Bruno, a political writer for *Newsweek* before joining ABC News. "You have an influx of people in journalism who are not journalists, who have none of the training, discipline, motivation, or ethics of journalism." True, print journalism also offers some of its most lucrative and high-profile jobs to untrained political operatives, but the practice is not nearly so widespread as in television, perhaps for the simple reason that television pays more and is a much easier and surefire path to fame.

Some network news stars say they find their fame a mixed blessing—opening doors but also making it hard for them to do their jobs. Chancellor often distinguished himself from other anchormen and television news celebrities by going out and covering presidential candidates himself. But, he would confide to newspaper colleagues, he was deterred from doing it more often because, egotistic as it may have sounded, he frequently would attract as much attention from the voters as the candidate did. Once, covering a speech Gary Hart gave in Maine in 1984, Chancellor was standing near the back of a crowded high-school auditorium when a young student turned and, pointing in his direction, shouted to her friends, "Look! The guy on television!" as she and her friends started pushing toward him. He was mortified, however, and the brunt of ribbing from his print colleagues thereafter, when the girl rushed by him without a glance to get to a local television anchorman standing behind him.

It has become commonplace for print reporters traveling with a presidential candidate to find political junkies and young press groupies standing at the door of a hotel pressroom looking for faces they know from television. Once a young girl was heard to say, as the reporters filed by: "He's nobody . . . he's nobody . . . there's Roger Mudd! . . . He's nobody . . . he's nobody . . . there's Sam Donaldson!" This reaction was understandable and inevitable, but in time once-obscure newspaper and magazine reporters began to be recognized, too, when they were recruited, or actively solicited opportunities, to appear on interview shows. Some of these hustlers were established print reporters eager to gain television's higher wages; others openly sought the attention and recognition that television offered—and, in time, opportunities for big lecture fees. At first, the television producers wanted experts on the subjects to be addressed; later they wanted glib, aggressive reporters, whether they really knew much about what they were talking about or not.

But nobody loves a know-it-all. Along with the newly acquired celebrity came considerable public disdain for these motormouth refugees from the obscurity of print journalism. That attitude did not, however, seem to diminish the zest with which many print reporters rushed to the television studios to convey their instant wisdom. The chief abomination in this regard is the weekend television talk show hosted by McLaughlin, a man who lost a race for the U.S. Senate in Rhode Island before going to the Nixon White House as an official fact-spinner by virtue of his abrasively offensive personality and then making himself a television celebrity. In the guise of serious political-issue discussion, he and his fellow panelists put on weekly entertainments that trivialize politics and cannibalize each other with their sound-bite shouting matches and off-the-wall predictions.

Presidential candidates who decline to master the skills of communication through television only jeopardize their own chances. They may deplore the "dumbing-down" to accommodate television, but they seldom buck the advice of their high-priced consultants to learn how to speak in sound bites. In 1984, Walter Mondale made no secret of his dislike of the demands television placed on him, and often resisted his strategists' efforts to hone his message and style more effectively for the omnipresent medium. He paid a price, for he was largely ineffective against Ronald Reagan, the old movie star and television host to whom the camera's eye had been a career-long companion.

At the same time, presidential candidates today shun the sort of close association with reporters, print or television, that they once enjoyed and that encourage a better mutual understanding of each other's roles. They have learned the hard way about how an offhand comment or gesture, captured on videotape, can come back to hurt them. Equally significant, television has lured candidates away from the old campaign trail to its studios, and the hierarchy of presidential campaign management has changed with it. That television has been a powerful and often positive mechanism for voter education cannot be denied, notably in the presidential debates, the single best opportunity for voters to assess the candidates. But it carries dangers with it that have damaged and even destroyed candidates, especially when they make ill-conceived or unwitting remarks during those debates. Written accounts of foibles and faux pas simply do not have as much impact as seeing them directly on television. When Governor George Romney, in a radio broadcast in Detroit in 1967, said he had undergone a "brainwashing" by American military authorities in Vietnam, the remark got very little attention at first, appearing far down in a story in *The New York Times.* There was no picture to illustrate it. Only later, when the comment was picked up in television commentary and other newspapers did it severely damage Romney's chance for the Republican nomination.

The television camera on occasion can do political harm to a candidate simply because of how he appears even when he says or does nothing. In 1960, a weary and ill Nixon looked pasty and sweated profusely during his first televised debate with Kennedy, and most voters polled afterward who had watched the debate said they thought Kennedy had "won." A majority of those who had listened on radio said they thought Nixon had been the winner.

In 1972 during the New Hampshire primary, Senator Muskie, who was the front-runner, in an angry harangue against a local newspaper publisher who had published derogatory remarks about Muskie's wife, appeared to have wept. It was snowing hard at the time and it was never established whether tears or, as Muskie's aides later insisted, melting snowflakes ran down his face as his voice broke. But the scene produced much comment and generated expressions of doubt about his temperament to be president.

"George Romney could say to the print guys, 'I was brainwashed,' and it was a big deal," Donaldson said. "And maybe [David] Broder [of *The Washington Post*] and others drove the idea that Edmund Muskie had cried in the snow. But we also showed him crying or apparently crying on that platform, and the pictures were very powerful. After '72, when you think of incidents that become the metaphor or the line of a national campaign, they almost always occurred on television, for good or for evil."

Another example he recalls: "Roger Mudd asks poor old Teddy [Kennedy] a simple question: 'Why do you want to be president?' [in 1980]. And nobody could really remember the substance of his nonanswer. He rambled. He looked like he hadn't thought about it, which I guess he hadn't."

In 1976, President Gerald Ford looked confused in a television debate with Jimmy Carter when he insisted that Eastern Europe was not under Communist domination. The episode reinforced the impression many voters already had that he was naive or ill-informed, and it took his strategists the better part of a week to get him to correct himself—a stumble that effectively destroyed a late surge in the polls that might have led to his election.

In 1988, television cameras caught a grim-faced Michael Dukakis, wearing a singularly foolish-looking combat helmet, as he drove a military tank at a manufacturing plant in Michigan; the scene sent the accompanying press corps into peals of laughter and ridicule, the sounds of which were duly picked up on the videotape and heard when the scene was shown on network news that night—and, unmercifully, often during the rest of the campaign. Also in 1988 was the televised scene of Dan Quayle on a New Orleans dock, freshly informed that he would be George Bush's vice presidential running mate. "He acted like he was on speed," Donaldson recalls, "and might have been about fourteen years of age. And that did it. The impression stays." The networks could rerun that tape whenever Quayle committed another gaffe, such as when he misspelled "potato" in an attempt to help a young boy in a school spelling bee.

Some veteran politicians with solid records of achievement can slough off such slips, but, Donaldson says, "the new guy out there slips on TV and it becomes a reel. We just keep playing it over and over again . . . [Print reporters] can report the quote and that can be very damaging, but when we show it again, every little nuance, the facial expression, every sort of awkward phraseology is right there to remind people: Oh, yeah, that guy."

In 1992, in the presidential debate in a town-meeting format in Richmond, Virginia, George Bush didn't do himself any good when at one point he glanced at his watch as if he couldn't wait for the debate to be over. And when a questioner asked how each of the candidates could understand the problems of the common people, Bush came off as confused and pathetic. Meanwhile, Bill Clinton stood by, visibly eager to answer. When the camera panned to him, Donaldson recalls, "he's just licking his lips." The moment Bush finished, Clinton walked over to the questioner and offered specifics on how his Arkansas friends and neighbors were hurt by high federal taxes and how they had lost jobs. "Little things like that, even if you had tried to play them up in print," Donaldson says, "wouldn't have had the kind of impact" which television immediately gave them.

In 1996, when Bob Dole, on a speaking platform in Chico, California, slipped and fell over a makeshift rail, the cameramen had another field day. Dole quickly hopped back up, but the incident served to remind many voters of Dole's age at the time, seventy-three, and to reignite speculation about his physical condition and ability to stand the rigors of the presidency. The witty Dole recovered nicely, laughing as he rose, and quipped, "I think I just earned my third Purple Heart going over the rail. But you can always say I've fallen for Chico." And in this instance, according to an Annenberg School for Communication review, the news media acted responsibly. Of the networks and seven major daily newspapers checked, only ABC News had mentioned Dole's age when reporting the fall and, according to the review, "most reports did not treat the fall as a symbol of a faltering campaign."

Such incidents have done nothing to dampen the interest of candidates and their handlers to get more and more television time and to dream up "photo opportunities" that will fill television's quenchless need for "visuals." On the simplest level, there was Jimmy Carter in 1976 carrying his own suit bag getting off a campaign plane. In the 1988 Dukakis-Bush campaign, the Bush consultants used Boston Harbor as a backdrop when their candidate contended that waterways in Dukakis' home state remained polluted in spite of his strongly expressed environmentalist views.

If television can sink a candidate, it also can save him. Clinton, after giving an interminable speech at the 1988 Democratic National Convention, salvaged the situation by going on a late-night talk show and poking fun at himself. "You do almost anything short of actually stealing money from the bank," Donaldson says, "but if you then use self-deprecating humor, we tend to give you a pass. 'Oh, what a great guy he is.' We think this is wonderful, but it's a technique."

Four years later, Donaldson notes, Bill and Hillary Clinton's performance on *60 Minutes* was "absolutely critical" to his political survival after Gennifer Flowers had made accusations of sexual misconduct against him (denied on that show but later admitted in 1998, in a deposition in the Paula Jones case). "If he had proved not to be so confident in that put-upon way," Donaldson says, "I think he would have been out of the race."

Failure to play constantly to television can be very costly. Also in 1988, Dukakis suffered badly when he decided to go back to Massachusetts after the convention in Atlanta that had nominated him and attend to gubernatorial business, while Bush began campaigning right after his nominating convention in Houston. Bruno recalls a Dukakis staffer calling him to complain about the imbalance in ABC's coverage. "Why don't you cover us?" the staffer asked. "Why doesn't your candidate go out and do something?" was the reply.

By 1996, candidates could pretty well forget the chances of getting a full-fledged campaign speech aired in anything approximating its entirety, except in opening and closing remarks at the televised debates. In terms of the voters, it probably didn't matter all that much, because by then they were conditioned to value appearance, performance, and style over substance. "It's the delivery, it's the demeanor," Donaldson says. Television "clearly diminishes the quality of the campaign, which is not the fault of the television camera or those of us who are along for the ride . . . It's the use of the camera itself by a skilled politician, or the misuse by an unskilled politician. What it does is reward performance over substance."

This public acceptance of, or even preference for, performance over substance poses a problem to the television reporter that Donaldson acknowledges is not solved. "I used to think that by bringing factual material to a television report I could, if not offset, at least present another view of what the situation was," he says. "But in 1984 I watched Ronald Reagan and his people get away with the balloons, the 'God Bless the U.S.A.,' the Bibles, and the American flag—and I'm not against any of those symbols—and just never answer questions like, How are you going to balance the budget? and How are you going to deal with deficits? We put those questions to him constantly. The record will not show that the White House press corps wasn't doing its job trying to hold the president to account. We were, and we were putting it on the air, but it had no impact compared to those pictures." By the same token, Donaldson says, efforts to focus on substance are undermined by the very fact that more and more Americans get their information from television. "People don't read as much as they did," he says, "but even if they read, the impression they remember from television is stronger. The pictures always outdo the words, at least in the short run."

Beyond all this, television has in a significant sense also become the political scorekeeper. The networks' repeated use of "horse race" polls—showing who's ahead and who's behind—simplify what an election is all about and can be most misleading. National polls that record popular support for candidates do not refer to the fact that presidential elections are determined by the electoral votes in each state, and they can create the impression that an election is close when it really is not. Worse, the networks, relying on surveys of voters as they leave the polling places during Election Day—"exit polls"—now project the outcomes state by state as if that were the real thing.

Gone is the dramatic presentation of actual election results posted by hand on huge chalkboards. In its place are graphics based on polling in selected precincts—"keys"—that may or may not be accurate in predicting the outcome. One practical result has been to discourage voters in late-voting time zones from going to the polls at all if they believe their votes will not affect the outcome. When Jimmy Carter early on election night in 1980 conceded the election to Ronald Reagan based on unofficial returns, local Democratic candidates in Oregon and California screamed sabotage.

From all this, it can be fairly said that instead of merely holding up a mirror to the campaigns for the viewing public, television in significant ways shapes them, sets itself up as the national vote counter, and produces information that itself can affect the turnout in some states. While generally enlightening the American electorate, it has undermined the ability of presidential campaigns to deal adequately with complex issues facing the nation when it chooses its president.

Cable television and the Internet have only heightened these effects, and have triggered a general lowering of reportorial standards, since now both print and television news outlets present electronically circulated rumor and inadequately sourced information as fact. During the 1996 campaign, the Internet had not yet appreciably affected politics, but what followed in 1998–99 does not bode well. In the Clinton-Jones-Lewinsky circus, newspapers and newsmagazines all too often abandoned or shaved their traditional standards to be first to post on their sites in cyberspace a rumor, or insufficiently sourced report, or even an error along with a fact. For example, *The Wall Street Journal* one day had an article ready to publish reporting that a White House steward had told the grand jury that he had seen President Clinton and Monica Lewinsky alone in a study next to the Oval Office. Concerned that some other news organization might publish the story before the *Journal*'s next morning edition, the paper's editors decided to scoop themselves by putting it on the *Journal*'s Internet Web site and its wire service the afternoon before. One writer of the story, Brian Duffy, later told *The Washington Post* that the reason the *Journal* didn't wait was that "we heard footsteps from at least one other news organization and just didn't think it was going to hold in this crazy cycle we're in." The explanation was an intonation of the old newsroom gag: "Confucius say, 'Reporter who sit on hot story get ass burned.' " In this case, it was the newspaper that didn't sit on the story that wound up with a singed posterior. Three days later, the *Journal* was obliged to report that the story had been wrong, that the steward had not told the grand jury any such thing.

Technological advances in the news media have in many ways greatly improved their ability to serve the viewing, listening, and reading public. But the obligation of press, radio, and television to be accurate as well as first with the news, and to be fair-minded in the process, remains the same. In journalism's traditional job of holding presidential candidates to account for what they say and do, the standards have changed. New rules have evolved that sharpen the adversarial relationship between those seeking or occupying the presidency and those who find out and publish personal information about them that may deny them their presidential goal.

8 Watchdogs and Lapdogs

In that distant time before television, print journalists found some of their most rewarding, prestigious, and glamorous work in reporting on presidential campaigns. Hobnobbing with incumbent and would-be presidents was both a choice assignment and a prime opportunity to delve into critical issues of the day and, in the process, to hold the candidates' feet to the fire of accountability.

In doing so, the press tried to observe high standards for its own behavior. Newspapermen were supposed to report as if they were flies on the wall—seeing but unseen, or at least unheard. They were supposed to be as objective as it was possible to be, and they were supposed to examine the candidates' promises made and kept, and their behavior as it affected their performance as officeholders or office seekers.

At first, television constructively assisted in these tasks, driving the print press to more extensive examinations of the campaign issues and the strengths and weaknesses of the men (and only occasionally the women) who held or sought high public office. As the new medium gained prominence, better newspapers and their reporters delved ever more deeply into investigation and analysis, into lengthy exposés and interpretative articles that television journalism, with its limitations of time and visual demands, could not hope to match. There was little serious dispute that quality journalism was to be found in the printed word, not on the television screen.

In reporting scandals, the print press seemed more suited to the task than television, for the printed word could best describe in detail the intricacies of a particular corruption or other malfeasance. Seldom was a politician caught on camera with his hand literally in a cookie jar or himself flagrante delicto, committing a misdeed that would look exciting on television. Network news divisions (headquartered in New York) undertook very little original political reporting, taking their leads instead from what was first printed in *The New York Times*, *The Wall Street Journal*, or *The Washington Post* or carried on the wires of the Associated Press. But as the networks began to appreciate the entertainment as well as the educational aspects of political campaigns, and as their technology more and more facilitated on-the-scene transmission of pictures, they committed themselves more and more to political reporting.

Political developments also affected the change in the functions of the print press. Senator Joseph R. McCarthy in the 1950s, waving papers that he purported were proof that there were this many or that many Communists in the State Department, finally convinced editors that their reporters had to be more than mere megaphones for politicians making such allegations. And pressure for more searching journalism was emphasized after World War II when tales of excess, corruption, and influence peddling by presidential cronies in the Truman and Eisenhower administrations needed to be examined. Then came the Vietnam War and Watergate, both of which pushed what now was called the news media—print, radio, and television—to ever greater intensity in investigative and interpretative journalism. Mushrooming public skepticism of and, eventually, cynicism about the trustworthiness of politicians and the news media itself led in turn to closer examination, in the print press especially, of the conduct and behavior of officeholders and office seekers. The searchlight began to be directed not simply on how they did their jobs but also on how they lived their lives, private as well as public.

Many politicians disliked this intrusion. In his 1996 political memoir, *Time Present, Time Past*, then Senator Bill Bradley, a celebrity ever since his days as an All-American college and professional basketball player and a conspicuous guardian of his privacy, wrote: "As a public figure, I believe that people are entitled to know my views on the issues of the day and why I hold them; they are also entitled to a full disclosure of what I own and some basic biographical material. The public has a right to know if you are a crook, but they do not need to know if you are a sinner, since we all are." For many years, and certainly before Watergate, that view was widely accepted by the mainstream of American journalism, and reporters took a careful approach with political figures generally and presidential candidates particularly. The rule of thumb was: any conduct that affected a candidate's ability to perform his official duties was fair game for investigation and disclosure; whatever didn't was his or her own business. The worst that might be reported about social behavior was that a politician had "an eye for the ladies" or "a fondness for the grape."

A prominent illustration given today of the difference in press ethics over the years concerns John F. Kennedy's womanizing as a presidential candidate and in the White House. Many reporters, notably those who were not around then, critically observe that there was a conspiracy of silence among their predecessors in the Washington and national press corps protecting Kennedy from having his activities disclosed. If indeed they were known at the time, the illustration would be certainly a key one, although as a reporter in Washington then, I never knew of Kennedy's womanizing myself nor did I hear of it from fellow reporters senior to me. Perhaps that fact only confirms the existence of a conspiracy of silence, but in any event a different code of journalistic ethics governed reporting in those days. Members of Congress could and did show up in their cups on the floor of the House and Senate, but if they did not fall on their faces or punch a colleague, nothing was written or said about it.

Disclosures of criminal wrongdoing that led to the resignation first of Vice President Agnew in November 1973 and of President Nixon nine months later were, however, indisputably legitimate products of enterprise investigative journalism, and they raised the standard of "character" as a measure of a candidate's or a president's worthiness to a new level. It seemed after these resignations, and the long and sorrowful saga of the Vietnam War, in which deception had been a handmaiden to military and political decision making, that this was a legitimate and necessary extension. Indeed, Jimmy Carter made "character" a centerpiece of his Democratic campaign in 1976, vowing to voters that "I will never lie to you," while making extravagant promises (which he failed to keep) to reduce the size of the federal government. And after the Agnew scandal and after George McGovern's unhappy experience with Tom Eagleton, Carter had aides undertake unprecedented interrogations of the backgrounds of the people he considered as a possible running mate, and conducted interviews himself with each of them.

At the same time the news media began to take a closer look at presidential candidates, applying the yardstick of "character," usually defined as moral fiber or lack of it as demonstrated by conduct in areas quite beyond the performance of official duties. This conduct, to be sure, had for years been the focus of scandal sheets peddled over the counter in supermarkets and corner drugstores across the country. But the mainstream press and television in general shunned their garish and sleazy stories, treating these newspapers and magazines as at best distant, unsavory cousins, not to be acknowledged as members of the family. Still, strains of the "gotcha" mentality that drove these journalistic outcasts began to seep into the mainstream media. The celebrity and riches that came to *Washington Post* reporters Bob Woodward and Carl Bernstein for their brilliant work in unearthing the Watergate cover-up and attendant excesses rejuvenated the interest of thousands of young Americans in print journalism, especially investigative writers. Inevitably, digging out dirt about political candidates, including those who wanted to be president, became part of the study of "character" or its absence.

In the 1984 presidential campaign, the search was undertaken in a rather innocuous way concerning Democratic presidential hopeful Senator Gary Hart of Colorado. Reporters discovered a number of minor facts about Hart's personal life that in themselves were insignificant but taken together suggested to some a pattern of, at the least, quirkiness and evasiveness. He had been born Gary Hartpence but had changed his name; he had changed the way he signed his name; he had listed his age in official and campaign biographies as forty-six but it appeared from other sources to be forty-seven. Beyond this, there were rampant rumors that he was a womanizer, but they did not appear in the mainstream press because they were insufficiently substantiated and a restrained code of professional ethics still prevailed. Within the traveling press corps, women reporters told their male colleagues of approaches he had made to them, but they were unwilling to say this publicly. Meanwhile Hart's political fortunes rose in Iowa and New Hampshire, then fell, yet left him as a strong presidential prospect for 1988.

At a private dinner in Washington in late 1985, at the home of a reporter and with a number of other reporters present, all of them well known to Hart and all of them acquainted with the rumors about him, someone asked him about the state of his marriage. The question was a more delicate way of touching on those rumors, as everyone present understood. He gave the rather unusual reply that he "expected" to be married to his wife, Lee, in 1988, when the next presidential campaign came around. People continued to raise questions privately about the subject, not only reporters but many people eager to work for Hart's election as president who didn't want to be blindsided by a scandal that would undermine their efforts. Hart assured them that there was nothing in his private life that if disclosed would damage his chances.

In early 1987, by which time he had emerged as the Democratic front-runner, Hart in the course of conversation at another private dinner, this one with three reporters at a Boston restaurant, was asked how he was going to handle "the character issue" this time around. The question was in the context of his name and signature changes and his age, and no mention was made of womanizing. Visibly irritated, he blurted, "You're the only ones who ever ask me about those things. I go all over and nobody ever asks me." As the conversation went on at length, he volunteered that he had nothing to hide from anybody. Then he produced a lengthy autobiographical article about his boyhood in Kansas, which, he said, he was trying to get printed somewhere but had been turned down. This was proof, he said, that nobody cared very much about his personal life—except political reporters like those of us sitting at the table with him. The article, which was subsequently published in the *Boston Globe*, included a brief reference to past marital problems. "Comment was made of the fact that Lee and I suffered short separations during those years," he wrote. "Coming in an age of divorced presidents, this seems to deserve no more attention than that. Lee is proud of reflecting, as she should be, that we were able to resolve those temporary stresses, where others were not. In 1988, we celebrate our 30th wedding anniversary."

Still the rumors persisted, in the press corps and in the Hart campaign itself. Hart's aides got tips that some news organizations were thinking of putting a tail on him, and reports came to campaign strategists that he and a prominent backer named Billy Broadhurst, who had a boat in Florida, had been seen in the company of some college girls. Hart told them it was all innocent. But a few days before his official announcement of candidacy in April 1987, *Newsweek*, in a profile about him, observed, "The Harts' marriage has been a long but precarious one, and he has been haunted by rumors of womanizing. Friends contend that his dating has been confined to marital separations—he and Lee have had two—nonetheless many political observers expect the rumors to emerge as a campaign issue." A 1984 Hart campaign insider named John McEvoy was quoted as saying, "He's always in jeopardy of having the sex issue raised if he can't keep his pants on."

Hart was livid but held his tongue. At his formal announcement in Denver, not a single inquiry about any of this came his way. John Emerson, a key aide, said later, "I thought we had crossed the bridge over from the Land of Womanizing and Personal Questions to the Land of Substance and Message." But he was wrong. On Hart's chartered campaign plane en route to Texas and Iowa that very day, he was pressed again about the rumors of womanizing. A reporter told him, he said later, that they were being spread by the campaigns of rival candidates, Senator Joseph Biden of Delaware and Governor Michael Dukakis of Massachusetts. Hart injudiciously passed this report on to another inquiring reporter, and when he did, Hart recalled later, "the plane went into orbit."

Hoping to quell the uproar this allegation of duplicity by his rivals had aroused, Hart walked to the back compartment of the plane, where reporters were demanding to talk to him. He told them he had only been commenting "off the cuff" about what he had been told and wasn't trying to "make news." He said he hoped and believed that other candidates weren't spreading rumors about him. But he had committed a political blunder. Going back to the reporters only aired the story of rival duplicity again. Even before the campaign plane had landed, reporters were abuzz, with Hart's remarks on their tape recorders and in stories on their computers about his "accusation" against his competitors. In the wink of an eye, his carefully crafted announcement in Denver was overwhelmed by the breaking story of how "the character issue" had been injected foursquare into the campaign by Hart himself.

"It was dumb on my part," he said later. "I should have said, 'No comment.' " At the time, however, he seethed at the way the press already was ignoring the substance of his campaign and choosing to focus on his personal life. He began not only to tell reporters he had nothing to hide but to invite them to find out for themselves. "Follow me around," he told E. J. Dionne, then of *The New York Times*, "I don't care. I'm serious. If anybody wants to put a tail on me, go ahead. They'd be very bored." Dionne quoted him in an article he was writing for the newspaper's magazine to be released the next Sunday.

In the meantime, other political reporters were considering the ethics of the situation. Far from going after Hart on the rumors, Tom Fiedler of the *Mi-*

ami Herald wrote a page-one analysis that raised thoughtful questions about "the nature of the modern campaign in a media-intensive age, where the scrutiny seems less intended to test a candidate's intelligence quotient than to expose his or her private life." The Hart case, he wrote, "raises real and serious questions about media ethics . . . Is it responsible for the media to report damaging rumors if they can't be substantiated? Or should the media withhold publication until they have solid evidence of infidelity? . . . Even if sexual adventures can be proven, do the media have a legitimate interest in a candidate's private sex life, assuming it doesn't interfere with doing the job?"

Fiedler, who had interviewed Hart earlier, noted that from nowhere did anyone come forward with evidence of any infidelity, and he quoted the candidate: "I've been in public life for fifteen years and I think that if there was anything about my background that anybody had any information on, they would bring it forward. But they haven't."

Fiedler concluded: "In a harsh light, the media reports themselves are rumormongering, pure and simple. So why have the media rushed the rumors to print? The answer appears to be that the rumors have achieved a critical mass, sustaining themselves through repetition and Hart's failure to categorically and convincingly deny them." Fiedler concluded with Hart's remark: "I think people are going to get tired of the question."

But on the night Fiedler's article appeared, he learned firsthand that at least one *Miami Herald* reader wasn't tired of the question. Working late at his desk, he received a phone call from a woman who told him irritably, "You know, you said in the paper that there were rumors that Gary Hart is a womanizer. Those aren't rumors. How much do you guys pay for pictures?" Fiedler asked the woman her name, but she declined. Instead, she went on: "Gary Hart is having an affair with a friend of mine. We don't need another president who lies like that." At first Fiedler dismissed the woman as a crank caller, cautioning her that she was making a serious charge. But she pressed on, saying she had pictures she could turn over, provided her name was not used. He told her that if he could verify the information to his own satisfaction he would not have to identify her. He told her to sleep on it and call him back the next day if she wanted to proceed. No one could accuse Fiedler of not acting responsibly in the matter.

The woman called again the next morning, sounding nervous. She was a liberal Democrat, she told him, and "she couldn't tolerate someone who would say one thing publicly and do another privately. The nation had just seen that happen with President Reagan and the Iranian arms sales." She then told Fiedler the whole story: she and her friend had met Hart at a yacht party in Miami, the friend had gone on an overnight "cruise" to a nearby port with Hart and later showed her pictures of the two together there. Hart had phoned her friend repeatedly from the campaign trail—the woman specified when and from what states the calls were made—and said her friend was going to Washington the next Friday to spend the weekend with Hart. She suggested that Fiedler travel on the same plane and talk to her. The caller described her friend as a very good-looking blonde with a rich Southern drawl who was "really outgoing" and would tell him all about it. Fiedler asked the caller for information about her friend's flight and she said she would call back, but she never did.

Then Fiedler checked Hart's earlier campaign travel schedule and found it matched with the dates and states the woman had supplied on his phone calls to her friend. He also determined that Hart was indeed going to be in Washington the next weekend, as a result of a late change in travel plans. On Friday afternoon, a *Herald* investigative reporter named Jim McGee got on the most likely nonstop flight from Miami to Washington and found aboard not one but three good-looking blondes, one of whom he subsequently spotted leaving Hart's Capitol Hill town house on the senator's arm. More than an hour later, Hart returned, still with the woman (later identified as Donna Rice). McGee and a colleague staked out the place all night, although in a lapse of reportorial judgment they left it uncovered from about three o'clock in the morning to five, while they went to get something to eat.

Earlier, McGee had reported to his newspaper that he had seen Hart and Rice. The next morning, Saturday, Fiedler and two other colleagues caught the first plane to Washington. En route, Fiedler perused newspaper clippings about Hart, including an advance copy of the story in the *Times* Sunday magazine in which Hart was quoted as "inviting" the press to put a tail on him. Later accounts attributed the *Herald*'s action to that invitation, but the anonymous phone calls to Fiedler were really the catalyst.

Once in Washington, Fiedler and the others joined the surveillance. That night, when Hart and the woman reappeared leaving Hart's house, the reporters confronted the senator, but he denied any wrongdoing. He said the woman was staying with a nearby friend, not in his house, and he declined to let them talk to her. With the newspaper's last deadline approaching, the *Herald* reporters wrote an account of what they knew, which appeared in what remained of the newspaper's Sunday morning run, bannered across page one.

Hart's campaign headquarters in Denver, alerted to developments by then, swung into a damage control mode. Hart's aides interrogated Rice at length by phone, then sent a woman campaign strategist to Washington to accompany and counsel her. Later, at a press conference in Miami, Rice denied any wrongdoing, though she did acknowledge that she had gone on an overnight trip aboard a yacht named *Monkey Business* with Hart and others to the island of Bimini, where a photograph, later revealed, showed her sitting on his knee. Hart's presidential candidacy was on the ropes.

Senator Hart tried to counterattack. In a previously scheduled speech to the American Newspaper Publishers Association in New York, he charged that the *Herald* had published "a misleading and false story that hurt my family and other innocent people and reflected badly on my character." He cited "a spotty surveillance" and charged the reporters had "reached inaccurate conclusions based on incomplete facts" and "most outrageously refused to interview the very people who could have given them the facts before filing their story, which we asked and urged them to do." (Members of the *Herald* team later pointed out that he had refused to let them talk to Rice when they faced deadline pressures.)

Hart acknowledged that he had made "a mistake by putting myself in circumstances that could be misconstrued." But, he went on, "did I do anything immoral? I absolutely did not." Nevertheless, the story was now irrefutably in the public domain. Reporters surrounded Fiedler after Hart's speech, peppering him with questions about the events leading up to and including the surveillance, and then demanded that Hart hold a press conference. Aides staved this off for a time, but finally decided he would have to hold one. The next day in a small lounge at the Hanover Inn at Dartmouth College in New Hampshire, where Hart had just delivered a foreign-policy speech, there unfolded one of the most bizarre and inquisitional meetings a presidential candidate had ever had with members of the traveling campaign press corps.

Hart began by saying, "I have nothing to hide." While he had made "a serious mistake" in judgment, the *Herald* had misread an innocent situation. "If I had intended a relationship with this woman," he said, "believe me, I have written spy novels. I am not stupid. If I had wanted to bring someone into a house, an apartment, meet with a woman in secret, I wouldn't have done it this way."

But Hart was not going to be let off so easily. A reporter for *The Washington Post*, Paul Taylor, rose and pointedly posed a series of specific questions:

Q. *"When you said you did nothing immoral, did you mean that you had no sexual relationships with Donna Rice last weekend or at any other times you were with her?"*

A. *"That is correct, that's correct."*

Q. *"Do you believe that adultery is immoral?"*

A. *"Yes."*

Q. *"Have you ever committed adultery?"*

A. *"Ahhh . . . I do not think that's a fair question."*

Q. *"Well, it seems to me that the question of morality . . . was introduced by you."*

A. *"That's right, that's right."*

Q. *"And it's incumbent upon us to know what your definition of morality is."*

A. *"Well, it includes adultery."*

Q. *"So that you believe adultery is immoral."*

A. *"Yes, I do."*

Q. *"Have you ever committed adultery?"*

A. *"I do not know—I'm not going into a theological definition of what constitutes adultery. In some people's minds it's being married and having relationships with other people, so—"*

Q. *"Can I ask you whether you and your wife have an understanding about whether or not you can have relationships, you can have sexual encounters with—"*

A. *"My inclination is to say, no, you can't ask me that question, but the answer is no, we don't have any such understanding. We have an understanding of faithfulness, fidelity, and loyalty."*

Another reporter, Tom Oliphant of the *Boston Globe*, asked, "Except for the times you and your wife were separated, has your marriage been monogamous?" Hart replied, "I . . . do not need to answer that question."

Through all this, Hart had maintained remarkable composure under the circumstances. Near the end, he pleaded for "fairness in our society" and without mentioning names he deplored those "who believe the way to get to the top is to tear down others . . . That is not the way you win, and it is not what the American people want. It is old politics, and you don't get to the top by tearing other people down."

Later, Hart said that a rehearsal for the press conference had anticipated the question about extramarital affairs in the past, and that he had replied that he didn't have to answer. But when the real questions came, he tried to respond, instead of flatly turning them away, in ways that seemed either incriminating or evasive. And in so doing, he set a precedent that would prove much harder for future candidates and reporters to ignore.

Hart's attempt to tough out the situation was in vain. Resuming his normal schedule later in the day, he was caught in a crush of cameramen and reporters, as the focus swung entirely on his personal life. That night, at dinner with staff members, he decided to pack up and go home to Denver the next morning. Meanwhile, Taylor of the *Post* told a Hart press aide he had details and photos of another Hart liaison of long standing with another woman in Washington and requested an interview with Hart to discuss the matter. The aide told the reporter that Hart was asleep and would be advised in the morning. But Hart was told soon after, and he decided then and there he could not continue. He gave orders for a small plane to be readied, and he and his wife, Lee, flew off to Denver shortly after daybreak, leaving aides to hand out a statement that "while running for president is important, right now my family is more important. Lee and I are returning to Denver, to our home and our family. We are going to take a few days, or a few weeks, to be together. This campaign will continue and our cause will succeed."

But it did not. The next morning, Hart came out swinging, charging in a Denver press conference that "if someone's able to throw up a smoke screen between me and the voters . . . you can't get your message across." He didn't say who had thrown up the "smoke screen" or offer further response to the allegations other than to say that "clearly under present circumstances, this campaign cannot go on. I refuse to submit my family and my friends and innocent people and myself to further rumors and gossip. It's simply an intolerable situation."

The whole system, Hart said, "reduces the press of this nation to hunters and presidential candidates to being hunted." It was a system, he said, "that has reporters in bushes; false and inaccurate stories printed; swarms of helicopters hovering over our roof, and my very strong wife close to tears because she can't even get in her own house at night without being harassed. And then after that, ponderous pundits wondering in mock seriousness why some of the best people in this country choose not to run for high office."

Hart bowed out, with a call to "those talented people who supported me," many of them now disillusioned by him, "to insist that the system be changed. Too much of it is just a mockery, and if it continues to destroy people's integrity and honor, then that system will eventually destroy itself." But, he said, "the events of this week should not deter any of you who are idealistic young people from moving on and moving up . . . the torch of idealism burns bright in your hearts. It should lead you into public service and national service . . . And whoever you are and what you do in that cause, at least in spirit, I will be with you."

Gary Hart was convinced, then and later, that "the system" rather than his own conduct had destroyed his chances for the presidency. And it is true that if the standards of press scrutiny had been the same as they were in the days of John Kennedy, Hart might well have become president. But the misinformation and deceptions of the Vietnam War and the Watergate scandal had left scars on the body politic, and there was a higher public demand for honesty, integrity, and the other personal qualities summed up in the word "character." And to gauge character, the news media believed it was justified in digging into the candidate's past and present social behavior—and the truthfulness or falsity of how those candidates dealt with their own.

In Hart's case, further revelations gave his protestations of innocence an ever more hollow ring. Some weeks later, the *National Enquirer*, the nation's best-known gossip tabloid, ran the picture of Rice sitting on Hart's knee on a pier, presumably one on Bimini; he was smiling, and wore a T-shirt that said "Monkey Business Crew." The paper ran another photo inside of Hart, Rice, and other companions clowning on the bandstand of a Bimini nightclub. *The New York Times*, which first tentatively dipped its toe in the Hart story and only later jumped into the swim, observed editorially, "A candidate's private morality may or may not be fair grounds for judging fitness for office, but a candidate's judgment is surely fair game . . . Reporters once treated candidates' 'personal' indiscretions discreetly. No longer, and that's to the good. Beyond the proper, debatable bounds of privacy, the public needs to know as much about a candidate as possible."

Not all voices in the *Times* agreed. The columnist Anthony Lewis wrote on the same day:

> *When I read about the* Miami Herald *story on Gary Hart, I felt degraded in my profession. Is that what journalism is about, hiding in a van outside a politician's home? Is it "investigative reporting" to write that a woman may have spent the night there—or may not, since we're not sure we watched all the doors? . . . Are we more hypocritical now than we used to be? Perhaps. But the real difference is that we no longer let politicians have a private life. We insist on knowing all. The loss of respect for privacy has exacted a terrible price in American politics. When anyone who runs for president knows that intimate details of his or her life will be shouted to the world, what sensitive person would run? . . . The way we choose presidents is a national disgrace and a cause of international concern. That is not the press's fault. But the* Miami Herald *stakeout of Gary Hart shows how the press can make it worse.*

Other voices of the *Times* weighed in. The columnist A. M. Rosenthal wrote: "I did not become a newspaperman to hide outside a politician's house trying to find out whether he was in bed with somebody." And his colleague William Safire claimed that had he been asked the adultery question he would have replied, "Go to hell." He called on other journalists "to blaze away at keyhole journalism."

At the same time, however, the *Times* undertook a survey of all prospective Democratic and Republican presidential candidates that asked artfully how "a hypothetical presidential candidate" who hasn't committed adultery should answer the question and how one who has should. Most of those who replied more or less took Safire's advice.

In the end, Hart acknowledged—speaking to Ted Koppel on *Nightline* months later—that he had not been "absolutely faithful" to his wife during their twenty-nine-year marriage, including during the two separations, but after all he hadn't been "running for sainthood," and whatever he did didn't compare with the *public* sins of other officials. He noted that "no laws were broken," that "no papers were shredded. No money changed hands. No one lied to Congress, and all of those things have happened in [the Reagan] administration."

On the Republican side, in the same 1988 race, then Vice President George Bush repeatedly dodged questions from reporters about what he really knew regarding the sales of arms to Iran to free American hostages and the use of profits from the sales to finance the Contras in Nicaragua. Bush defended his silence on the grounds that he could not divulge the content of privileged conversations with President Reagan. Then, whenever he was asked a question about Iran-Contra, he would unfailingly say he had already answered it, except for anything touching on his conversations with the president, which were sacrosanct. In a celebrated interview by Dan Rather on the CBS Evening News during the Iowa caucuses, Bush stonewalled again, suggesting he had been sandbagged by Rather's bringing up the old issue. Afterward, Bush told a campaign audience he should have gotten "combat pay" for his confrontation with Rather, observing, "It's tension city when you're in there."

Thus the "character issue" was seldom raised against Bush concerning his honesty or lack of it about a matter of public policy, but it was raised, again in the same campaign, to the detriment of another candidate, Senator Joseph Biden. Once again reporters found what they considered serious character flaws not in deceitful policymaking, as in Iran-Contra, but in Biden's speechmaking and personal biographical data.

It so happened that William Schneider, a political scientist at the well-known conservative think tank the American Enterprise Institute, who doubled as a columnist and television analyst, had been in London in the spring of 1987 observing the campaign between British Prime Minister Margaret Thatcher and her unsuccessful challenger, Labour Party leader Neil Kinnock. Schneider had been taken with a television commercial by Kinnock in which he alluded to his ancestry of Welsh coal miners with great emotional effect, so he got a videotape of the commercial and gave it to Biden's campaign. Such, apparently, was Schneider's notion of journalistic neutrality.

Biden was impressed with Kinnock's remarks and began to incorporate them almost verbatim into his basic campaign speech. He adapted the rhetoric to his own ancestry and history, using considerable literary license but usually crediting Kinnock. In a debate at the Iowa State Fair in August, however, he launched into the exposition without any attribution to the British leader.

Not much notice was taken at first, until reporters from *The New York Times* and the *Des Moines Register* received copies of a videotape from a source not at first disclosed. Using the split-screen technique, it showed Kinnock and Biden delivering their versions of the same basic pitch. Both newspapers then published articles about the striking similarities between the words of the two men. Biden's camp tried to brush off the matter, noting that Biden had attributed his remarks to Kinnock on several other occasions, but allegations of plagiarism soon filled the air, and reporters began to shop around for other Biden "borrowings." After Biden gave another speech in Sacramento, the *San Jose Mercury News* found one: almost precise echoes of a speech of Robert F. Kennedy's in 1968, again used without attribution. The similarity was duly reported by a growing band of character police.

On the heels of all this, it was disclosed that as a first-year law student at Syracuse University, Biden had been given a failing grade and was forced to repeat a course because he had included in a paper of his own five pages from a law-review article without crediting it. On top of that, a C-SPAN videotape showed Biden being needled at a New Hampshire event by a persistent questioner about his academic credentials, charging he had grossly exaggerated his record. He had claimed that he had gone "to law school on a full academic scholarship" when in fact it was based half on need, and that he had finished "in the top half of my class" in law school when he actually was ranked 76th in a class of 85 in his final year.

As far as Biden's presidential aspirations were concerned, it didn't matter that the similarities between the Kinnock and Biden speeches first came to light because two aides of a rival Democratic candidate, Michael Dukakis, had prepared the split-screen videotape and circulated it to certain reporters. Coming soon after the "character issue" had driven Hart from the campaign, the charge of plagiarism against Biden gained immediate currency and potency, and he too was forced to withdraw. In this case, there had been little press sleuthing involved of the sort that nailed Hart and triggered endless journalistic soul-searching about the ethics of gathering damaging information by questionable means. The damaging evidence had been handed out on a silver platter by a political rival, which raised a different ethical question: should the news media willingly be a partner to an effort by a rival campaign to undercut an opponent, and must they disclose where the ammunition had come from?

Protection of sources is a bedrock axiom in all aspects of journalism, and in this case the recipients of the tape protected their sources. When the furor continued, the two Dukakis aides finally owned up, resigned from the campaign, and Dukakis apologized to Biden. But the damage was done. Dukakis had known nothing about any of this when the tape was distributed, so his character was not in serious question, but Biden was deemed suspect. It didn't matter that on many other occasions he had attributed the relevant remarks to Kinnock, or that he hadn't known that a speechwriter had appropriated a phrase or two from Robert Kennedy or that he let his temper get the best of him once in defending his academic record. Given the political climate, he had sinned and had to be banished.

In both the Hart and Biden cases, damaging information had become public via the mainstream news media. Only afterward did the gossip tabloids join in. But that journalistic pecking order was reversed in the next presidential campaign, to the great discomfort of Democratic candidate Bill Clinton.

Like Hart, Clinton in earlier years had been the subject of widespread but unpublished rumors about womanizing. According to David Maraniss in *First in His Class*, they had started as far back as 1974, in Clinton's first (unsuccessful) political campaign for a seat in Congress, when he was still a bachelor. They continued when he became governor and, again according to Maraniss, the allegations were discussed by Clinton and his aides when he first considered running for president in 1987, after Senator Dale Bumpers of Arkansas announced he would not run for the White House in 1988. Clinton began to assess his own chances, and when Gary Hart withdrew in early May 1987, the young Arkansas governor explored how the Hart episode was likely to affect the political climate. At one point Clinton asked a trusted aide whether there was "a statute of limitations on infidelity—whether you get any credit for getting it [one's marriage] back together." The aide told Clinton not to count on it. Another aide confronted him with specific allegations about his own conduct and advised him not to run. He decided not to, but the rumors continued.

In 1990, near the end of Clinton's successful bid for a fifth term as governor, a disgruntled former state employee held a press conference and said he was filing a lawsuit against him, charging that he had used a slush fund to entertain at least five women with whom he had had affairs. The man offered no proof and the Arkansas press corps wrote nothing about the allegations or the suit. Clinton was reelected. But still the rumors flourished.

In the summer of 1991, the *Washington Times* reported unverified rumors that Clinton had had "extramarital affairs, illegitimate children and used drugs," and *The New Republic* and the right-wing columnist George Will made references to similar rumors when commenting on how the press should deal with them. Clinton once again conferred at length with aides to consider this potential roadblock to a presidential nomination. According to Frank Greer, one of Clinton's strategists at the time, Clinton argued, "What we're really doing with the standards that journalism and politics have set today, we're encouraging people to split up and divorce. If you're divorced, then nobody will ask any questions about you. But if you have some difficult times and work things out, you make a real effort to keep your marriage together, then you have to pay a price."

In the course of those discussions, Clinton's lack of military service also came up. "He always said," Greer recalled, " 'You know, I didn't serve in the military. Basically I got a high lottery number. But, Frank, I opposed the war in Vietnam. I didn't want to serve and I was really thankful when I got a high lottery number. But it's never been an issue here [in Arkansas] because every time it's come up, the people involved, they all said I did nothing wrong and that they'd back me up.' " And so that matter, too, was shunted aside.

The prospective candidate's wife, Hillary, herself raised the question of how to deal with the womanizing allegations. It finally was decided to confront the rumors directly in some press forum; the hope was—as Clinton had often said—that since he had preserved his marriage he should get some credit for it. The forum chosen was a popular breakfast meeting of Washington reporters organized by Godfrey Sperling of *The Christian Science Monitor* in late September 1991, with both Clintons attending. Greer tipped off a reporter that the couple would be ready to discuss the whole issue.

With Hillary sitting at his side, Clinton said he had declined to discuss the rumors in the past because they had been "sparked by a disgruntled state employee who was working for my opponent. Those were false, and I said so at the time." Then he launched into his carefully crafted response. "What you need to know about Hillary and me," he said, "is that we've been together nearly twenty years. It has not been perfect or free from problems. But we're committed to our marriage and its obligations—to our child and to each other. We love each other very much." That answer, he said, "ought to be enough" to put the matter to rest. In this hope, Clinton was relying on the news media to adhere to the old journalistic standard: that you reported verifiable facts, not unproved rumors. That was what had happened in Hart's case, with the *Miami Herald* writing its story only after its investigation. The mainstream news media viewed gossip sheets with attitudes ranging from indifference to contempt; they certainly did not take their lead from them.

Shortly after Clinton declared his candidacy for the Democratic presidential nomination, the sex magazine *Penthouse* ran a raunchy paid interview with a self-described rock star groupie from Arkansas named Connie Hamzy, in which she alleged that she had had a near-encounter with Clinton in a North Little Rock hotel back in 1984. The interview became fodder for local talk radio. Clinton's embryonic presidential campaign office swung into action, gathering affidavits from several Clinton associates who could swear to have seen the woman approaching Clinton and Clinton rebuffing her. CNN's *Headline News* mentioned the interview once but dropped the story after the affidavits were produced.

In mid-January 1992, as Clinton was campaigning in New Hampshire for the state's traditional kickoff presidential primary, the *Daily Mail* of London printed a story about the old Arkansas lawsuit filed by the disgruntled former state employee. It was largely ignored in the United States, but a few days later a supermarket tabloid, *The Star*, ran an account of its own, and it was off to the races thereafter. Although the Clinton campaign could provide denials from all five women mentioned in the suit, two New York newspapers latched on to the story: first the *New York Post* featured it with a headline declaring "Wild Bill," and then the *Daily News* proclaimed it with the headline "I'm No Gary Hart." Another paper, the *Boston Herald*, and the Fox television network, with its growing reputation for tabloid journalism, joined in. Clinton, at a New Hampshire hotel, dismissed the stories as "old news" that had been "thoroughly investigated" and found to be "totally bogus," stories that had emerged "as I start to do a little better" in the campaign, and were the work of a gossip sheet "that says Martians walk on earth and cows have human heads."

Nevertheless, the stories were beginning to seep into the journalistic mainstream. Some newspapers questioned the ethics of printing such stories, and others published pious articles discussing the ethical questions as a sort of backdoor way of reporting the allegations. The verbal combat known as *Crossfire*, on CNN, had the editor of the *New York Post*, Jerry Nachman, defending his paper's publication of the charges and a Democratic television consultant, Mandy Grunwald, taking the opposite position.

Then came a televised debate among the Democratic presidential candidates. The moderator, Cokie Roberts of ABC News and National Public Radio, asked Clinton to comment on "concern on the part of members of your party that these allegations of womanizing, that the Republicans will find somebody and that she will come forward late, and that you would lose the all-important Democrat women's vote." Clinton's pollster, Stanley Greenberg, later called the question "a fairly scurrilous form of journalism." Clinton replied that the allegations were "an example of what the Republicans have been trying to do to me for years." He said he didn't believe they should be rewarded at the polls for "the kind of rumormongering negative and totally irrelevant stuff that they won on four years ago. I don't think the American people are going to fall for it again."

But the allegations, now greatly embellished, kept coming. *The Star* in its next weekly edition ran a detailed, spicy first-person account by one of the five women mentioned in the original Arkansas lawsuit, Gennifer Flowers, under the headline "They Made Love All Over Her Apartment." Flowers said that from 1977 to 1989, Clinton had frequently jogged over from the state capitol to her apartment, where he had outdone himself in various sexual exploits. The tabloid said that Flowers had turned over to its editors fifteen taped telephone calls with Clinton from December 1990 to recent days. On one, dated a week before Clinton's formal declaration of candidacy, Flowers was heard to express concern about pressures from the news media, and a man's voice that Flowers identified as Clinton's replied, "If they ever hit you with it, just say no and go on. There's nothing they can do. I expected them to look into it and come interview you. But if everybody is on record denying it, no problem."

ABC News got an advance copy of this article and privately asked Clinton about it. While declining to verify that it was his voice on any particular tape, he later acknowledged that he had talked by phone to Flowers, whom he had helped get a state job. She told him of the tabloid press offering her as much as $50,000 to say she had had an affair with Clinton, he said, and that was what he was referring to in the remark she attributed to him. Clinton's headquarters in Little Rock had a year-old letter from Flowers' lawyer threatening to sue a local radio station because a talk-show host had "wrongfully and untruthfully alleged an affair between my client, Gennifer Flowers, and Bill Clinton." Damage control aides set about duplicating the letter for distribution to the press.

By the time Clinton arrived in the midst of a bleak winter storm at a small plant that made paintbrushes in Claremont, New Hampshire, the reporters traveling with him had also obtained copies of the incriminating story, and he was peppered with questions as he squeezed into a small foyer at the front of the plant. He insisted that "the story is not accurate, the story is just not true. She's obviously taking money to change her story." Clinton said that each time Flowers had called him in distress he had told his wife, and she had advised him to return the calls. "I did call her back every time she called me," he said. "She said she was frightened, she felt beleaguered, she felt pressure, she felt that her life was being ruined by people harassing her" and later "offering her bribes to change her story." He had told her, he said, "to just tell the truth."

Clinton then proceeded to tour the plant and make some remarks to the workers as if nothing untoward was happening. But when he was finished with the tour, he made a beeline for the plant's upstairs offices, where he closeted himself with two political advisers, George Stephanopoulos and Paul Begala.

We reporters accompanying him had our own dilemma. Here was a scurrilous, very damaging story printed by a supermarket gossip sheet in general disrepute among mainstream journalists. In the past, we would have ignored such a story. But here was the Clinton campaign making a public response to it, circulating copies of the woman's denial to a Little Rock radio station a year earlier, and putting Clinton's daily schedule on hold while he and his political strategists met behind closed doors to figure out what the next step should be. There clearly was a campaign crisis going on, and for us to have ignored it would have left us open to allegations that we were covering up or showing favoritism toward the candidate. In a highly competitive situation, we reporters dutifully lined up at the single pay phone in the plant cafeteria and transmitted our accounts of the fiasco to our news organizations. It didn't seem to matter at this point that the initial story had come from a supermarket gossip sheet. Circumstances dictated that attention be paid.

Some paid more attention than others. *The New York Times*, which had stepped gingerly into the Hart story four years earlier, did the same again this time. While other newspapers headlined the Flowers allegations on page one, the *Times* relegated them to eight inches on an inside page under the headline "Clinton Denounces Report of Affair." But New Hampshire's top television station, WMUR-TV in Manchester, carried a vivid report of the scene in Claremont with Clinton being bombarded by questions. The major networks, however, ignored the story that night, except for a brief reference in a Clinton profile on NBC—and an artful dodge by ABC News's *Nightline.*

ABC's news executives, having decided not to touch the story in their regular evening news roundup show in spite of having had a copy of *The Star* in hand early in the day and having questioned Clinton directly about it, now dragged the supermarket report into the mainstream with a carom shot. *Nightline* decided to devote itself to an analysis of the ethics of publishing this story. Efforts to get the Clintons themselves to appear on the show fell short, so the executives agreed to invite Mandy Grunwald, the television advertising consultant who earlier had appeared on *Crossfire* and who subsequently joined the Clinton campaign.

An aggressive young woman who had prepared many of her own clients for television appearances, Grunwald was more than a match for Ted Koppel. When he asked her in his lofty style if it was possible to put this kind of story in proper "perspective, or does it develop a momentum of its own?" she immediately went on the attack. She noted that until this time *Nightline* had not done any programs about Clinton or any of the other presidential candidates. "But here we are just a couple of weeks before the New Hampshire primary," she continued, and "people are about to go out there and vote . . . They have real concerns. And you're choosing with your editorial comment, by making this program about some unsubstantiated charges that . . . started with a trashy supermarket tabloid . . . You're setting the agenda and you're letting *The Star* set it for you."

Grunwald's scolding of Koppel made her an instant heroine not only in the Clinton campaign but for many viewers who had had their fill of his all-knowing prosecutorial manner. A gossip-journalism story that apparently had been deemed too questionable for the network to present as "news" was seized upon by the same network as a legitimate subject for "analysis."

For all of Grunwald's gutsy counterattack, the Clinton campaign decided that a direct response from the candidate could not be sidestepped. Its strategists finally decided on CBS News's *60 Minutes* as the best opportunity, especially because it was scheduled for the next Sunday night right after the Super Bowl, with its huge audience.

Both Clintons taped the interview with CBS correspondent Steve Kroft on Sunday morning. Before the taping began, according to a key Clinton adviser who was present, the show's senior producer, Don Hewitt (who had helped produce the historic first 1960 Kennedy-Nixon debate), knelt at Clinton's side and said, "When he asks you if you committed adultery, say yes. It will be great television. I know. I know television. The last time I did something like this, Bill, it was the Kennedy-Nixon debates and it produced a president. This will produce a president too." Clinton, the adviser said, simply "listened impassively."

Clinton made no such blanket admission; he denied having had an affair with Flowers, but he did say he had been responsible in unspecific ways for "wrongdoing" and for "causing pain in my marriage," while Hillary sat supportively at his side. As for the question about adultery, he was "not prepared tonight to say that any married couple should ever discuss that with anyone but themselves."

Near the end of the interview, Clinton said, "I think most Americans who are watching this tonight, they'll know what we're saying, they'll get it, and they'll feel that we have been more candid. And I think what the press has to decide is, are we going to engage in a game of 'Gotcha'?" Recalling a time "when a divorced person couldn't run for president, and that time, thank goodness, has passed," he asked, "Are we going to take the reverse position now that if people have problems in their marriage and there are things in their past which they don't want to discuss which are painful to them, that they can't run?" And Hillary added, "I don't think being any more specific about what's happened in the privacy of our life together is relevant to anybody besides us."

The Clintons' performance was widely judged a success, but the story was far from over. The next day in New York, Flowers at a televised press conference insisted that Clinton was "absolutely lying" in saying they had not had an affair, and she played twelve minutes, out of an hour or more, of tapes she said she had made available to *The Star.* Nothing on the tapes, however, definitively established that such an affair had occurred. Nevertheless, CNN carried the press conference live and the other network news shows showed portions that night. The old line between supermarket and mainstream journalism had vanished.

According to Clinton's chief strategist, James Carville, the Clinton campaign did its best to make the mainstream news media squirm about taking a lead from the gossip sheets. "After everybody went through it, no one felt very good about it. It was my job [to foster that feeling]. I was out there trying to make [press and television] people feel bad about it." An ABC News poll subsequently found that 80 percent of the people surveyed said they didn't think whether or not Clinton had had an extramarital affair should have been an issue in the campaign.

Nor, indeed, did the mainstream press surrender its watchdog role entirely to the supermarket tabloids. Only days after Flowers' press conference, the eminently respectable *Wall Street Journal* quoted a retired army recruiter in Arkansas as saying that Clinton, during the Vietnam War in 1969, had signed up for the Reserve Officers Training Corps (ROTC) at the University of Arkansas to avoid the draft and then "was able to manipulate things so that he didn't have to go in."

At the time, Clinton had been at Oxford on a Rhodes Scholarship, and as an ROTC enrollee had a further deferment to finish there. He had said then that he intended to enter the University of Arkansas Law School and the ROTC program but later decided not to enter that program and asked to be put back in the draft; after being reclassified 1-A, he received a draft number too high to be called up and went on to Yale Law School, not Arkansas. The retired recruiter explained to the *Journal* that had it been known Clinton wasn't going to go to law school in his native state, he never would have received the deferment that enabled him to continue at Oxford.

Once again the Clinton campaign was thrown into a damage control mode as the result of a newspaper story, this time in a pillar of mainstream journalism. Still in New Hampshire, Clinton was bombarded with questions about his draft history. He insisted he had not signed up for the ROTC in Arkansas to avoid the draft and when he pulled out had no way of knowing he would have a draft lottery number too high to be called up. "I put myself into the draft when I thought it was a hundred percent certainty that I would be called," he said. And later: "I did not do anything wrong, and I certainly didn't do anything illegal."

But the whole notion of a presidential candidate avoiding military service, whether legally or not, was a political bomb waiting to go off. Once again, ABC News provided the spark, disclosing a letter written by Clinton in Oxford in December 1969 to the ROTC recruiter in Arkansas thanking him for "saving me from the draft." In the letter, written only days after Clinton had received the high draft number, the then twenty-three-year-old poured out his deep opposition to the Vietnam War and to the government's right to "make its citizens fight and kill and die in a war they may oppose." He praised two Oxford friends who were conscientious objectors and said he had considered that option but "decided to accept the draft in spite of my beliefs for one reason: to maintain my political viability within the system," having prepared himself for "a political life." He hoped his explanation "will help you to understand more clearly how so many fine people have come to find themselves still loving their country but loathing the military, to which you and other good men have devoted years, lifetimes, of the best service you could give."

Many people in the Clinton campaign and the news media concluded that publication of this letter was the kiss of death to the Arkansas governor's presidential dreams. But with deft handling, including an appearance on *Nightline* by Clinton himself, the candidate once again survived. Afterward, Clinton said the letter was "consistent with everything I've said for the last eighteen years [about his draft record] . . . although it is a true reflection of the deep and conflicted feelings of a just-turned-twenty-three-year-old young man."

Although neither the womanizing allegations nor the draft controversy shot down Clinton's candidacy, together they kept a cloud over his head throughout the campaign, and kept the news media—both mainstream and gossip tabloid—on the trail of his personal life. The question of his draft record, Clinton said, "came to have legs partly because the press thought that there was still more to come out. And frankly, my opponents felt more comfortable raising questions about it [than about the allegations of womanizing]." Damage control by this time had become a standard aspect of campaign strategy and management: part of it the marshaling of facts and arguments to counter allegations; part of it the questioning of the news media's motives and conduct. The credibility of the news media had become a casualty of journalism peering into corners previously ignored or left unexamined out of taste, ethics, and a sense of a candidate's right to privacy.

It cannot be fairly said, however, after Clinton's election in 1992, that the voters had not been informed about issues concerning his "character." There was a lengthy documentation of the man's record for deceiving and dissembling at the time when voters were called upon to make a judgment of him. And in the campaign of 1996, one old episode in the history of Bill and Hillary Clinton (their failed Whitewater land deal), one tragically new one (the suicide of White House aide and close personal friend Vincent Foster), and a new allegation of old sexual misconduct haunted Clinton and kept the searchlight of both the mainstream and gossip tabloid press on the First Couple.

Although a long-drawn-out investigation of Whitewater by independent counsel Kenneth Starr produced no formal charges of wrongdoing against either of the Clintons throughout the course of the 1996 campaign, a constant tug-of-war between the White House and Starr about documents sought by Starr kept the story, and various other allegations, in the news. Inquiries by the police and others into the circumstances of the suicide of Foster, who had been the White House lawyer in charge of overseeing the Whitewater case, fanned new allegations—and wild, unproven speculation aired by radio talk-show hosts as fact—that Foster and Hillary Clinton had had a personal relationship that went beyond friendship. More embarrassing, however, was a civil suit brought by a former Arkansas state employee named Paula Corbin Jones, charging Clinton with sexual harassment and deprivation of civil rights. She alleged that Clinton had ordered state troopers to bring her to a Little Rock hotel room, where he proceeded to lower his trousers and ask her to perform oral sex, which she refused. She sought $700,000 in damages and pressed for a trial.

Clinton's lawyers argued that such a trial would seriously interfere with his conduct of the presidency and should be put off until after he left office. The Supreme Court ruled against him, but White House lawyers succeeded in fending off a trial until after he had been reelected, entering into negotiations with Jones's lawyers. They reportedly offered to have Clinton pay the $700,000 but balked at Jones's insistence that the president apologize. Clinton steadfastly denied any wrongdoing and declined, so the case dragged on well into his second term. The judge in the case, Susan Webber Wright, finally threw it out on grounds that whether the allegations were true or not, Jones had not been damaged in her job or in her advancement opportunities, as she had charged. Jones appealed, but before the appeal was heard, Clinton through his lawyers decided to settle for $850,000. (Later, Judge Wright found the president in contempt of court, anyway, for testifying falsely and obstructing the Jones case.)

If it seemed strange that Clinton would settle a case he had won at such a high cost, his action became clearer in light of another, much more serious allegation of sexual misbehavior that posed a much greater challenge for reporters trying to meet the dual responsibility of informing the public and doing so within the bounds of fairness and professional ethics. In January 1998, another revelation of a sexual affair by Clinton, as president in the White House itself, ushered in a new era in the history of the news media as character police. New players now joined in, not just supermarket tabloids whose reports had already been dragging the mainstream press into purveying rumor and gossip. Scandalmongering found a new home in cyberspace by way of the Internet and in expanded cable television, with repeated reports that the president had had a sexual dalliance with a twenty-one-year-old White House intern named Monica Lewinsky in the Oval Office.

Clinton quickly denied these reports, but they triggered a frenzy of investigation, gossip, and rumor that obliterated the distinction between the mainstream press and the gossip sheets. A *Newsweek* reporter, Michael Isikoff, had been diligently investigating reports of sexual misbehavior by Clinton for months, but it fell to a wildly irresponsible trader in rumor on the Internet named Matt Drudge, a cartoon character out of the Walter Winchell era, to break the story. He learned of Isikoff's investigations and co-opted him as a result of an excess of caution by *Newsweek*'s editors. As the newsmagazine let its weekly deadline go by in order to check out the story further, Drudge's report turned loose an avalanche of other accounts, first in *The Washington Post* and the *Los Angeles Times.* At once, everyone else jumped in, pressed now by every other manner of information-conveying and rumor-spreading outlets, particularly on the Internet and cable. Starr's Whitewater investigation was expanded to look into the Lewinsky matter, and in short order allegations of perjury, subornation of perjury, and obstruction of justice were hanging heavily over the sitting president, jeopardizing completion of his second term.

The first days of the frenzy were marked by an uncommon seizing upon, publishing, and airing of unsubstantiated, unsourced, or weakly sourced reports either without attribution or with the use of the naked word "sources." In a pell-mell determination not to be left in the dust, news organizations everywhere repeatedly seized on unattributed or nominally attributed stories told by others and compounded their circulation with little or no attempt to verify them. Along with this came reckless predictions of Clinton's political demise. For example, Sam Donaldson observed, "If he's not telling the truth, I think his presidency is numbered in days. This isn't going to drag out . . . Mr. Clinton—if he's not telling the truth, and the evidence shows that—will resign, perhaps this week."

Despite a gag order against leaks issued by federal judge Norma Holloway Johnson in the Lewinsky case, it became apparent early on that the lawyers involved were talking to certain reporters who, operating on the time-honored practice of shielding their sources, were leaving the reading and viewing public to speculate as to where—if anywhere—their information was coming from. The most sensational and damning early report came from ABC News correspondent Jackie Judd, attributing her information to "a source with direct knowledge of" Lewinsky's allegations to Starr. She told her audience, "Lewinsky says she saved, apparently as a kind of souvenir, a navy blue dress with the president's semen stain on it. If true, this could provide physical evidence of what really happened." Judd's report hit a wall of public and press criticism as a new low in the abandonment of taste in journalism. In time, however, she was vindicated, when Lewinsky turned over just such a dress to Starr's office, and DNA testing by the FBI corroborated her story that Clinton had indeed been engaged in a sexual relationship of some kind with her.

Many other reports, however, proved to be fictional or unverifiable, as rumor and fact became interwoven in the tabloid press, on the Internet, and in the traditional news media. In this case, it was not a matter of mainstream journalism being dragged reluctantly to cover a story: the scandal became so big so fast, and of such seemingly catastrophic consequences for the political life of the president and the country, that the "responsible" news media, the stately *New York Times* included, were obliged to join the competition or be swept away.

(It was in this context that Clinton admitted, in a sealed deposition, that he had indeed had sex with Gennifer Flowers when he was governor of Arkansas—but, he testified, only once. Michael McCurry, Clinton's press secretary, contended that candidate Clinton had not lied in his *60 Minutes* appearance in 1992, presumably because his encounter with Flowers had been a one-night stand, not the twelve-year affair that Flowers had alleged and about which Clinton had been explicitly asked.)

The whole matter was not concluded until more than a year later, with the impeachment of Clinton by the Republican-controlled House of Representatives and his subsequent acquittal in a Senate trial; solid Democratic support frustrated the requirement of a two-thirds vote to convict him. Despite that outcome, Clinton's "character" lay shattered by the experience and, along with it, the reputation of the news media.

Accordingly, in any discussion of the news media's watchdog function in presidential politics, it is clearer than ever that part of it must be to provide, *before* a presidential election, as much information—substantiated, not just rumored or gossiped—as possible about the candidates' conduct of their lives. Timely presentation is imperative, so that voters can make informed decisions about whether such candidates are fit for the presidency. And fitness means having not only the experience and intelligence for the job but also the moral fiber and behavioral judgment to stand as a role model for the citizenry.

Acquiring the facts on which to make that appraisal must be done within the bounds of fairness and sensitivity to individual rights of privacy. This caveat was well illustrated in the furor over rumors of cocaine use by George W. Bush that began building in the summer of 1999.

In focusing on matters of "character" regarding Clinton, the news media in the 1996 campaign failed to uncover or largely ignored another, equally significant scandal—the outrageously excessive fund-raising by Clinton, Vice President Al Gore, and the Democratic National Committee to finance the reelection of the national Democratic ticket. Usually, Republicans far outdid Democrats in siphoning money from their supporters, but they had not done so with quite the audacity displayed by the Clinton crew in the 1996 election cycle. News reports and Senate hearings after the election chronicled Clinton's use of White House perks including overnight stays in the Lincoln Bedroom for big campaign contributors, and aggressive fund-raising within the White House walls, all of which placed a cloud over him and Gore as well.

Clinton's Attorney General, Janet Reno, had the Justice Department investigate whether there was enough evidence of wrongdoing to justify appointment of an independent counsel; then, during the course of the impeachment of Clinton she ruled there was not. Still, the allegations were politically dangerous for the vice president—particularly his involvement in a fund-raising event at a Buddhist temple in Los Angeles—as he planned for his own presidential campaign in 2000.

As in the election campaign twenty-four years earlier, when Richard Nixon's reelection committee committed wretched excess to obliterate a weak challenger, Clinton and his campaign went overboard to turn back a bland challenge from the opposition. The "anything goes" mentality that drove the Nixon campaign in 1972 was alive and well in the Clinton campaign of 1996—but most of the American press did not focus on it until after the campaign was over and Clinton had won. With a few notable exceptions, the press corps chased the presidential candidates around the country as they had always done, and monitored their television ads as they more recently had done, but largely missed the most important story. This failure did nothing to enhance the public's already limited respect for the news media.

Many news organizations spend hundreds of thousands of dollars sending out reporters on exorbitantly expensive press planes following the candidates for the entire long primary campaign season, and following the presidential and vice presidential nominees every day of the fall campaign. There had been a time when such coverage was fruitful, when reporters shared the same planes with candidates, had chances to interview them and their aides, and could observe some of the inner workings of the campaigns. But it is a different story when reporters are confined to press planes and, except for a few selected pool reporters, have no opportunity for direct contact. When the press plane lands, the reporters are kept away from the candidate, herded behind ropes where they can only watch as the candidate greets VIPs and voters. What they usually see and hear is the candidate giving the same stump speech he has given many times before, to audiences to whom it may seem new, but to them has become mind-numbing.

In 1996, Bob Dole says, "I don't think I went back to visit with reporters over three or four times, because there might be two people in the whole plane who didn't agree with the other fifty-some that this was off the record. So you couldn't have any fun or sit down and talk to somebody." The advice from his strategists, he says, was: " 'Don't talk to the media. Stay back. Don't answer any questions.' You know this theory—'You've got a message to get out, stay on your message.' And if you let the media talk to you off to the side, your message will be reported, but it'll be a footnote instead of the story. Ten years ago you could still get the message out."

The more recent practice of monitoring the candidates' television commercials and printing "truth watch" analyses and commentaries on them has been a most helpful development. But the old reportorial habits continue to focus on the "death watch" aspect: the term has a literal connotation—for editors who fear that their news organizations may miss the biggest of stories: an assassination or assassination attempt on an incumbent president or challenger. But the death that reporters watch for is a political one—the gaffe that buries a candidate's chances.

News organizations with ample money and the willingness to spend it—*The New York Times*, *The Washington Post*, the *Los Angeles Times*, *The Wall Street Journal*, and a few others—have the resources to do both the political death watch and independent reporting on key campaign issues, including how and how much money is being raised and spent. But most either don't have the money or won't spend it, preferring to make do with sending their reporters chasing candidates around the country doing work that could be performed just as well and much more cheaply by the Associated Press. Their justification and imagined reward is having the byline of their own reporter on a presidential campaign story, though this is noticed by the reporter himself, his wife, his editors, and probably very few others.

The credibility of the news of presidential campaigns has been further eroded by a deplorable development within the press corps itself. As we have seen, reporters' pursuit of their own celebrity at times can both overshadow and diminish their ability to do the work for which they are paid, and increasingly paid quite well. Indeed, print reporters sometimes find their reputations inflated for no other reason than having become television celebrities. It is long past the time when reporters confined themselves to reporting and politicians to politics. Reporters, commentators, and columnists with the greatest of ease cross over into politics as press secretaries or as various other political and governmental functionaries, even into political candidacy—and sometimes back over again. A prime example is Patrick J. Buchanan, two-time Republican presidential candidate, with a victory in the 1996 New Hampshire primary to his credit, who after the campaign went back to performing on television and writing a syndicated newspaper column, then again entered the presidential race for 2000.

It works in the opposite direction as well, with prominent politicians and their aides crossing over into journalism while overtly or covertly continuing to carry water for their old party or political bosses. William Safire, Richard Nixon's speechwriter, publicist, and apologist, was hired as a columnist by *The New York Times*; from time to time he defends his late, disgraced boss and tries to diminish the significance of Nixon's Watergate fiasco by referring to nearly every new scandal that comes down the pike as a new "gate"—as in Koreagate, Billygate, Contragate, Nannygate, and so on. Then there are columnists like George Will, a former Republican senatorial aide who boasts that he has never ridden on a press bus and thumbs his upturned nose at any pretense of evenhandedness as a precept of honest journalism. Embracing the cause of limiting congressional terms, for example, he twice testified in favor of the idea before congressional committees. On at least one occasion, in 1980, he helped to prepare a presidential candidate, Ronald Reagan, for his debate with his Democratic opponent, President Jimmy Carter, and then, in a postdebate television analysis, playing the part of press critic, praised Reagan's performance.

Editors, publishers, and television producers reward years of propagandizing by political principals and hangers-on with choice jobs in the news fraternity they have labored to manipulate and even mislead over the years. A prime example is Chris Matthews, onetime press secretary for the late House Speaker Thomas P. O'Neill and a notorious self-promoter. Matthews collared a job as Washington correspondent for the *San Francisco Examiner* and then parlayed it into a cable television talk show that, with his glibness and its noise level and tabloidization of the news, rivals the news-as-entertainment *McLaughlin Group.* In this way the once-clear distinction between those who practice politics and those who report on them is eroded, especially when so many reporters seem as interested in their own public persona as they are in chronicling the performances and personae of the politicians they cover—and join as partners in making television entertainment. No wonder the public has trouble sorting the practitioners of one discipline from those of the other. The sense that Washington politics is one big closed club is inevitable under these circumstances.

It is probably unrealistic to expect or hope for a return to the old days when members of the American press stayed out of the limelight, especially at the level of presidential politics, and concentrated on their job of holding candidates' feet to the fire, rather than striving for celebrity status of their own. But when reporters forget who they are and what their job is, or when they willingly put that knowledge on the back burner and pursue celebrity, both journalism and politics suffer. When they transform themselves into entertainers, instead of giving voters reason to participate in the process, they give them reasons to shun it.

9 A Process Gone Berserk

The major new "improvement" of the 1996 presidential election cycle—bunching up thirty-two state primaries and caucuses within the first six weeks of the political calendar, from early February through mid-March—proved to be a disaster. This "front-loading" was driven by the state political parties' desire to have a more decisive voice in selecting the presidential nominees, and to cash in on the greater publicity, press attention, and spending by candidates' campaigns and the hordes of news organizations covering them. One body of Republican opinion also thought that the earlier the party decided on its nominee, the faster intraparty wounds incurred during the primary competition would heal and the quicker the nominee could focus on the campaign against the Democratic nominee.

All this was academic to the Democrats in 1996 because their nominee was already established. President Clinton was certain to bid for reelection, and any Democratic primaries and caucuses were meaningless. But for the Republicans, who had a full field of contenders, the front-loading was not. So in 1996 the candidates raced from one state primary or caucus to the next at a maddening pace, and voters got only the briefest glimpses of them if at all. As could have been predicted, campaign resources were stretched to the limit, handicapping the poorest of the candidates and giving an additional advantage to the multimillionaire Steve Forbes, whose only inhibition was an unwillingness on his part to write his own personal checks.

Phil Gramm, who had labored for two years raising money for

what he thought would be a long haul in 1996, was wiped out early, as a result of poor showings in Louisiana and Iowa. "Front-loading meant you had to get off to a fast start," Gramm lamented later. "I kept saying [it would be a] marathon, not a sprint, but it turned out to be a sprint."

Bob Teeter agrees. While "ideological candidates" like Gramm, whose appeal lies in the issues they embrace rather than in their personalities, can continue to raise money for a time, what matters for most candidates is momentum, he says. "You guys [the press] are not going to let some guy stay alive when he's finished third in two primaries in a row." One, Lamar Alexander, did in fact continue after finishing third in Iowa and New Hampshire, but he had to drop out of the race shortly afterward. Dole, who nailed down the Republican nomination five months before the convention, had plenty of time to focus on Clinton. But in part because of the financial demands of the front-loaded calendar, especially in light of the free-spending Forbes's challenge, he had little money to spend until the August convention, when full federal financing would begin. "We went around with a tin cup," Dole recalls. "All we could do was fly around and hold news conferences and try to get on the evening news shows. When you're broke, you have to sit around and wait for the convention to get your check. April to August is a long, hot summer, especially when you're running against an incumbent."

The front-loading was clearly a mistake on at least two other counts. It did produce an early Republican nominee, but after Iowa and New Hampshire none of the other primaries or caucuses drew the kind of extensive news media attention the parties wanted, even in the states that had voted before the nomination was nailed down. The primaries and caucuses simply came too thick and fast. And when a number of states were bunched on a single day, the largest one inevitably got what attention could be parceled out by the hard-pressed candidates, with the press and television inevitably focusing only on the front-runners.

Worse, the lack of time between the various primary and caucus dates handicapped responsible voters. They had little chance to see and hear enough of the candidates to make thoughtful judgments about them, and little time to digest whatever constructive analysis reporters and other newspeople could contribute in that abysmally brief period.

"Front-loading and the compression of the primaries into a few weeks is a gigantic advantage to the front-runner and the candidates with the most money," says Haley Barbour, Republican National Chairman during the 1996 campaign, "and a disadvantage to voters, because they have no time to adjust to the winnowing process. If your candidate drops out after three weeks and you have only a week [before the next primary] to pick another one, the best-known and 'safest' candidate benefits. There's a natural shunting of the losing candidates' support to the front-runner." That is what happened when Gramm quit the race and his backers moved to Dole, he says.

Front-loading made it impossible for the news media to keep voters adequately informed. Scarcely had one day's vote in several states occurred than the candidates had to move on to others. An intelligent understanding of the results by press and voters was a continuing challenge. Members of the traveling press and television are criticized under normal circumstances for making snap judgments, for prematurely anointing front-runners and burying others. The insane calendar driving the candidates pell-mell from one state to another made for even greater confusion, uncertainty, and error.

Although many states moved their primaries and caucuses forward, only a handful had a significant say in the Republican outcome, and according to Curtis Gans of the Committee for the Study of the American Electorate later, less than 7 percent of all eligible Republicans bothered to vote. California, which moved its presidential primary from early June to late March, nevertheless found its primary irrelevant, even though about 20 percent of the national convention delegates needed for nomination were to be chosen there.

Barbour later advised California "to go back to the first Tuesday in June and be the hammer" that would nail down the nomination in a more deliberative process. That way, he said, the parties would choose a stronger nominee, because "the longer voters have to look, the better they're going to feel about who they do nominate. It is in the parties' interest for Republican voters to have the most meaningful and effective participation."

Instead of following Barbour's advice, however, the California legislature in 1998 moved the state's presidential primary even earlier, to the first Tuesday in March. The law, signed by retiring Republican governor Pete Wilson, himself then regarded as a 2000 presidential prospect, immediately threatened to change the chemistry of the process. As a state so huge that wholesale politicking, via costly television, and high-name recognition are essential for a winning candidate, California's move was good news for well-heeled, well-known early favorites like Gore among the Democrats and Governor George W. Bush of Texas among the Republicans. But it was bad news for the long shots—short on campaign funds and public recognition. New York and eight other states also moved their primaries to the same date, March 7, compounding the advantage for the well-heeled front-runners and also threatening to minimize the effect of the earliest important delegate contests in Iowa and New Hampshire. Several states also moved their dates to late February.

Had there been competition in the Democratic Party for the presidential nomination in the 1996 election, these destructive aspects would have been doubled. Even with only a Republican nomination race to examine and endure, it was little wonder that voters were overwhelmed—and repulsed. They were inundated every day with election results, analyses, exaggerated candidate claims of success, and rationales for defeat.

The effects of front-loading will be even more important in the 2000 presidential election, when candidates of both parties will have to deal with an even more jammed-up calendar, and so will the already hard-pressed news media. It can only be hoped that by 2004 national and state leaders of both parties will come to acknowledge not only that front-loading is a colossal mistake but also that the whole schedule of primaries and caucuses requires major overhauling. Much more needs to be done in restructuring the preconvention process of delegate selection to make it comprehensible, fair, and conducive to greater voter interest and participation.

Lack of uniformity in the way states choose their delegates—when and where primaries and caucuses are held and under what ground rules—remains a source of confusion and competition among the states. Why do some states use a caucus-convention process and others a primary election, under a dizzying array of differing rules and regulations? And why does the process always have to start off, for all practical purposes, in Iowa and New Hampshire, two small and atypical states?

Actually, the process starts well before the first primaries and caucuses. Long before then, prospective candidates have begun their exhausting quest for campaign money and for ways to generate favorable publicity that will attract contributions. At the same time, state parties vie for early attention by scheduling fund-raising events and straw polls to lure presidential hopefuls.

The straw polls particularly have been a plague on the nomination process. Candidates pour much too much money and time into what are essentially meaningless and often misleading exercises, which give false impressions of their strengths or weaknesses and often drain their resources, lessening their chances in the later, significant primary and caucus votes. The classic example was a straw-poll effort (and victory) for Democratic hopeful Senator Alan Cranston of California in Wisconsin in 1983, which turned out to be the high point of his campaign and a harbinger of exactly nothing in 1984. In 1996, Senator Phil Gramm tied Bob Dole in a much-ballyhooed straw poll in Iowa, but was an also-ran in the state's caucauses six months later. The Republican consultant Charles Black, whose candidates have competed in costly and fruitless straw polls, calls them "horrible" distractions. The national parties, he suggests, should tell the state parties that they will receive no money from the national party committees if they hold them in the future.

Still, some candidates, particularly the less well-known ones, believe they cannot pass up any opportunity to become better known or to get their campaigns going. The cycle for the 2000 election began for all intents and purposes almost immediately after the 1996 election, with White House aspirant Lamar Alexander reconstituting his 1996 campaign operation as a political action committee. Called the Campaign for a New American Century, it really should have been labeled the Lamar Alexander Fund for Gathering Friends and Allies for the Year 2000. He held a large fund-raising dinner in Nashville that yielded more than a million dollars and thereafter peppered news organizations around the country with his views on every large or small political development to come down the pike. The self-financing Steve Forbes also revved up almost before Bob Dole's political body was cold, announcing his Americans for Hope, Growth and Opportunity and immediately hitting the political hustings.

Both Alexander and Forbes joined the stampede to the first major candidate "cattle show" at a Republican regional meeting in Indianapolis. More such events followed, condemned by candidates and the news media as meaningless and a waste of campaign resources but attended religiously by both. They looked to them as a way to affect the candidate pecking order.

By August 1999, a Republican straw vote in Iowa took on the dimensions of an election itself, some underfunded candidates looking to it as a test of whether to continue in the race. George W. Bush and Steve Forbes, the two best-financed candidates, finished first and second—Bush at 31 percent and Forbes at 21 percent—in a field of nine. Two days later, Alexander, who ran sixth, did indeed drop out.

The caucus approach—precinct caucuses being the first stage of a process that also includes subsequent county and state conventions—clearly is on the wane. Only eight states in 1996 selected national convention delegates in whole or in part through caucuses and conventions, and except for the precinct caucuses in Iowa, they were ill-attended and sparsely reported. Even the Republican caucuses in Iowa were poor examples of the "living-room democracy" they were touted to be. In fact, they're not really caucuses at all, but merely a series of neighborhood straw polls, sometimes but not always with a little prevoting conversation about candidates and/or issues thrown in. Voters drop into a neighbor's living room or go to a local school, church, or other public building, maybe listen to a few words spoken by a representative for each of the presidential candidates, then write down a candidate's name on a slip of paper—a secret ballot, just as in a primary election.

The main difference between voting in a primary and in one of these caucuses is that in the caucus the voting must occur only at one designated time in the evening in somebody's home or public place, whereas a primary provides a public polling place open for most of the day—and there can be no politicking on the premises. At the GOP precinct caucus I attended in a private home in Des Moines in 1996, representatives of some but not all of the candidates showed up to make brief pitches, but there was virtually no discussion among the caucus attendees before they were asked to mark their ballots.

When the Democratic Party holds precinct caucuses in Iowa in a presidential election year, the meetings can fairly claim the name. Democratic voters who attend them actually discuss the pros and cons of the candidates, then divide themselves up into camps clustered in different areas of the room. Thereupon delegates to the next voting level—the county convention sometime later—are allocated on the basis of strength. For a Democratic candidate to gain a delegate to the county convention, he has to have at least 15 percent of the attendees on an initial division, the measure of whether his candidacy is "viable" at that point. Voters supporting a candidate who does not reach the 15 percent "threshold" then have an opportunity to regroup, either joining another group supporting a candidate who has reached the threshold or binding together in support of a "nonviable" candidate and giving him the needed 15 percent for a delegate.

This procedure very often stimulates lengthy discussion about the candidates and their stand on important political issues. It is a true exercise in democracy, complete with wheeling and dealing, raised voices, and sometimes even fights.

The drawback is that while many voters have little reluctance to go behind a curtain and pull a voting lever in a primary, they have qualms about going into the home of a neighbor, often a stranger, or into a schoolroom or church basement full of strangers, and standing up in open support of a specific politician. In Iowa, this procedure more often than not occurs on a frigid February night, further discouraging voters. As a result, a caucus turnout is almost always much lower than for a primary. Even with all the national news media attention focused on Iowa, and the chance that you might see Peter Jennings, Tom Brokaw, or Dan Rather in your neighborhood, more than 10 percent of eligible voters seldom show up.

Primary elections, especially in New Hampshire and other states that hold them early in the year, draw much larger crowds. Voters are more familiar with the procedure, don't have to go into a stranger's house, and don't have to engage in political discussion and identify themselves publicly for a given candidate. Even with guaranteed anonymity, however, turnout for presidential primaries, except in New Hampshire and a few other states early on the calendar, is also low compared to the turnout for the general election.

The proliferation of primaries has been the product of reform measures in the Democratic Party designed to generate more grassroots political activity. Primaries as a practical matter call for less voter initiative than caucuses, and since they more closely resemble general elections and preserve the national tradition of the secret ballot, they are more easily understood by voters.

Whether voters choose presidential candidates in precinct caucuses, county and state conventions, or primaries, the consequence has been in most states to shift decision making from local and state party leaders to the voters directly. Caucuses, with their lower turnout and greater demands on organization and persuasion, still enable party leaders to exert considerable influence. But they don't always dominate, as the results in the first two delegate-selection caucuses of 1996, in Louisiana and Iowa, amply demonstrated. Louisiana Republican leaders, who strongly supported Phil Gramm and badly wanted national media attention, in effect "stole" Iowa's traditional role as the caucus kickoff state in 1996. They had the additional hope of giving Gramm an early lead in the delegate count; in early 1995, in a straw poll at a state party convention, Gramm had won 72 percent of the vote, so his supporters in the

Republican hierarchy in Louisiana confidently scheduled statewide "caucuses" six days before what was usually the election year's first caucuses in Iowa.

The move was a fiasco, ineptly planned and executed. Makeshift polling places were set up in only forty-two poorly advertised locations, with the polls open for only four hours. And because there were no provisions for prevoting discussion, it was really a primary, not a caucus. Gramm thought he had Louisiana sufficiently well organized so that he did not have to campaign there until caucus day itself. All the other candidates except Pat Buchanan and Alan Keyes boycotted the Louisiana voting in deference to outraged Iowa Republicans, who zealously guarded their first-in-the-nation tradition. To be sure, they were "encouraged" to do so by a demand from Iowa Republican chairman Brian Kennedy, to which they adhered, that they pledge not to compete in caucuses that Louisiana had "stolen" from Iowa. Buchanan had no support from the Louisiana party establishment except for renegade Governor Mike Foster, whom he had endorsed, but he exploited Gramm's miscalculations and campaigned hard in his absence. When he won the makeshift "caucuses" Gramm started on his downhill slide.

In the Iowa caucuses, six days later, despite strong support from Governor Terry Branstad and the state party organization, Bob Dole managed only a narrow three-point victory over Buchanan, which generated more comment about Dole's weakness than about his success. And a week later, he lost the New Hampshire primary to Buchanan. Still, by then he had enough campaign money and organization, as well as a storehouse of goodwill in his party built over many years of loyal service, to survive the setback and sew up the Republican nomination in a matter of weeks.

Iowa and New Hampshire have always been regarded as the states where serious contenders for the party nominations are separated from the rest. Candidates who meet or exceed expectations there, and hence can raise the campaign money needed to go on or already have the money to persevere, survive to continue the marathon run. The others are said to have been "winnowed out"—a description that prompted long-shot Democratic senator Fred Harris in 1976 to proclaim on the basis of a weak third-place Iowa finish in a field of ten that he had been "winnowed in." But he too in time was winnowed out of the race by poor showings in later primaries and a consequent lack of funds.

All this began to change, however, in 1988, when other states contested

Iowa and New Hampshire for the windfall of candidate time, national publicity, and heavy spending by campaign and news media brought to them because of their early place on the election-year calendar. The two kickoff states began to feel a time squeeze. Iowa, which once had held its first caucuses in March, moved them up to February, and New Hampshire moved its primary up to only eight days after the Iowa voting. There was less time for a candidate who had made an unexpectedly good showing in Iowa to capitalize on it. Bob Dole upset then Vice President Bush in Iowa, but he couldn't withstand a heavy, and negative, late television advertising campaign against him in New Hampshire and his campaign faded.

Still, Iowa and New Hampshire have remained the early focus of presidential aspirants. In the 1996 election cycle, the contenders spent record amounts of time and money courting Republican voters there for more than a year. In no other states did the candidates do such intensive and serious campaigning that would enable voters to cast truly informed and reasoned votes—based on knowledge and understanding of the candidates' intellect, experience, personality, character, and in-depth positions on the major and minor issues of the day.

The effort of Louisiana Republicans in 1996 to usurp Iowa's tradition of being first failed mostly because the candidates had already invested much time and money in Iowa in 1995, and because they were unwilling to buck the tradition. Also in 1996, New Hampshire governor Steve Merrill, another Dole national campaign leader, extracted from most of the candidates a pledge not to compete in the Delaware primary, scheduled only four days after the first primary in New Hampshire. Forbes refused to sign it, though, and, by dint of his campaigning virtually unchallenged in Delaware and his expensive outlays for advertising there, he won the primary—and the resentment of Merrill and presumably many other Republicans in New Hampshire, where he finished a dismal fourth.

Despite these attempts by Louisiana and Delaware to lure Republican candidates away from Iowa and New Hampshire, the traditions survived. Reporters were once again able to write in 1996 about voters in the two customary kickoff states telling them that they hadn't made up their minds yet because they had only met so-and-so personally three or four times. Voters in most of the forty-eight other states did not get much of a look at the 1996 Republican field, however, especially as a result of the front-loading. The most absurd illustration of the folly came shortly afterward in New York, where the 102 delegates at stake were the largest convention prize yet offered in a primary or caucus. By then, the only "serious" contenders left were Dole, Forbes, and Buchanan, and none gave even two full days to this megastate. New York City, the nation's largest, was bypassed almost completely by Dole and Forbes—and completely by Buchanan, as old charges of anti-Semitism against him were renewed and trumpeted there. Instead, Dole and Forbes braved heavy snowstorms in brief upstate swings. In the end every single New York delegate went to Dole, thanks to the organization of Senator Alfonse D'Amato, his national chairman, and a process he rigged to benefit Dole. New York's state party leadership was so strong and the primary election mechanism so undemocratic that the voters' opportunity to express their will was severely hampered. D'Amato and Governor George Pataki fought costly court efforts by Steve Forbes to open the process, requiring that one had to have hard-to-get voter signatures on petitions to qualify for ballot position in each of the state's thirty-one congressional districts. At the eleventh hour, a judge ruled in favor of Forbes (and Buchanan, who joined the suit in selected districts), but by that time it was too late for effective political activity.

In most states, however, the proliferation of primaries has meant—or has been intended to mean—that more Americans will have more to say directly in the identity of their party's presidential nominee. State party leaders can still try to use the party apparatus and manpower to deliver the state's delegates to their favorite candidate, and in 1996 did so impressively for Dole after his initial setbacks, though in generally low turnouts.

If a stronger challenger had been able to mobilize higher turnouts in his favor, and had more campaign money to persevere, the machinery was in place to enable him to score upsets, but none could do so in any consistent fashion. Dole swept to the Republican nomination in 1996 not because the process was stacked in his favor everywhere, as it was in New York, but because he had the money to endure despite early setbacks. After voters had a chance—however brief—to consider the alternatives, he was the clear choice.

Not everything about this presidential nominating process is wrong. That some states choose their delegates by primary and others by caucus and convention doesn't matter too much so long as voters have an adequate opportunity to express their will. In Iowa, the precinct caucuses as the Democrats do them have worked quite well, but the quickie system created by the Louisiana

Republicans in 1996 was a farce. It got the paltry public attention it merited, not because Iowa deserves always to hold the first caucuses but because the process in Louisiana was ill-conceived and ill-executed, discouraging rather than encouraging public participation.

Generally speaking, however, if the objective is greater voter participation, the primary system usually offers the better chance for success. True caucuses of the sort conducted in Iowa may be best suited for smaller, rural states where neighborhood gatherings are more traditional and easier to conduct than in major cities and other heavily populated areas. Whichever method is used, common sense demands that while uniformity in rules for delegate selection is not essential and probably not achievable, a more practical and manageable national framework to guide state legislatures must be established if the chaos of recent preconvention politics, and especially of 1996, is to be eliminated.

Some argue that as of now the nominating process is much too long, that the money-raising aspect begins too early, and that there are too many state primaries. Former Democratic National Chairman Don Fowler says that "the American people are not particularly political people. They believe most things that are important to them take place in the private sector of their lives. They're just not interested." With a process that stretches from February to November, plus lead-up time before that, "people get tired and alienated." He suggests that there would be much greater public interest and involvement if the first primaries were not held before June of the election year, if there were fewer of them, and, in fact, if there was a return to the old days of the smoke-filled room. Having party leaders, who know the candidates well, "go to the convention and bargain" over the selection of the nominee might not be, Fowler says, "any worse than what we have now."

The Republican consultant Stuart Spencer agrees. "With all this democracy [of more primaries], it's not better than the old days when we sat in a room [and picked the nominee], because we knew who a winner could be," he says. Democrat Bob Shrum notes that "the peer review process led to some very good nominations," but adds that Ronald Reagan "never would have been nominated under the old process [in 1980] because he wouldn't have passed the peer review. He was not the choice of the political elites. They thought he was too old and didn't know enough. The only way he could have won was in winning the primaries."

Fowler contends that the current nomination system "lacks rationality," having been developed through "trial and error" from state to state, with states guarding their independence and candidates picking and choosing which primaries and caucuses they will enter. Congress, he says, should step in with an entirely new, more abbreviated process, though he doubts that it could ever overcome the resistance by states and politicians to basic change.

Republican consultant John Deardourff advocates less sweeping but significant alterations in the existing system. He would prohibit raising campaign funds until later in the cycle and encourage more states to go back to the caucus process. This, he says, would "reinvigorate the parties and take the process out of the hands of professionals like me." Another old Republican hand, John Sears, notes that while the proliferation of primaries was supposed to broaden voter participation in the nomination and minimize the impact of special interests, it has actually worked the other way. Primary voting has become the activists' game, he says, and "only the special interests take a real interest in voting." Also, he suggests, the length of the campaign only breeds voter contempt. "By June," he says, "voters say they don't like either one of these guys" slated for nomination, but it's too late then to do anything about it.

The current system gives too much attention to the desires of the state parties and not enough to the needs of the public. There must be provision for breathing room between each primary or caucus day, so that candidates can campaign adequately in every state about to vote and voters and the news media can digest what has gone before. Also, candidates who do well in the earliest contests need time to reap the benefits of their success, in wider publicity and stronger fund-raising.

Ideally, a presidential nomination campaign should permit a progression in the discussion of issues and ideas. The present front-loading instead too often has candidates bouncing from one state to another simply repeating what they've said in earlier states. In these circumstances, what escalates is not the substantive value of the dialogue but the intensity of the negativism. As already noted, when candidates don't campaign in a state, the vacuum is filled more and more by radio and television advertising, itself increasingly negative.

Many proposals have been made to change the preconvention calendar: to have a single national primary day or a series of regional voting days. The first would allow for a long campaign period during which issues could be aired, but the drawbacks outweigh that advantage. For one, such a primary would greatly favor independently wealthy or famous candidates who can easily raise money. It would effectively shut out long shots and as a practical matter concentrate campaigning in the most populous states. And it would amount to a very high, single roll of the dice, with no possibility for reflection or reconsideration.

A series of regional primaries spaced several weeks apart has the obvious advantage of reducing candidate (and news media) travel, thus saving time, energy, and money. It would also allow everyone ample time to hear and see the candidates and assess developments of the whole campaign. Theoretically at least, it could encourage more discussion of regional issues. But it might give undue advantage to whichever candidate came from the region that held its primaries first, and penalize others whose background and strength with voters lay elsewhere. Also here, too, the larger states doubtless would get the most attention. The National Association of Secretaries of State has adopted a proposal for the 2004 presidential election that would group all state primaries into regions—East, South, Midwest, and West—with their primaries to be held on or about the first Tuesday of March, April, May, and June. The regions would rotate going first every four years, with Iowa and New Hampshire continuing as the leadoff states. Chances of the states agreeing, however, seem slim.

This regional approach might have made more sense in earlier years, when travel distances were more of a factor than they are today. But in the era of the jet plane, candidates now can and do campaign on the East and West Coasts in a single day, and in between as well. There is no reason nonregional groupings could not be created that would give adequate time to campaign and to be seen and heard widely. The most important factor is an orderly, less frenetic process that does not give undue benefit to any candidate or region.

Under the present system, campaigning starts long before the election year, takes a breather during the December holidays, then intensifies in January for the first voting in February. The front-loading in 1996 turned February and March into political madness and then, abruptly, the nominating process for all practical purposes was over, with voters in eighteen states, 36 percent of the total (including California and Pennsylvania), having had no say in the choice. Then came more than four long months of political shadowboxing leading to the August conventions. The same pattern, only more so, was put in place for the 2000 cycle. To what end?

With the major parties holding their conventions in August and launching the general election campaign on or around Labor Day, there are seven months in a presidential election year leading up to this period in which to select the party nominees. January is impractical for voting, for the simple reason that December holidays inevitably intrude on campaign activities and voter attention. That leaves six months. If the first caucuses and primaries were delayed until March, there would still be ten two-week periods between then and the second week in July during which voting could take place in five selected states on every other Tuesday. This schedule would give ample time for candidates to visit all five states, for voters to gain exposure to them and their ideas, and for everyone to reflect on the results of earlier primaries and caucuses and to consider what it all meant.

Limiting each of the ten every-other-Tuesday voting days to five states would also have the advantage of stretching out the decision process. That might not please Republican leaders, who were so eager to settle on an early nominee in 1996, but it would make life much easier for the candidates and make the campaign much more informative for the voters.

To enable long-shot and underfunded candidates to compete, it would be important to have smaller states lead the parade. This would also have the virtue of delaying the actual clinching of the nomination to later in the process, which might persuade larger states like California, New York, Illinois, and Pennsylvania to move their primaries to the late spring. If they were assured by the sheer arithmetic that no candidate would be able to clinch the nomination before they had their say, they might be more receptive to such a schedule.

Iowa and New Hampshire have not only traditions of being first in the process but also a logical argument. Brian Kennedy, chairman of the Iowa Republican Party during the 1996 caucuses, has observed that the two states "have served as equal-opportunity level playing fields where the political Goliaths must stand toe to toe with the little-known or under-financed Davids seeking to become the party's standard-bearer." Testifying before the national party's task force in San Diego, he reported that the Republican candidates in 1996 had spent a combined total of more than 500 days campaigning in Iowa for the caucuses, of which 90 percent were spent in "retail politics" out of "the glare of TV lights and the watchful eye of the press corps . . . For months the campaign was marked by quiet days riding in vans from small town to small town, meeting with potential caucus attendees in cafes and living rooms. Iowa and New Hampshire may be the only places where voters expect the candidates to meet with them and discuss issues, not sound bites."

Political leaders in Iowa and New Hampshire always claim, with considerable validity, that their seasoned caucus and primary voters take their special responsibility most seriously. But they might have to sacrifice it in order to let other smaller states have a crack sometime at leading off the election year. However, the Democratic Party protects the kickoff voting in Iowa and New Hampshire in its charter, and changing that protection would be difficult. The Republicans have no such provision, making it possible for Louisiana to "steal" Iowa's leadoff caucus tradition again in 2000, which it planned to do.

One practical way to schedule state caucuses or primaries would be to have two pools, of smaller and larger states, then to hold a lottery every four years to determine which in each pool goes first, second, and so on, with the larger states starting later on the calendar. Voters in other states surely could be counted on to take the responsibility of heading the parade as seriously as voters in Iowa and New Hampshire do, guaranteeing especially thoughtful appraisal of the candidates and a seasoned skepticism that makes the candidates toe the mark. In fact, voters in new states holding the first delegate selection might be even more motivated than many of those in Iowa and New Hampshire who over the years have become somewhat blasé about the exercise.

Extending the primaries into mid-July would sharply reduce the gaping "intermission" between the end of delegate selection and the opening of the national conventions that occurred in 1996. To be sure, this would not guarantee that voters in the later-voting states would have a say in selecting party nominees, who might well clinch the nominations before the process had run its course. But a rotation of states by lottery in each presidential election year would avoid shutting out the same states at the end of the delegate-selection calendar, and give different smaller states a turn at kicking off the process.

At the Republican National Convention in San Diego in 1996, the Republican National Committee task force on presidential primaries recommended a delegate bonus system to reward states that delayed their primaries and caucuses, with bonuses of from 5 to 20 percent of a state's original delegation, depending on how late the vote came. But the convention reduced the top bonus to 10 percent, not enough to persuade many early-voting states to push their events back to May or June. In any event, the number of delegates a state has to a national convention is largely irrelevant for states with a very early caucus or primary date. What they are after at that stage of the nomination process is not voting power at the distant convention. They are seeking early national attention and a key role in determining which of the candidates will be taken seriously, will draw the news media spotlight, and attract the contributions required to press on. The name of the game at this early stage is expectations met, exceeded, or fallen short of, not delegates won. And in this game, the news media is inordinately important, declaring which candidates have come up to expectations and which have not.

Iowa and New Hampshire, and Louisiana in 1996, held their delegate-selecting processes first in order to cash in on this expectations game—with money and publicity brought to the states. They have known that the first actual phases of convention delegate selection are a strong magnet for presidential hopefuls and the army of reporters following them. Louisiana, snubbed by most Republican candidates in 1996, indicated it intended to be first again in 2000. The massive press coverage that the New Hampshire primary has enjoyed at least since 1952 (when Estes Kefauver upset Harry Truman and drove him from the race for the Democratic nomination) and the Iowa caucuses at least since 1976 (when Jimmy Carter came out of nowhere) has made it virtually impossible for any serious candidate to bypass either state without paying a price. Senator Henry M. Jackson of Washington State ducked New Hampshire in 1976 and Senator Al Gore of Tennessee in 1988 skipped the Iowa caucuses, to the detriment of both their candidacies. When Senator John McCain elected to duck the Iowa GOP straw vote in August 1999, expectations grew that he would skip the Iowa caucuses too in 2000.

In 1976, when there were five weeks between the Iowa caucuses and the New Hampshire primary, Jimmy Carter had ample time to capitalize on his Iowa success. In 1980, the same was true but to a lesser extent for George Bush, who upset Ronald Reagan in Iowa that year; he fell to Reagan in New Hampshire, but for lack of message and campaign performance, not lack of time. In 1984, Gary Hart was able to parlay a rather weak but nevertheless surprising second-place finish to Mondale in Iowa into a media and fund-raising bonanza that helped him upset Mondale in New Hampshire eight days later.

But the shorter the time between Iowa and/or Louisiana and New Hampshire, and between New Hampshire and the rush of other state caucuses and primaries, the less significant will be the windfall of winning or exceeding expectations in the kickoff states. So, too, the chances will diminish for candidates who stumble in the earliest tests to recover and regroup.

What matters most to average voters is the question of how long the whole process takes, not which state gets to be first. For all practical purposes it now lasts for at least a year or more before the presidential election year itself, and then it plods on until Election Day in November. The federal campaign finance law, which stipulates that only contributions raised in the calendar year preceding the election year can qualify for the matching-fund subsidy, dictates that candidates start fund-raising—and campaigning—in January of that preceding year to take optimum advantage of the law. Moreover, the $1,000 limit on individual contributions, unchanged in the twenty-five years of the law's existence, puts extraordinary demands on candidates' time and efforts to raise sufficient money to compete, especially in the front-loaded schedule.

If for no other reason than the ever-increasing costs of television advertising and travel, the limit should be raised. Increasing the individual contribution limit to $5,000 would allow moving the starting date for raising money eligible for matching funds to July 1 of the year preceding the election year, shortening the campaign by six months. Also, persuading or requiring television networks and local stations to provide free time to candidates who have qualified for the federal campaign subsidy, and limiting their purchase of additional time, would cut costs substantially and free the candidates to focus more on live campaigning and discussion of the issues.

John Deardourff proposes laws to ban all paid television commercials once the presidential nominees are selected. At that point, he says, "there is no good argument for ads using public money. The candidates are very well known and there is nothing [new] you can tell us about them in paid ads, so they only highlight the negative aspects of their opponents." The ban could be applied as the price for receiving the federal subsidy for the fall campaign, and the candidates would also be required to agree to at least three debates. The proposal is an excellent one, but one that would be fiercely opposed by the army of campaign professionals who now dominate the election process and enrich themselves from it. Candidates, too, would be reluctant to forgo paid advertising if convinced by their hired guns that it was critical to their election chances.

All the changes suggested here will be resisted on many fronts—by some candidates, by many states, by the television industry and political professionals. Many of the paid consultants are interested less in creating a level playing field than in taking maximum advantage of the system as it is, in behalf of the candidates who hire them or of themselves. Left to their own devices, the various states will continue to jockey for positions most advantageous to their own interests on the political calendar, and the losers, as in the past, will be the voters.

It is time for the national parties, in an era in which their influence seems less and less significant, to cooperate to eradicate the disgrace that is the current process. Only by convincing political leaders in the fifty states that they must make a concerted effort to bring order out of the current chaos can we restore public comprehension of, and confidence in, the process.

10 Coronations, Not Conventions

The Republican National Convention in San Diego and the Democratic National Convention in Chicago in 1996 were only the latest examples of the disintegration of the quadrennial meetings as decisive instruments in selecting the major parties' presidential nominees.

The Republican gathering that anointed Bob Dole was the twelfth in a row over the previous forty-eight years in which the party's decision was confirmed on the first ballot. And the Democratic affair that crowned Bill Clinton marked the eleventh straight time that only one roll call of states was needed. Not since Thomas E. Dewey went over the top before a third Republican ballot in 1948 and Adlai E. Stevenson was chosen on the third Democratic ballot in 1952 has either party had anything like a prolonged contest on the convention floor.

The reasons are obvious. The proliferation and increasing front-loading of primaries produce presumptive nominees well before the conventions. Since 1948 and 1952, circumstances, usually contrived by an eventual loser, have occasionally injected a modicum of uncertainty, but none has ever prevented a first-ballot decision. In 1972, Democratic opponents of Senator George McGovern challenged the legitimacy of the delegates he had won in that year's California primary. They argued that its winner-take-all rule was unfair, although it had long before been approved by the national party's Commission on Delegate Selection; the opposing forces of Hubert Humphrey, in control of the convention's credentials committee, obtained a ruling against McGovern. But in a critical roll-call vote on the convention floor, McGovern prevailed, held on to all of California's delegates, and was nominated on the first ballot.

In 1976, President Gerald Ford appeared to have a majority of the delegates heading into the Republican convention, but Ronald Reagan's campaign manager, John Sears, a veteran of the 1968 Nixon campaign, temporarily threatened Ford's first-ballot nomination with a clever gambit. Sears persuaded Reagan to announce his choice of a running mate in advance—Senator Richard Schweiker of Pennsylvania, then regarded as a moderate. One rationale was that Schweiker might shake loose some Ford delegates in his own state for Reagan, but there was much more involved. Sears reasoned that Ford would come under pressure to disclose *his* running mate from both conservatives and moderates in the party. Whomever he picked, Sears figured, Ford would offend one side or the other. At the convention, he pushed for a rule requiring candidates to name their running mates in advance of the presidential roll call. He lost in committee but got enough votes to bring the issue to the convention floor, by which time he had created the impression that Ford's nomination hung in the balance. The proposed rule finally was voted down, but Sears had kept alive the idea that Reagan was still a viable candidate until shortly before Ford's first-ballot nomination.

In 1980, strategists for Senator Ted Kennedy, challenging President Carter, also tried an eleventh-hour ploy to bar the incumbent's first-ballot renomination. They proposed a "freedom" rule; it would have relieved delegates of the party-approved obligation to vote for the candidate under whose banner they had been chosen as delegates in their state primaries and caucuses. Carter was slipping in the polls at the time, and the Kennedy forces hoped many of his delegates might be having second thoughts. Instead, resentment of Kennedy among Carter supporters deepened, and the strategy failed.

The idea of a rule that freed delegates at the convention of any commitment to support the candidates with whom they were aligned in the primaries or caucuses should not be dismissed out of hand, however. It would protect the parties against the nomination of a standard-bearer about whose qualifications or ability to win there were widespread doubts by convention time. It would offer at least the possibility of restoring a true nominating role to the convention and inject much more uncertainty and hence public interest in the proceedings.

With the choice of the presidential nominees already made before the conventions start, the only major piece of business that remains is the selection of running mates. And in that, the delegates' work almost always is to rubber-stamp the personal choice of the presidential nominee. Not since 1956, when Adlai Stevenson threw the matter open to the Democratic convention and Senator Estes Kefauver was chosen over Senator John Kennedy, did the delegates truly make the decision.

In defense of party conventions that are little more than coronations, many party leaders, such as the Republican consultant Charles Black, argue that when smoothly conducted they can enhance party unity and in the convention platforms make clear statements of party policy and goals. For the only time in four years, it brings together party officials and officeholders from every state for exchanges of ideas as well as conviviality.

All that is true, but the catch is that sometimes the gatherings do not go smoothly. Conflicts are played out under the glare of television lights, party unity is impaired, and defeat in November is risked. At the 1968 Democratic convention in Chicago, the raucous fight over a platform plank about the Vietnam War triggered an uproar on the convention floor and spilled out with rare brutality into the city's streets. War protesters, including some delegates, were beaten unmercifully by the city's police in an ugly paroxysm that contributed to Humphrey's narrow election defeat at Nixon's hands later that year. And at the Republican convention in Houston in 1992, an exclusionary and bellicose harangue by the defeated candidate Patrick Buchanan struck such a discordant note that many Republicans blamed it for the defeat of President Bush by Bill Clinton.

In 1996, on the other hand, the party conventions were so carefully orchestrated to avoid any show of conflict, and to accommodate sharply scaled-back network television coverage, that viewership plunged, although millions of Americans still watched. A low-key fight to remove or change the Republican platform plank opposing abortion was shunted to a preconvention committee session that was not permitted to mar party harmony. With the Democrats, the only matter that temporarily caused a ripple was the sudden resignation of Dick Morris, close to the convention's end, in the wake of the disclosure of his indiscretions with a prostitute.

The notion of antiseptic party conventions whose principal function is to present the parties in their best light to fewer and fewer members of the public is a far cry from what the Founding Fathers intended. There is no mention in the Constitution of either political parties or conventions for them. From the start, it was the Founders' clear intention that the selection of the president be what the later American underworld would call an inside job—a choice by the political elite in each state of one of their own, through the electoral college, which we shall examine in Chapter 14. The precursors of national conventions were congressional caucuses in the various states, first roughly divided among Federalists and Anti-Federalists. The first semblance of a convention took place in 1812, when sixty-four Federalist delegates from eleven states met in New York and nominated James Madison, who was subsequently elected. Local, county, and state political meetings and conventions of various sizes and under various rules were not uncommon by then. In New England, the nonpartisan town meeting was the forerunner, and small states like Delaware and New Jersey were able to hold state conventions without undue travel inconvenience to participants. They were effective counters to the less democratic congressional caucuses.

The first real national political convention was held in 1830 in Philadelphia, when opponents of President Andrew Jackson calling themselves Anti-Masons sent 96 delegates from ten states. They produced a host of anti-Jackson resolutions but no consensus on a presidential nominee to challenge him in 1832. They met again in Baltimore in late 1831, with 116 delegates from thirteen states, and after much casting about settled on William Wirt, Attorney General under President James Monroe, as their candidate. Wirt was a former Mason himself, however, who promptly testified that he never found the society's practices to be offensive or subversive, and his candidacy quickly crumbled. The first national political convention in American history became the first and last of the new party that had convened it.

The first Democratic National Convention also met in Baltimore in May 1832. Curiously, its main business was the nomination of its vice presidential candidate, since Jackson had already been renominated by several state legislatures, and the convention simply concurred. The convention adopted the unit rule—obliging each state delegation to cast all its votes for the candidate who had a majority—and required a two-thirds majority for nomination. Both rules plagued the party often thereafter, until they were finally abandoned.

By the 1840s, national party conventions had become fixtures of the political landscape, and with them came increasing intraparty intrigue. In the celebrated convention of 1844, party power brokers in a "smoke-filled room" denied another nomination to former President Martin Van Buren, and after nine exhausting ballots, a dark horse was chosen, James K. Polk, a former governor of Tennessee.

Independent groups like the Liberty Party, the American Anti-Slavery Party, and the Free Soil Party also held conventions in this period, but could not gain a toehold. In 1856, the new Republican Party met in Philadelphia with more than 600 delegates from all the free states and four border states and picked the forty-three-year-old former army officer and explorer John C. Frémont as their nominee. He ran a creditable race, winning eleven of the sixteen Northern states, but lost to Democrat James Buchanan of Pennsylvania.

Through all this, states selected delegates to the major-party conventions by various means, with third-party conventions coming and going. It was not until the turn of the twentieth century that a state primary election to choose delegates began to be favored. In 1901, the Florida legislature passed an optional primary law that allowed state or local party officials to pick their candidates by this direct means. In 1905, the Wisconsin legislature, led by Robert M. La Follette, Sr., leader of the Progressive movement, also provided for direct election of national convention delegates. In 1906, the Pennsylvania legislature did the same, with the added proviso that candidates for delegate could put the name of the presidential candidate they favored on the ballot next to their own. Finally, in 1910, the Oregon legislature approved the first "pure" presidential preference primary; winning delegates had to support the presidential candidate who won the primary.

The idea quickly spread. By 1912, twelve states had adopted direct election of national convention delegates or a presidential primary, or both. Three more gave their voters the option to do either or both. By 1916, a total of twenty-six states had passed primary laws as part of the Progressive movement's electoral reform, which also included many state laws providing initiative, referendum, and recall provisions, all to require greater accountability to the voters.

But this proliferation of primaries and other processes to enhance grassroots voter participation ran into obstacles. One was the distraction of World War I, which diminished voter turnout; another was the high cost to the states of maintaining these political innovations; a third was the growing disinclination of prominent politicians to risk their futures in the less controllable, less predictable primary process. By 1935, eight of the twenty-six states had repealed their primary laws and they fell into disuse in others.

In the meantime, the development of big-city political machines produced more political bosses and other party bigwigs at all levels of politics. The most notable and conspicuous example of bossism and the decline of the primaries' influence came in 1920, when Warren G. Harding of Ohio, after weak showings in two primaries, was anointed in another convention of "the smoke-filled room" in Chicago. Harding was summoned to a hotel suite and interrogated by a small group of party bosses and leaders who finally gave him their blessing. He was nominated on the tenth ballot (with women delegates participating in some numbers for the first time). Four years later the Democrats in a much more prolonged version took 103 ballots to nominate John W. Davis.

The presidential primary meanwhile had slipped largely into eclipse, with presidential hopefuls relying more on the backing of party bosses and officeholders to get them delegates. Politicians had little use for primaries in states where they had a firm grip on the party and election apparatus; they didn't want to have their nominees selected by average voters, who would have to be courted not simply in the general election but also in assembling the party ticket. Primaries often became the resort to which candidates with little or no formal party support were obliged to turn to contest for nomination.

Doing so was risky, as the 1940 Republican presidential nominee, Wendell L. Willkie, found out in 1944. Having won the nomination without entering any primaries in 1940 but having been defeated in November by President Franklin D. Roosevelt seeking an unprecedented third term, Willkie took the primary route four years later, lost in Wisconsin, and quickly withdrew.

In 1944 and again in 1948, however, the Republican primaries contributed to the nomination of Thomas E. Dewey against Harold Stassen, General Douglas MacArthur, and Senator Robert A. Taft. In these cases, though, only a handful of primaries served as a testing ground of popular support; the primary was not yet a certain means in itself to achieve nomination.

In 1952, Democrat Estes Kefauver demonstrated the renewed efficacy of the presidential primary when he challenged an aloof President Harry S Truman in New Hampshire. Kefauver raced around the small state shaking hands and greeting voters, and beat the absentee incumbent by 4,000 votes. Truman dismissed primaries as "eyewash," but within three weeks he announced he would not seek reelection. The primary may have driven Truman out but it failed to usher Kefauver in. Adlai Stevenson, who entered no primaries, was eventually nominated with little overt effort on his part.

In the Republican Party the same year, General Eisenhower had his name placed in the New Hampshire primary and was an easy winner. But he and his chief opponent for the party nomination, Taft, skipped later competitive primaries and sought support from party leaders. In a lively and contentious convention in which the Eisenhower forces, led by Dewey, outmaneuvered Taft in fights over contested delegations from Georgia, Louisiana, and Texas, Eisenhower won a first-ballot nomination.

The year 1952 marked the practical beginning of the television era in politics. Both party conventions were heavily covered by television news teams. Credentials committee hearings at the Republican event illuminated the strong-arm tactics the Taft forces were using and worked to the advantage of the Eisenhower camp. Millions of voters around the country were engrossed by the proceedings; from front-row seats in their own living rooms, they could watch the entire presidential campaign unfold. Presidential politics, it was clear, would never be the same.

In 1960, John Kennedy, still not the choice of most power wielders in the Democratic Party, used the presidential primaries to end-run them. As a popular New Englander, he kicked off his campaign with a victory in neighboring New Hampshire, then beat Hubert Humphrey in Wisconsin and West Virginia, the latter a victory in a state thought to be strongly anti-Catholic. Kennedy's other chief rival, Senate Majority Leader Lyndon Johnson, chose to skip the primaries and rely on his support in the Senate and elsewhere in the party hierarchy. This strategy didn't work, but had LBJ taken the primary route the chances are that Kennedy, a most appealing candidate in person, would have beaten the often haughty Johnson anyway.

In 1968, Eugene McCarthy's near-victory over Johnson in New Hampshire and Robert Kennedy's string of primary successes thereafter, interrupted only by McCarthy's upset over him in Oregon, all signaled a revitalization of the idea of going directly to voters. So did Richard Nixon's demolition of his earlier "loser image" when he chased Governor George Romney out of the Republican race even before the primary in New Hampshire, and thereafter piled up one primary victory after another.

Nevertheless, the Democrats in 1968 nominated Vice President Humphrey, a man who had not entered a single primary. Anti-war activists and other liberals, including many Humphrey supporters, decided that something had to be done to respond more effectively to the growing demand in party ranks for "participatory democracy." At the 1968 convention, they succeeded in inserting the stipulation that Democratic voters in 1972 would have "a full and timely opportunity to participate" in selection of convention delegates and "all feasible efforts [would be] made to assure that delegates are selected through . . . procedures open to public participation within the calendar year of the national convention." This commitment led in 1969 to the appointment of Senator George S. McGovern as chairman of a commission to reform delegate selection and party structure. Its decisions effectively opened the process to broader grassroots participation than ever before. Its requirements that delegates be chosen by the most open means feasible, that they be allocated through a proportional representation system, and that women and minorities be given adequate representation had the practical effect of encouraging primaries. It was easier for state parties to use primaries than to have closed conventions that might lay them open to charges of discrimination. Party officials and elected officeholders had to win seats as delegates in the same way everyone else did—by getting elected in a primary, caucus, or state convention.

As a result, many officeholders in 1972 made early decisions to support leading candidates as their means of becoming national convention delegates. One outcome was a rush of endorsements for the early front-runner, Senator Edmund S. Muskie of Maine. When his candidacy collapsed, the party leaders who had signed up to be Muskie delegates were out in the cold. Still, the primary was the easiest way for a state to comply with the mandate to keep delegate selection open and to include women and minorities.

When so many Democratic officeholders were shut out as delegates to the 1972 convention, modifications were made before the 1976 convention. But there was no doubt that the reforms, and the proliferation of primaries that resulted, had shifted power from state parties and organizations to voters. By 1976, thirty states and the District of Columbia had passed one sort or another of presidential primary law. A grueling obstacle course had been created, which presidential aspirants had to cover to reach the nominating convention.

Despite dire warnings that the increasing resort to primaries and the use of proportional representation in the Democratic Party would lead to indecisive outcomes and brokered conventions, this did not happen. But as more and more states held primaries, states that held theirs late in the preconvention season began to feel they were being cut out of any meaningful participation. Iowa's caucuses and New Hampshire's primary were still receiving an inordinate amount of attention, and their voters were still having an unwarranted voice in the nominations. And candidates who failed to meet or exceed expectations in these two states saw their campaign money quickly dry up.

After Jimmy Carter's 1976 coup in the Iowa caucuses, they drew a record number of participants in 1980, to the point that the state's caucuses were deemed "the functional equivalent of a primary." Although neither of the winners there that year—Carter for the Democrats and George Bush for the Republicans—was ultimately elected, the argument continued against Iowa's and New Hampshire's holding their delegate selections first. On the Democratic side, these states' kickoff positions were protected by party rules; on the Republican, they were sheltered by custom.

But in 1984, nine states decided to hold their processes earlier than in the past, two weeks after the New Hampshire primary, in what came to be called Super Tuesday, in the hope that the earlier dates would bring them more influence and more attention in the nomination. But Democrats Gary Hart and Walter Mondale split the results; the expectation that their contests would be decisive, particularly in the Southern states involved, wasn't borne out.

In 1988, Super Tuesday grew to twenty Democratic primaries and caucuses, fourteen of them in the Southern and border states, as Dixie party leaders hoped they could bring about the nomination of someone from their region, or at least someone acceptable to the South. But bunching so many states together put a premium on campaign money available and made it impossible for the candidates to spend much time in any but the largest states. The two politicians who would naturally have found the South most hospitable, Richard Gephardt of Missouri and Al Gore of Tennessee, saw their candidacies shattered; two of the least likely beneficiaries turned out to be two Northerners, Michael Dukakis of Massachusetts and Jesse Jackson of Illinois. In 1992, a somewhat diminished Super Tuesday in the South helped Bill Clinton of Arkansas recover after a series of knocks in Iowa and New Hampshire, but other sections of the country continued to feel left out.

Then the dike broke. More and more states, including giants like New

York and California, decided they were tired of being afterthoughts in the critical business of picking the presidential nominees. By 1996, thirty-seven states in every region of the country had decided to hold their caucuses and primaries between the first week in February and the last week in March. Iowa and New Hampshire once again were slated to begin the process, and therefore would be the early testing grounds, in spite of a feeble attempt by Louisiana Republicans to replace and overshadow Iowa's hold on the first-in-the-nation caucuses. But this time the candidates could not ignore the incredibly imposing schedule that lay beyond, which was certain to consume whatever money they had left, and more time than any of them could muster to do justice to it. For 2000, even more states advanced their contests into February and March. By contrast, the earlier years, when candidates spent the year before the actual campaigns leisurely mending their fences with party leaders who would deliver state delegates to the conventions, or when only a few primaries or caucuses had to be contested, seemed a pushover.

Back in 1952, the military hero Dwight Eisenhower still was on active duty as commander of North Atlantic Treaty Organization (NATO) forces in Europe when the presidential election year began. And in 1960, Kennedy did not formally announce his candidacy until January 2. In the year before, Kennedy and Theodore C. Sorensen, his closest personal aide at the time, traveled the country alone, quietly conferring with party leaders and attracting little notice as they labored to build support for the 1960 nomination.

With the summertime conventions no longer determining the party nominees, should they be abandoned? That would amount to a surrender to the shortcomings of the modern-day convention, when there are still opportunities to rehabilitate it. Its secondary functions, including strengthening the personal and ideological ties among party members and leaders, and writing the party's statement of purpose, continue to justify holding the party gathering. So is the opportunity to garner extensive free television coverage that will promote not only the nominees but the party's policies. But unless the prime function, nomination of a national ticket, can somehow be restored, national political conventions will never again have the significance—and generate the interest and excitement—of old.

Most candidates and their strategists and supporters do not view the restoration of the conventions as desirable, and many think it would be destructive. Multiballot, "brokered" conventions conjure up old images of corruption and party bosses, of divisions laid bare, and ill will generated. Yet at the same time they could show a political party as vibrant and open—an image conspicuously lacking today.

Reform of the delegate-selection process is essential. Stretching out the primaries and caucuses, and putting the smaller states with the fewer delegates earlier in the political calendar, would at least delay identification of the nominee. But unless some means is found to keep one candidate from amassing a majority of the party delegates before the first roll call, the convention will continue to be merely a confirming event, not truly a nominating one.

If two or more candidates in a multicandidate field remain sufficiently competitive through the primaries and caucuses, then the convention becomes critical again. But to achieve this end, the candidates need to have both the public appeal and the financial resources not simply to win victories but to survive primary defeats. History has not been cordial to such a possibility. While the measurement of campaign treasuries may seem unfair and arbitrary in determining which candidates can survive, it does have the merit of showing a candidate's ability to attract and hold public support. Candidates with great personal appeal like Ronald Reagan in 1980 or those representing popular or high-intensity causes—Eugene McCarthy as an anti-war candidate in 1968 comes quickly to mind—can manage to stay afloat. But for most others, the ability to remain in contention is directly proportional to their campaign bank accounts. Unfortunately, the political viability of wealthy candidates like Ross Perot in 1992 and Steve Forbes in 1996 rests with their wealth, and not with their ability to maintain any particular level of public support.

Most of the ideas broached about denying a candidate a pre-convention majority are impractical. If voters are dissatisfied with the choices, as many often say they are, they can vote for uncommitted-delegate or favorite-son slates, and if the practice is widespread enough, a majority can be withheld from any one candidate until the convention. But getting millions of voters to band together in support of such slates is unlikely. Perhaps if someone were willing to make the kind of organizational effort Perot made for himself in 1992 and 1996 on behalf of uncommitted slates pledged to bring about change in one or both parties, a majority could be denied any candidate. But Perot showed little interest in practicing civics rather than self-aggrandizement, all his rhetoric to the contrary.

Don Fowler, the former Democratic National Chairman, suggests that the parties could eliminate pledged delegates or prohibit delegates from being firmly committed to a specific candidate. This notion of permitting or encouraging delegates to be free agents at the party conventions flies in the face of the motivation that gets them there, however.

John Sears, who was a Reagan campaign manager, says presidential nominations could be kept open into the national conventions by making some of the primaries and caucuses advisory only, leaving the delegates uncommitted until the conventions. That would be better than the situation now, when "we effectively pick the presidential nominees in March for a race that isn't decided until November," he notes. James Carville yearns for an old-fashioned convention but confesses he doesn't know how it will come about. With a national primary and a rule that a nominee had to win 50 percent of the vote in it, or with an increase to two-thirds of the votes required to be nominated under the state-by-state system, it might happen, he says, but neither seems likely. Bob Shrum, who was part of Ted Kennedy's failed campaign scheme in 1980 to open up the Democratic convention, says nevertheless, "I believe that sometime in the next two cycles we will have a convention that will actually determine the nominee."

Even if a truly open convention could be achieved, what is the deeper political justification for it? The strong virtue of primaries is that they give the choice of the party's nominees to millions of voters. But it can be argued that voters, unlike party leaders, do not know the candidates well and don't make much effort to learn more about them.

This was the argument made after the 1968 election when the Democratic Party drastically reformed the way it selected delegates. Every Democrat who hoped to be a delegate to the 1972 convention had to run for the position; the process was undeniably more open and democratic, but in the end it froze out many elected officials who either didn't run or supported a losing candidate. The party subsequently and partially corrected the problem by providing for so-called superdelegates—party leaders and elected officeholders awarded automatic seats at the next convention. The results of the primaries still affect the choice of the party nominee more than these superdelegates do, but their presence assures that considerable political experience and knowledge of the candidates are available in the unlikely event that the nomination falls to the convention itself.

The Republican Party has no similar provision for superdelegates, nor stipulations that party members must be elected as convention delegates in the primaries and caucuses, nor any requirement for equitable representation by gender and race. Party leaders and officeholders still attend the convention by virtue of their positions.

Perhaps the best that can be achieved regarding the national conventions is to streamline them, to make them more useful and honest. A lively convention can focus the spotlight on the party nominee and provide a positive kickoff to his fall campaign. The Democratic nominees Clinton and Gore, bursting out of their convention in New York in 1992 with a dramatic bus tour across half the country, provided a sense of energy and motion that gave the presidential campaign real electricity.

But it would be a mistake to focus on politics as entertainment. Both parties bent themselves out of shape in 1996 in responding to the television networks' irresponsible decision to abandon gavel-to-gavel coverage in favor of a narrow one-hour window of prime time (actually five hours over four nights). The networks arbitrarily chose to cover some convention speakers and ignored others, cut them short, or had their own analysts and reporters substitute their own wisdom for straight coverage of the speakers and events of the convention. The networks, Bob Teeter remembers, "didn't take their cameras off Christopher Reeve," the movie actor confined to a wheelchair after a riding accident, when he addressed the Democratic convention, "and never showed Ford and Bush," the two former Republican presidents, when they spoke to their party. The ultimate in television chutzpah came when Ted Koppel of ABC News declared the Republican convention unworthy of further coverage, packed up, and went home to New York. If some major unforeseen development had occurred, he would have been left with a large omelette on his face. But his ABC News colleague, Sam Donaldson, says it's the parties' fault. "If they return to a convention where the nomination is up for grabs," he says, "we're going to be back there gavel to gavel."

An orderly national political convention, by its very nature, is a contradiction in terms, or should be. There is nothing inherently wrong with conventions that run smoothly, but clashes are inevitable. The activists who are drawn to conventions are by and large very sensitive to political and social issues and figures of the day, and committed to advancing their views and positions on them. To shoehorn them into a convention that is carefully crafted to avoid or neutralize conflict and to reduce the whole event to show business does them and the political process they are involved in a huge disservice. Will Rogers, who used to say, "I belong to no organized party—I'm a Democrat," would have felt at home in Chicago at the Democrats' convention in 1968, but lost at the sanitized version there in 1996.

Short of the contest for the presidential nomination occurring on the convention floor, party leaders need to think less about the public-relations aspects of their conventions—putting the best face on their party, to make it seem as harmonious as a church choir—and more about breathing life into them with candor and honest conflict. The parties need to lighten up, to air their competitions and controversies more openly and with fervor unrestrained by the glare of television lights.

11 Rolling the Dice

The one remaining piece of convention business that still generates great public interest is the selection of the vice presidential nominee. This decision is also the single most important one confronting the presidential nominee, since tradition and practical politics have almost always left the choice of his running mate to him. (There have been exceptions, as in 1956, when Adlai E. Stevenson threw the choice to the Democratic convention and Senator Kefauver of Tennessee was selected over Senator Kennedy of Massachusetts, in an exciting competition that introduced Kennedy to American voters.) The party recognizes that the choice could affect the presidential nominee's chances of election and, if elected, the ability of the two to work together harmoniously. More important—although regrettably not always well factored in—is the imperative of having a vice presidential nominee who could perform well the duties of the presidency if fate were to call on him to do so.

In 1997, five years after President George Bush's defeat for reelection, the presidential historian Herbert S. Parmet quoted a Bush diary entry in which Bush confessed "I screwed up" in choosing Senator Dan Quayle of Indiana to be his running mate in 1988. Although Bush later denied this sentiment and called Quayle a "great" vice president, his original comment squared with the widely shared view that Quayle had been woefully over his head as vice president for eight years. What made Quayle's selection, which startled Republicans, so irresponsible was that Bush himself, in the first weeks of his own vice presidency under President Ronald Reagan, had come within a heartbeat of succeeding to the Oval Office, when Reagan narrowly escaped death in an assassination attempt. Yet Bush's cavalier manner of choosing his running mate was more routine than exceptional in American political history.

From the beginning of the Republic until relatively recent times, the vice presidency had largely been a subject of inattention, and more often than not of derision and ridicule. Creation of the office by the Founding Fathers was almost accidental; it was first proposed in a speech by Alexander Hamilton and eventually was a by-product of the original double balloting for president. Electors in each state were obliged to cast two votes for president, only one of which could be for a candidate from an elector's home state. That caveat would avoid their voting only for favorite sons and keeping any candidate from gaining the requisite majority. The candidate with the most votes would become president, and the runner-up vice president. From this arrangement, it was clear that the intent was to have two individuals of the highest esteem in those two offices, and indeed that was the case in the early years, when John Adams and then Thomas Jefferson served as vice president before being elected president.

During the Constitutional Convention, however, James Madison had warned of the danger that each elector "after having given his vote for his favorite fellow Citizen [of his own state] would throw away his second on some obscure Citizen of another state, in order to ensure the object of his first choice [becoming president]." At the same time, in an excess of idealism, he added that "it could hardly be supposed that the Citizens of many States would be so sanguine of having their favorite elected as not to give their second vote with sincerity to the next object of their choice." Another framer, Hugh Williamson of North Carolina, later observed that "such an office as vice president was not wanted. It was introduced only for the sake of a valuable mode of election which required two be chosen [for president] at the same time."

Hamilton's original proposal was for an elected president of the Senate to be vice president, but this idea was rejected out of fears that it would blur the separation of executive and legislative powers and give the Senate an undue role in presidential succession. It was argued somewhat incongruously but successfully, however, that if the vice president were himself elected and permitted to vote in the Senate only to break a tie, there would be little damage to the separation-of-powers concept. In all this, notably, the Constitutional Convention seemed much more concerned about the vice president's function as president of the Senate than about the possibility that he might succeed to the presidency. John Adams understood the frustrating dilemma, though, as noted in his famous commentary on being vice president: "In this I am nothing, but I may be everything." In a letter to his wife he added: "My country in its wisdom has contrived for me the most insignificant office that ever the invention of man contrived or his imagination conceived."

Jefferson's vice presidency spotlighted the political pitfall in double balloting for president. As a leader of the Anti-Federalists, he was basically at odds with Federalist President Adams, who tried to neutralize him by sending him on a diplomatic mission to France, where he earlier had served as American minister. Jefferson declined on grounds that as president of the Senate he was a legislative, not an executive, officer, given that his sole constitutional function was to break a Senate tie vote.

The double balloting promised to create still more mischief. In the 1800 election, the Anti-Federalist ticket of Jefferson and Aaron Burr finished in a tie for first, with seventy-three votes each. The broad intention of the Anti-Federalists was that Jefferson be president and Burr vice president, but Burr had other ideas. He refused to bow out in Jefferson's favor and under the Constitution the choice fell to the House of Representatives, which took thirty-six ballots over a week's time to select Jefferson. As vice president, Burr bucked Jefferson and made clear he was not the president's agent, even voting against an administration bill to break a Senate tie. Something drastic had to be done. In 1803, Congress finally passed the Twelfth Amendment, which ended double balloting for president and provided for the separate election of the president and vice president—but not before a considerable debate about abolishing the vice presidency altogether. Representative Roger Griswold of Connecticut argued that the office, under separate election, "will be carried to market to purchase the votes of particular states," which turned out to be true enough in many elections thereafter.

In 1804, Jefferson's Anti-Federalists, now called Republicans, not surprisingly replaced Burr as his running mate, choosing the aging former New York governor George Clinton as their vice presidential nominee. At sixty-five, Clinton was four years older than Jefferson, and there was no sense in grooming him for a presidential bid four years later. Rather, he was there to give geographical balance to the ticket. When Jefferson decided not to seek a third term, Clinton was bypassed as the party's presidential nominee in favor of Madison, Jefferson's effective and loyal Secretary of State. But in a measure of how insignificant the vice presidency was then regarded, Clinton—a man summarily dismissed as presidential material—was kept on the ticket at the age of sixty-nine. Elected with Madison and sworn in as vice president for a second term in 1809, he died in office in April 1813, with two weeks short of a year left in his term. For the first time in the young Republic, the vice presidency was vacant, with no provision for a replacement until the next presidential election seven months later.

Another such vacancy occurred in Madison's second term, with the death of Vice President Elbridge Gerry after only twenty months in office, this time leaving the post vacant for two years and three months. Nobody seemed to notice, or at least care. After Adams and Jefferson, the vice presidency had become a ticket to nowhere.

In 1836 Martin Van Buren did in fact use the vice presidency as a stepping-stone to the presidency, the first to do so since Jefferson and the last until George Bush 152 years later. But during that century and a half, no fewer than nine vice presidents were elevated to the Oval Office after presidential deaths—John Tyler, Millard Fillmore, Andrew Johnson, Chester A. Arthur, Theodore Roosevelt, Calvin Coolidge, Harry S Truman, and Lyndon Johnson—or presidential resignation—Gerald R. Ford.

Tyler's succession to the presidency in 1841 when the first Whig president, William Henry Harrison, died of pneumonia only a month after his inauguration was the first test of the constitutional language that stipulated that upon a president's "death, resignation or inability to discharge the powers and duties of the said office, the same shall devolve on the vice president." Did that mean Tyler would become president or merely assume his powers and duties in some acting capacity? Tyler made the point academic by quickly having himself sworn in as president.

In all the cases of vice presidential ascension except Ford's, the vice presidency remained vacant until the next election with little public concern, although debates recurred about what the line of succession should be if anything happened to the newly elevated president. Six other vacancies occurred with the deaths of little-remembered vice presidents—William R. King, Henry Wilson, Thomas A. Hendricks, Garret A. Hobart, and James S. Sherman—and the resignation of much-remembered Spiro T. Agnew. In the latter case, the vacancy was quickly filled by President Nixon's nomination of Ford and his confirmation by Congress. These actions were the first applications of the Twenty-fifth Amendment, ratified in 1967, about filling presidential and vice presidential vacancies. When Ford himself became president upon Nixon's resignation in disgrace, he nominated Governor Nelson A. Rockefeller of New York to the vice presidential vacancy.

In spite of all the vice presidents who attained the presidency, being nominated or elected to the position was still widely considered, until fairly recently, akin to getting a gold watch for long service rendered. Those in whose power it was to offer the office by and large treated it with contempt. The classic example was in 1880, which had the Collector of the New York Custom House, Chester A. Arthur, running with Representative James A. Garfield of Ohio, a former Union general, on the Republican ticket, in an exercise of internal party strife and spite. President Garfield, at forty-eight, was in robust health, which encouraged E. L. Godkin of *The Nation* to write that there was "no place in which [Arthur's] powers of mischief will be so small as in the vice presidency." But only six months after the two men took office, Garfield was dead of an assassin's bullets and the former port collector and party hack, who had broken with his predecessor, was president of the United States.

When the next vice president, Thomas A. Hendricks, died less than nine months after his inauguration, Congress decided a change in the line of presidential succession was in order. President Grover Cleveland was a Democrat, but under a succession law enacted in 1792 the president pro tem of the Senate, who happened to be a Republican, was next in line after the vice president. A new law put members of the cabinet behind the vice president, starting with the Secretary of State. That order continued until 1947, when an elected official, the Speaker of the House, was placed immediately behind the vice president.

President William McKinley's vice president in his first term was another nonentity, former Republican National Chairman Garret A. Hobart, who died in office. So McKinley had to find another running mate when he ran for reelection in 1900, and he threw the choice to the Republican convention, a move frowned upon by his highly political campaign manager, Mark Hanna, who saw a boom building for a man he feared and despised—the hero of San Juan Hill in the Spanish-American War and now governor of New York, the irrepressible Theodore Roosevelt.

Roosevelt originally shared the view that the vice presidency was indeed a political dead end, observing that "I would a great deal rather be anything, say professor of history, than vice president." But he changed his mind and decided to go to the national convention in Philadelphia, adding fuel to the drive to select him. And with McKinley reiterating (against Hanna's wishes) that he had no recommendation to make to the delegates about his running mate, the die was cast. Hanna was irate. According to Donald Young, in his book on the vice presidency, *American Roulette*, he exploded to Henry Payne, a Wisconsin national committeeman: "Do whatever you damn please! I'm through! I won't have anything more to do with the convention! I won't take charge of the campaign! I won't be chairman of the national committee again!" When the startled Payne asked what was the matter, Hanna shot back: "Matter? Why, everybody's gone crazy! What is the matter with all of you? Here's this convention going headlong for Roosevelt for vice president. Don't any of you realize that there's only one life between that madman and the presidency? . . . What harm can [Roosevelt] do as governor of New York compared to the damage he will do as president if McKinley should die?"

Roosevelt "reluctantly" told the convention, "I cannot seem to be bigger than the party," and was easily nominated to run with McKinley. A grim Hanna told McKinley: "Now it is up to you to live." Hanna swallowed hard and put his organization to work, delivering a wider margin for McKinley than he had enjoyed in 1896. Then, only six months into his term, McKinley was assassinated in Buffalo by a deranged anarchist. Hanna reportedly proclaimed: "Now look! That damned cowboy is president of the United States."

By now, presidents seeking reelection were routinely changing their running mates, to suit their perceived reelection needs or to bestow the political gold watch on some other faithful party functionary. When Vice President James S. Sherman ran for a second term with President William Howard Taft in 1912, he was the first holder of that office in eighty-four years to be renominated by either major party.

Woodrow Wilson's running mate in 1912, Governor Thomas R. Marshall of Indiana, not only personified the low public opinion of vice presidents but also openly joined in the general view of the office. The vice president, he said, "is like a man in a cataleptic state; he cannot speak; he cannot move; he suffers no pain; and yet he is perfectly conscious of everything that is going on about him." Wilson agreed: "The chief embarrassment in discussing this office is that, in explaining how little there is to be said about it, one has evidently said all there is to say."

Marshall endured his plight as vice president in good humor, joking that his job was "to ring the White House bell every morning and ask what is the state of health of the president." But the joke was beyond laughing when debilitating illness struck Wilson in their second term. After he collapsed while campaigning for Senate ratification of the League of Nations, the public had little idea of the degree of his incapacitation, nor did most members of his official family.

The president's wife, Edith, made up her mind there would be no resignation and no delegation of presidential authority as provided in the Constitution. She kept Marshall in the dark about the president's true condition, and he declined to press the matter. When, tortured, he finally went to the White House in the hope of discussing directly with Wilson whether it was time to invoke the constitutional authority to take over the presidency or at least the acting presidency, Mrs. Wilson refused to admit him to the sickroom.

The low esteem of the vice presidency continued. In 1920, when the Republicans nominated Senator Warren G. Harding of Ohio, a man known more for his handsome countenance than for his brains, Senator Hiram Johnson of California was approached to be his running mate. He took the offer as an insult, remarking, "We're living in a day of strange events, but none so strange as that I should be considered second to Senator Harding." Thus rebuked, the party picked a drab man more fitted to the role, Governor Calvin Coolidge of Massachusetts. Coolidge's opposite number on the Democratic ticket with Governor James M. Cox of Ohio was a relatively obscure former Assistant Secretary of the Navy named Franklin D. Roosevelt, a young cousin of Teddy Roosevelt. He campaigned vigorously, but Cox and Roosevelt lost, and Coolidge joined the ranks of vice presidents seldom seen or heard, until the sudden death of Harding from bronchial pneumonia in 1923. Coolidge served out the term as president, marking the fourteenth time there was a vice presidential vacancy.

Yet the office still did not seem to be perceived by ambitious politicians as the most promising route to the Oval Office. In Coolidge's subsequent full term, his vice president, Charles G. Dawes, distinguished himself by making the worst mistake for an official whose only constitutional duty was to break a Senate tie. Before a key vote, he had slipped back to his hotel for an afternoon nap and he missed the roll call, causing the defeat of a controversial Coolidge cabinet nominee. That episode didn't do much for the public esteem of the vice presidency either. Neither did the election of Senate Majority Leader Charles Curtis of Kansas as Herbert Hoover's vice president in 1928. Approaching the age of seventy, he was anointed as "the apotheosis of mediocrity" by the well-known writer Oswald Garrison Villard and was such a conspicuous protector of the poultry industry that his nickname was "Egg" Curtis. (He was reputed to be the model for Alexander Throttlebottom, the vice presidential candidate in *Of Thee I Sing*, the Broadway musical hit by George S. Kaufman and Morrie Ryskind, played by the ever-forlorn Victor Moore. Throttlebottom worries throughout the play that his mother will learn of his nomination, and he busies himself trying to find two references to obtain a library card.)

When Franklin D. Roosevelt was nominated for president in 1932, the man he accepted as his running mate, House Speaker John Nance "Cactus Jack" Garner of Texas, was able enough but reluctant, having only a year before attained the House leadership he had long coveted. Three weeks before the victorious Roosevelt and Garner were to take office, fate brushed Garner when an unemployed and disgruntled bricklayer fired on President-elect Roosevelt and Mayor Anton Cermak of Chicago in a Miami motorcade. Cermak was killed and four others were shot, but the assassin missed Roosevelt. Had he not, and had the president-elect died, Vice President-elect Garner under the Constitution would have been sworn in as president on March 4. Once again, the importance of making a responsible choice in selecting a running mate was illustrated by the actions of a madman. Even Garner, however, continued to demean the vice presidency, with his famous, and reportedly sanitized, remark that the office was "not worth a bucket of warm spit."

In their second term, Garner broke with Roosevelt first over his scheme to pack a Supreme Court that was frustrating important aspects of his New Deal agenda and then with Roosevelt's decision to seek an unprecedented third term. Indeed, Garner declared his own candidacy for president against him. Roosevelt was renominated easily but threatened privately to refuse to run when the convention appeared to balk over his choice for a successor to Garner—Secretary of Agriculture Henry A. Wallace, an Iowa farmer with a reputation as a fuzzy-thinking social philosopher. A direct appeal at the convention by the president's wife, Eleanor, to give her husband the strong right hand he wanted quelled the prospective rebellion and Wallace was nominated on the first ballot. The spectacle of Roosevelt ramming Wallace down the convention's throat was a significant milestone in establishing the presidential nominees' "right" to name their own running mates, even over the opposition of party leaders.

With the United States at war in 1944, resistance to a fourth term for Roosevelt crumbled, but opposition to Wallace grew. Party leaders told Roosevelt that he would have another fight on his hands if he tried to keep Wallace on the ticket. They also appreciated, as did Roosevelt, that the president's health was rapidly deteriorating under the pressures of his wartime leadership, and that he might well not live out his next term. In a series of small private meetings with the ailing Roosevelt, they convinced him that Wallace had to go, and by a process of elimination persuaded him that his best bet was Senator Truman of Missouri, a man Roosevelt did not know well but respected as an effective chairman of a Senate watchdog committee on defense contracting. Over the previous four years, Roosevelt had gone from being a commanding figure who insisted to the point of threatening to refuse renomination himself if he did not get his choice of his running mate, to being a physically tired and pliable man willing to listen and act on his advisers' recommendation. Yet the choice of Truman was hardly based on a consensus that he was the best man in America to meet such a challenge; rather, the argument for him was that he was not Wallace and was acceptable to most party factions.

Just eighty-two days after they were sworn in on January 20, 1945, as Truman put it later, "the moon, the stars and all the planets" fell on him. With the war still raging in Europe and the Pacific, he was summoned suddenly to the White House, where Eleanor Roosevelt put her arm around him and told him, simply, "Harry, the president is dead." Truman quickly took the oath of office, summoned the cabinet, and asked all of its members to stay on. As the meeting broke up, Secretary of War Henry Stimson stayed behind for a private word with the new president. As Truman later told the oral historian Merle Miller: "He said the most destructive weapon in history was being built, and that is about all he said that night." It was not until twelve days later that Stimson elaborated: as vice president, Truman had been kept completely in the dark about the development of the atomic bomb, whose use it would soon fall to him to decide upon. No single factor more pointedly illustrates the inadequacy of the vice presidency as presidents had treated it up to that time, as an office preparing its occupant to assume the responsibilities of the presidency.

In 1947, at Truman's urging, Congress changed the line of succession again, reverting to the idea that any successor should be someone elected by the people. The House Speaker was placed first behind the vice president, then the Senate president pro tem, and only after him the ranking cabinet members, starting with the Secretary of State. In 1948, however, Truman first looked to an unelected official as his running mate, Justice William O. Douglas, but he was turned down. Hearing about a boomlet at the Democratic convention favoring the presidential nomination of the seventy-year-old Senate Majority Leader, Alben W. Barkley, Truman acquiesced in taking him as his running mate if that was what the convention wanted. Deplorably, he told a White House aide, Eben Ayers, according to an entry in Ayers' diary, that he "never did care much about who was nominated to run with him."

Barkley came close to becoming yet another accidental president in November 1950, when two Puerto Rican nationalists bent on assassinating Truman opened fire on security guards on the steps of Blair House, across the street from the White House, where the president and his family had moved while the official residence was undergoing extensive remodeling. Truman was napping in his underwear at the time and rushed to the window when he heard the shooting, in which one assailant and a guard were killed and the other assailant wounded.

In 1952, when the Republicans nominated Dwight D. Eisenhower, the general, a political neophyte, expressed surprise when his advisers informed him that he could choose his own running mate. Senator Richard M. Nixon of California, who had pledged to support his state's favorite son, Governor Earl Warren, had been surreptitiously advancing Eisenhower's nomination in the hope that he would be chosen on the ticket with Eisenhower. Thomas E. Dewey, the loser to Truman in 1948, and Herbert Brownell, Jr., running the Eisenhower campaign, had been talking to Nixon, and after conferring with Eisenhower they summoned a small group of party leaders to tell them that in Dewey's judgment Nixon as a Californian would help the ticket most. Eisenhower barely knew the running mate who had been selected for him.

Later, when reporters ascertained that Nixon had had a "secret fund" given him by his right-wing California supporters, Dewey and Brownell had second thoughts about their choice; Nixon had to explain and defend himself, in the famous, nationally televised "Checkers" speech in which he piously acknowledged that a dog had been given to his daughter Tricia but that he wasn't going to return it. The reaction was resoundingly in his favor, and Eisenhower summoned him and declared, "Dick, you're my boy." The Eisenhower-Nixon ticket won in a landslide.

As vice president, Nixon gave the office greater public visibility than any predecessor had. Eisenhower had him preside over cabinet and National Security Council meetings in his absence and used him extensively as a foreign emissary—and as his political hatchet man on the campaign trail, a role for which Nixon had considerable experience. But when in late 1955 Eisenhower suffered a severe heart attack, Nixon deftly stayed out of the spotlight, avoiding any appearance of power grabbing; he presided over important White House meetings but gave the Oval Office a wide berth.

Nevertheless, Eisenhower was not impressed with Nixon and, with some prodding from Dewey and others, called him in to suggest that he might serve his own future better by not seeking reelection in 1956 but rather by taking a cabinet post. When Nixon dug in his heels, Eisenhower did not press him, and eventually said he would be happy to have Nixon run with him again.

Nixon tried to use his eight years in the vice presidency as evidence that the experience had prepared him to assume the responsibilities of the presidency. But Eisenhower, perhaps unwittingly, undercut the effort when he answered a press-conference request for an example of "a major idea of [Nixon's] you had adopted." Eisenhower replied: "If you give me a week, I might think of one. I don't remember." Those of us sitting in front of the president in the cramped Indian Treaty Room of the old Executive Office Building, adjacent to the White House, greeted this response with open mouths. Surprisingly, at the next presidential press conference nobody asked Eisenhower whether in the intervening time he had thought of any "major idea" contributed by Nixon.

The year 1960 also saw another fateful vice presidential choice, at the Democratic convention in Los Angeles. Kennedy, prior to being nominated on the first ballot, had his aides shop around the vice presidential nomination in hopes of gaining support. In the end, he offered the nomination to his last serious opponent, Senate Majority Leader Lyndon B. Johnson, in one of the most revisited and written about political maneuvers in the annals of American history.

Postmortems on Kennedy's decision have varied. Some have said that the offer was intended to be a gesture that Kennedy expected Johnson to decline. "My God," Robert Kennedy afterward told James Rowe, once an FDR adviser and now a Johnson intimate, "this wouldn't have happened except that we were all too tired last night." He also told Rowe that John Kennedy's "first thought after his own nomination [was] how terrible it was that he only had twenty-four hours to select a vice president. He really hadn't thought about it at all." Johnson, however, proved to be a very effective campaigner, especially in the South, and despite his earlier contention that he would never trade his Senate vote and leadership "for a gavel," that was what he did. He was elected as standby for a new forty-three-year-old president who was expected to occupy the Oval Office, with luck, for the next eight years. Lyndon Johnson, a man used to being in charge and used to being busy, was headed for frustrating days. He told friends he felt like a "cut dog"—politically neutered.

As 1964 approached, the prospect of another four years in political Siberia pressed on Johnson ever more heavily. He mused to friends that he might not seek reelection, even if Kennedy wanted to keep him on the ticket, and instead go back to Texas and run for the Senate again. But Kennedy, though much more popular by this time than he had been in 1960, could not take Texas for granted, as a result of a severe intraparty rift there; LBJ could once again be a key in carrying the state, as he had been in 1960. It was this circumstance that brought both men to Dallas on the fateful day of November 22, 1963, that shockingly and abruptly ended the Kennedy presidency, and elevated Johnson to the White House.

John Kennedy's death and Johnson's ascendancy left the vice presidency vacant for the sixteenth time. Dealing with the problem was long overdue, and in 1967 the Twenty-fifth Amendment was ratified, part of which at last provided for the president in the event of such a vacancy to nominate a new vice president, subject to approval by a majority of both houses of Congress.

In Johnson's ambition for a full term of his own, one fellow Democrat seemed an obvious choice to be his running mate—Robert Kennedy, who had agreed reluctantly to stay on as Attorney General for a time. It was obvious, that is, to everyone but Johnson. "I don't want history to say I was elected to this office because I had Bobby on the ticket with me," he told Kenneth O'Donnell, an old Kennedy hand, three weeks after John Kennedy's death. Nobody was under any illusion that anyone but the strong-willed Johnson himself would make the choice, but many Kennedy supporters, dreaming of a rebirth of Camelot, began talking of Robert as a vice presidential nominee, even to the point of urging him actually to run for the nomination, against all tradition. A write-in campaign for him blossomed in New Hampshire but he disavowed it. Still, the speculation continued, and polls indicated that Kennedy was the most popular choice to be Johnson's running mate.

Johnson was determined not to have Kennedy foisted on him, but neither did he want to antagonize Kennedy followers. He struck upon a most transparent device, announcing after a meeting with Kennedy, "I have reached the conclusion that it would be inadvisable for me to recommend to the convention any member of my cabinet or any of those who meet regularly with the cabinet." Few were fooled by this subterfuge. Kennedy said his only regret was "that I had to take so many nice fellows over the side with me." In the end, Johnson chose the ever-loyal Hubert Humphrey as his running mate, but only after another charade in which he appeared to dangle the job before several others, including Senators Eugene J. McCarthy of Minnesota and Thomas Dodd of Connecticut.

Humphrey at least had compiled an impressive and honorable record in the Senate to warrant his selection. On the Republican side that year, presidential nominee Barry Goldwater chose a sharp-tongued journeyman congressman serving as national party chairman, William E. Miller of New York, because, Goldwater said, "he drives Lyndon Johnson nuts."

Humphrey as vice president might have hoped to be treated better by Johnson than LBJ had been treated by Kennedy. Instead it often seemed that Johnson was visiting upon Humphrey the short shrift he thought he had been given by the Kennedy White House. If the loquacious Humphrey ventured to express a view, Johnson would often summarily cut him off. One insider compared LBJ's treatment of Humphrey with "the old system of hazing a college freshman." But Humphrey fell obediently in line, becoming one of the Johnson administration's staunchest defenders, including its pursuit of the war in Vietnam, about which he in fact had silent reservations.

For his efforts and loyalty, Humphrey was widely expected to remain as Johnson's running mate in 1968, when first McCarthy and then Robert

Kennedy decided to oppose Johnson. But on the morning of March 31, 1968, as he prepared to fly to Mexico City on an official visit, Humphrey received a visitor at his apartment. The president showed him a draft ending to a speech about Vietnam he was to make that night, two days before the Democratic primary in Wisconsin. Humphrey was shocked: the text said that Johnson had decided he would not seek reelection. Suddenly Humphrey, who had been facing the prospect of four more years of humiliation at Johnson's hands, saw the road to the Oval Office open to him.

Without entering a single primary, Humphrey benefited from a division of the anti-Johnson vote between McCarthy and Kennedy, and then from Kennedy's assassination, and won the nomination on the first ballot at a riotous convention in Chicago. With none of the charade that had marked his own choice by Johnson in 1964, Humphrey selected a popular senator, Edmund S. Muskie of Maine, as his running mate.

Nixon chose a rather novel way to select his running mate on the Republican ticket. He had his pollster test how he would run with various other Republicans and found that he would fare better running alone than with any one of them. That being impossible, he settled on the next-best thing—an individual about whom very little was known: Spiro Agnew. Before naming him, Nixon asked party leaders for their recommendations, just to let them think they were having some input. Agnew's name was not mentioned except by Nixon, and then it generated no interest. But in short order Agnew made a name for himself as a political hatchet man. If he hurt Nixon in the campaign, he didn't hurt him enough to lose the election. And in the vice presidency, Agnew continued to function as a political hit man, while grousing about the lack of significant responsibilities.

Although Agnew became popular with voters, his freewheeling style caused Nixon at one point, according to *The Haldeman Diaries: Inside the Nixon White House*, to consider ways to remove him from the line of succession. On one hand contending that Agnew was not fit to be president, on the other Nixon weighed the possibility of moving him aside by appointing him to the Supreme Court! In the end, however, Agnew stayed and remained on the Republican ticket in 1972.

On the Democratic side that year, the process of vice presidential selection had its most embarrassing modern episode: the Democrats' presidential nominee, George McGovern, designated Senator Thomas Eagleton of Missouri as his running mate, only to learn that Eagleton had once undergone electrical shock treatment to deal with mental depression. The revelation threw the Democratic campaign into a tailspin.

It was the old axiom that a running mate did not necessarily have to help the presidential nominee, but should not bring anything to the ticket that might hurt him. On postconvention vacation in Custer, South Dakota, McGovern agonized about whether to dump Eagleton, and then about how. Eagleton was in Hawaii at the time, and McGovern decided to leak his intentions to me in the expectation—correct enough—that I would write an article about them in my newspaper at the time, the *Los Angeles Times*, which Eagleton probably would see on his return to the mainland. McGovern called me to his cabin and advised me, in veiled terms, that Eagleton would have to go.

If Eagleton saw the front-page story in the *Times* the next day, he didn't seem to take the hint, and McGovern, frustrated, eventually had to seek Eagleton's withdrawal more directly. The political damage was compounded when he spent an inordinate amount of time finding someone of stature to replace him. He finally settled on Sargent Shriver, one of John Kennedy's brothers-in-law, for a ticket doomed to a landslide defeat at the hands of Nixon and Agnew.

Little more than a year later, however, Agnew was removed from the line of succession by a means never dreamed of by Nixon. An investigation that began in Maryland of corruption in the awarding of government contracts when Agnew had been Baltimore County Executive, then governor of the state, and that carried into the vice presidency itself, forced his resignation. It was the first time a vice president had been driven from the office in disgrace as a result of criminal charges against him. Agnew was permitted to plea-bargain down to a single count of income-tax evasion, to which he pleaded nolo contendere—no contest, but an acknowledgment that the serious allegations of corruption were true. The Justice Department had built an airtight case against him about taking payoffs, even in his office in the basement of the White House, but as part of the deal, Agnew was not sent to prison. Nixon's Attorney General at the time, Elliot Richardson, deemed that for the sake of the country the prime objective was to eliminate the very real possibility—since Nixon himself was facing possible impeachment in the Watergate scandal—that Agnew might become president before the trial against him could be completed. Agnew insisted thereafter that he had been railroaded, brushing aside the explicit observation of the sentencing judge that Agnew's plea of nolo contendere, "so far as this criminal prosecution is concerned, is the full equivalent of a plea of guilty."

For the first time in American history, the provision in the Twenty-fifth Amendment regarding a vice presidential vacancy applied. Nixon, already facing a hostile Congress as a result of Watergate, recognized that he would have to choose a replacement for Agnew who could win swift congressional approval. The choice was easy—one of the most popular men in both parties on Capitol Hill, House Minority Leader Gerald R. Ford, Jr.

One aspect of the choice was not complimentary to Ford—that he might be an "insurance policy" against Nixon's impeachment. Although Ford was extremely well liked among his congressional brethren, he was not highly regarded as an intellect. According to *Newsweek*, Nixon, in the Oval Office, was reported to have asked Nelson Rockefeller after Ford was confirmed, "Can you imagine Jerry Ford sitting in this chair?" As the Watergate disclosures mounted, however, that prospect did not seem so outlandish.

As the case against Nixon deepened, Ford, America's first unelected vice president, played the good soldier, defending Nixon almost to the last after being assured face to face that he was innocent. Ten days before the roof caved in on Nixon—with the disclosure of a taped conversation in which he acknowledged his role in the Watergate cover-up—Ford told me in a late-night chat aboard Air Force Two that although he wasn't kidding himself about the gravity of Nixon's situation, he was not going to abandon the man. At the same time, he was having his closest aides prepare for a Ford presidency. On August 9, Nixon resigned and left for California; when Ford was sworn in as the country's first unelected president, he remarked, "If you have not chosen me by secret ballot, neither have I gained office by secret promises." But barely a month later, Ford made a decision that put that observation under severe scrutiny. He issued a blanket pardon to Nixon, leading to wide speculation that he had made a deal to do so in order to gain the Oval Office, which he denied.

It fell to Ford to nominate his own vice presidential successor under the Twenty-fifth Amendment. In a poll of important Republicans, George Bush, then the party's national chairman, got the most votes, with Rockefeller next. But Ford was not comfortable with Bush. Many Republicans considered him a lightweight who had flitted from one appointive job to another and who lacked leadership qualities. Some Republicans urged Rockefeller's cause, with the argument that his selection would remove him as a challenger to Ford in 1976 and in the meantime make him a lightning rod for conservative critics. In the end, Ford did choose Rockefeller, who earlier had said repeatedly that he was not "built to be standby equipment." But Ford was already sixty-six years old, and history had by now established that the vice presidency was no longer a certain ticket to political oblivion, so Rockefeller decided to take his chances.

Ford's hopes for a presidential term in his own right looked bleak almost from the outset. The first bloom of public support for him at the end of what he had called "our long national nightmare" of Watergate began to fade with his pardon of Nixon. It soon became clear that he would not get a free ride to his party's 1976 presidential nomination. Supporters of Ronald Reagan, former governor of California, were pressing him to challenge Ford. A Ford campaign manager, Howard (Bo) Callaway of Georgia, fearful of defections by GOP conservatives, suggested that Rockefeller should take himself off the ticket, warning that he was the Ford reelection campaign's "number one problem."

Ford, however, saying that Rockefeller "has been a good teammate" and "I don't dump teammates," vowed to keep him. But after two assassination attempts against Ford within two weeks in California, conservatives raised the pressure on him to get Rockefeller out of the line of succession. Soon after, Rockefeller bowed out, amid contradictory reports about whether he jumped or was pushed. In any event, if the hope was that Reagan could then be persuaded to be Ford's running mate, it was a futile one. Reagan made a serious and divisive challenge to Ford that clearly contributed to his eventual narrow defeat (with Senator Bob Dole of Kansas as his new running mate) at the hands of former Governor Jimmy Carter and his running mate, Senator Walter Mondale of Minnesota.

Of all presidential nominees, none probably made such a public extravaganza out of the vice presidential process as Carter. Where most others had used smoke-filled rooms or their own personal counsel to decide, Carter conducted a very deliberate, visible talent search. Bearing in mind the fiasco that had resulted from McGovern's inadequate vetting of Eagleton in 1972, he was determined to select a fellow Democrat who not only would not lessen his chances to win the election but also could help him govern if elected. Carter's chief political adviser, Hamilton Jordan, had a list of more than four hundred leading Democrats compiled, from which Carter culled about two dozen names, together with recommendations from staff aides. Jordan pointed out that Carter's decision would be the first "of presidential magnitude that you will make" and would give voters their best indication of the quality of his judgment. Because of Watergate and the damage it had done to public confidence in politics, he wrote, in 1976 "the best politics is to select a person who is accurately perceived by the American people as being able and qualified to serve as president if that became necessary."

Each of seven finalists, all from Congress, was asked to fill out a seventeen-point questionnaire with detailed questions about tax returns, campaign contributions and other matters of finance, health, and personal life. With the Eagleton affair clearly in mind, the designers of the form explicitly asked whether the prospect "ever had psychiatric or similar treatment" and concluded: "Without details, is there or has there been anything in your personal life which you feel, if known, may be of embarrassment in the presidential election this year in the event you should be a candidate? What about any near relative?"

Compared to past screenings, this one was not only thorough but, many thought, downright humiliating. Carter also insisted on the subjects' going to his home in Plains, Georgia, for private interviews, or to submit to them at the convention in New York. One finalist, Mondale, prepared for his interview much as Jordan had worked up his list: an aide, Richard Moe, analyzed what Carter might be looking for in a running mate and vice president and urged Mondale to tell Carter "the kind of arrangement you would want to have with him if elected."

Later, Carter said that he picked Mondale because "he had really done his homework about me and the campaign . . . [and] had excellent ideas about how to make the vice presidency a full-time and productive job." Mondale also happened to fill a practical need. He had one thing that Carter lacked—Washington experience.

It was debated later whether the selection of Mondale had indeed made a difference. In their one televised debate, Mondale outscored Dole on discussion of issues and, more important, maintained his confident composure, in contrast to Dole. The Republican nominee was first casual, then flippant, then angry and combative, calling the previous four armed conflicts in which

American soldiers had served "all Democrat wars." He recounted bitterly the severe wounds he had suffered in World War II, which left him without the use of his right arm and hand. Mondale shot back: "I think that Senator Dole has richly deserved his reputation as a hatchet man tonight. Does he really mean that there was a partisan difference over our involvement in the fight against Nazi Germany?"

This exchange clearly hurt Dole, and Mondale helped Carter, but Ford's pardon of Nixon probably damaged the Republican ticket more than anything else. In any event, the Democrats won narrowly, and Carter in fact did make more productive use of his vice president than any previous president had. He gave him a key voice in administration appointments and an office in the White House, integrated his staff with the president's own, opened all cabinet and National Security Council meetings to him, and gave him an explicit invitation to attend any meeting in the Oval Office, including those with foreign chiefs of state.

In 1980, when Ronald Reagan won the Republican nomination, he inadvertently gave the vice presidency another boost, when at the party's national convention he entertained the idea of putting together what some advisers called "a dream ticket" by bringing Ford back as vice president. Ford had titillated Reagan with a convention speech in which he said, "I'm not ready to quit yet," and pledged he would do everything in his power to elect Reagan president. "This country means too much to me to comfortably park on the bench. So when this convention fields the team for Governor Reagan, count me in."

That was all Reagan needed. With advice from his pollster, Richard Wirthlin, that Ford could make the difference between victory and defeat, Reagan asked Ford to consider joining him on the ticket. At the same time, Reagan aides began to consider sweeteners that would give Ford a special role in budget writing and National Security Council deliberations. But at the same time they realized the danger in handing over presidential powers; maybe this wasn't such a good idea after all.

Meanwhile, Ford in an interview with CBS News anchorman Walter Cronkite allowed, "If there is to be any change [in his resistance to the vice presidency] it has be predicated on the arrangements that I would expect as a vice president in a relationship with the president. I would not go to Washington . . . and be a figurehead." When Cronkite mentioned the term "co-presidency" and Ford did not object, the fat was in the fire. Reagan, hearing this, was shocked. Ford took Reagan off the hook by saying the idea of putting him on the ticket would not work. Reagan breathed a sigh of relief, and agreed to George Bush, who had challenged him for the nomination and whom he had initially not wanted.

When Bush's own 1980 campaign was falling short, I began asking him at news conferences in the late primary states whether he was persevering in the hope that Reagan would select him as his running mate. Bush answered with what seemed to be the disavowal of interest to end all disavowals of interest: "Take Sherman and cube it," he would say, referring to the legendary response of General William Tecumseh Sherman, when asked if he would run for president: "If nominated I will not run and if elected I will not serve." But once Bush's 1980 presidential hopes were completely dashed, he stopped denigrating the vice presidency, accepted Reagan's reluctant selection of him, and served as one of the most loyal and uncomplaining presidential standbys in American history. So utterly and transparently resilient to Reagan's wishes was Bush as vice president that the conservative columnist and Reagan supporter George Will called him a "lapdog" in print.

Bush learned early in his first vice presidential term the truth of the saying that a vice president was only "a heartbeat away" from the presidency. Only six weeks after he and Reagan were inaugurated, Reagan was seriously wounded in an assassination attempt. And Bush had another reminder when Reagan later underwent cancer surgery.

But basic political considerations continued to dominate the selection of running mates. Even Mondale, who through his own experience as Carter's vice president appreciated the importance of choosing someone with the experience to take over the presidency if necessary, succumbed in 1984. As the long-shot Democratic presidential nominee against the overwhelmingly popular Reagan, he accepted the counsel of advisers who said he needed to make a daring choice to have a chance. After emulating Carter in an open quest for his running mate, Mondale selected the first woman to be nominated for vice president, a relatively little-known congresswoman from New York, Geraldine Ferraro, in the hope that the women's vote would produce an upset for the Democratic ticket. It didn't. Ferraro more than held her own in a debate against Bush, but allegations of financial improprieties in her husband's business affairs undermined her effectiveness as a candidate.

When it became Bush's turn to select a running mate of his own, after eight super-loyal years as Reagan's obedient vice president, he did no surveying of sentiment within the party, did not interview any prospective running mate, and in fact did not discuss the matter much even with his closest aides. Bush, of all people, after the assassination attempt against Reagan and his subsequent cancer surgery, should have appreciated the importance of having a vice president who would inspire confidence, against the time he might have to assume the presidency. Instead he chose someone who would once again make the vice presidency the brunt of jokes and, in sober moments, the cause of trepidation. Advised by his chief media consultant, Roger Ailes, to use the Republican convention in some dramatic way to establish himself as his own man after being in Reagan's shadow all those years, Bush made a bold vice presidential choice, which haunted him thereafter. His selection of Senator Dan Quayle of Indiana as his running mate, a junior member of the party widely regarded as a lightweight, set off endless criticism and ridicule, which Quayle himself only added to with injudicious, at times downright silly comments.

In a vice presidential debate with his Democratic counterpart, the senior and experienced Senator Lloyd Bentsen of Texas, Quayle made a colossal mistake. Asked what he would do if he became president, he did not answer but instead talked about his qualifications, observing among other things that "I have far more experience than many others who sought the office of vice president of this country. I have as much experience in the Congress as Jack Kennedy did when he sought the presidency."

Bentsen broke in. "Senator," he said in the manner of a schoolmaster reproaching a student, "I served with Jack Kennedy. I knew Jack Kennedy. Jack Kennedy was a friend of mine. Senator, you are no Jack Kennedy." In a sense, Quayle never recovered from this exchange, either as candidate or as vice president.

One who understood the political ramifications of Quayle's drawbacks was Robert Teeter, the veteran Republican pollster and strategist from Detroit who became Bush's campaign chairman in 1992. Teeter polled voters on how Quayle's presence on the ticket would affect the outcome. It was inconclusive, but the mere taking of the poll, and the talk about dumping Quayle, led key conservatives to rally around him, and Quayle stayed on the ticket. But because he was still regarded as a potential problem, Bush seldom campaigned with him.

By contrast, the 1992 Democratic nominee, Bill Clinton, and Al Gore, the latter selected after the presidential nominee interviewed five finalists, were inseparable. Clinton realized that Quayle was something of a drawback for Bush; by making a responsible vice presidential choice and advertising it, he reasoned he could make that choice more important in the election than it had been in the past.

From the outset, Clinton instructed his chief talent scout, Warren Christopher, to use one criterion only: "If something happened to me, who would make the best president of the United States?" At the same time, other aides compiled lists and screened them for possible disqualifying factors. According to Clinton's campaign press secretary, Dee Dee Myers, Clinton's "overriding concern was, he was not going to be a nominee who picked Dan Quayle. He thought that that was just a crass political decision. He blamed Bush totally . . . For him, it was an irresponsible decision on Bush's part to choose this man who was clearly incapable of being president." But Clinton also felt that the selection processes used by Carter and Mondale, while careful and deliberate, were too public and undignified for those asked to undergo scrutiny. So he went to great lengths to keep his own interviews secret.

His selection of Gore, Clinton said in an Oval Office interview later, "had a lot to do with my election . . . somehow it made a statement to the American people about me. I took them seriously because I took the job [of vice president] seriously." In Clinton's first term, he made Gore a partner in his administration more than any previous president had done. And in keeping Gore on the Democratic ticket in 1996, he proclaimed him to be "the best vice president in our history." The Clinton-Gore team was easily reelected, but when it was learned Gore had solicited questionable campaign contributions from his office in the White House and elsewhere, a cloud was cast over his obvious ambitions to be in the White House himself.

Bob Dole, in selecting former New York congressman and Bush cabinet member Jack Kemp as his running mate in 1996, expressed his own admiration for the way Clinton had chosen Gore in 1992. Like Clinton, Dole kept his deliberations secret; knowing most of the Republican prospects personally, he felt no need to interview them or trot them out. "I thought it would have been a little embarrassing," he said later. "I thought it sort of demeaned the process." It was widely assumed that because he and Kemp had not gotten along particularly well in the past, and had basic differences on budgetary and tax policies, Kemp would not be on Dole's list. But the surprise choice was very popular at the Republican National Convention, because Kemp had experience and stature. In the end, however, it could not save Dole's weak campaign.

The very fact that the selection of running mates can swing from the ridiculous to the not quite sublime and back again from one presidency to the next underscores the need to assure more consistently good choices. There has been no shortage of ideas about what needs to be done, ranging from abolishing the office of the vice presidency altogether to obliging presidential candidates to select their running mates before the primaries and have them seek public approval as a team.

In May 1988, a Twentieth Century Fund Task Force on the Vice Presidency lauded the evolution of the office into "a more useful and valuable institution," with a more attentive electorate teaching politicians "that they cannot increase their chances to win the election except by applying governance criteria to the selection of vice-presidential candidates."

That optimism was soon shattered with Bush's choice of Quayle, which gave new fuel to a minority report of the same task force, led by Arthur M. Schlesinger, Jr., the eminent presidential scholar and former Kennedy White House aide, which declared the vice presidency "beyond redemption" and called for its abolition. "Far from preparing the occupant for the presidency, the frustrations inseparable from the office have made it as often a maiming as a making experience, a process of emasculation rather than of education."

Since the Mondale vice presidency, though, occupants have increasingly been involved in the work of the administrations they have served, beyond their simple constitutional role. Getting rid of the vice presidency now is not in the cards, nor should it be. In the two most recent and dramatic cases of presidential vacancy, upon the assassination of Kennedy and the resignation of Nixon, having two experienced men as vice president provided a smooth transition and considerable stability to the country in times of national trauma.

The vice presidency itself is no longer simply a token for years of service. Sixteen of the last twenty vice presidents have sought the presidency, and the time when ambitious politicians ran for cover when presidential nominees set out to find running mates is long gone. The advent and reach of television have diminished geography as a factor in the selection, and the prospect for a politician from any state or region is broad.

The question no longer is how to attract worthwhile candidates for the vice presidency, but how to enhance the chances that they will be selected. One idea would be the separate selection in the primary process of presidential and vice presidential nominees in each party. But that concept would have the same drawback as the original double-ballot scheme for electing presidents, with the runner-up becoming vice president. The sort of ideological mismatch that resulted in 1796 with Federalist John Adams as president and Anti-Federalist Thomas Jefferson as vice president could occur again. The procedure might also eliminate meritorious candidates who had been defeated for a presidential nomination and could not be considered as the vice presidential nominee.

Another proposal is to require presidential candidates to identify their running mates early on, or even have them run as a team in the primaries. Voters could then make up their minds about the ticket as a whole. The late Senator Muskie, a former vice presidential nominee, favored this idea. Former Vice President Mondale has pointed out, however, that a long-shot presidential candidate, "at the nadir of his bargaining power," or for that matter any other candidate except an early front-runner, would find it hard to recruit a strong running mate. Also, a strong presidential candidate might be reluctant to risk giving his foes two targets to shoot at, rather than just one.

Still, early identification of the whole ticket would provide some voter protection against a disastrous vice presidential choice; presidential candidates might feel obliged to spend more time and thought on that choice. Had Bush proposed Quayle early on as a possible running mate, the uproar of protest would have come earlier, before the convention, cautioning Bush against it. Choosing a running mate well in advance of the convention might also reduce the practice of peddling the vice presidential nomination to a number of party colleagues in an effort to corral support at the convention.

In any event, as we have seen, the choice almost always comes down to the judgment of one individual. That outcome in itself is not perilous so long as it is followed by some review or confirmation process—by voters, convention delegates, or political peers. It has been well demonstrated almost from the outset of the Republic that a president and his vice president must have a personally and ideologically harmonious relationship to be effective, and to assure continuity of policy if destiny dictates elevation of the vice president to the Oval Office.

One obvious improvement would be to slow down the process. George McGovern, whose 1972 presidential candidacy was shattered by his original selection of Tom Eagleton and the subsequent ragged search for a replacement, acknowledged in his autobiography, *Grassroots*, that fatigue—his own and that of his staff, obliged to fight for the nomination right into the convention—had contributed to the fiasco. At a minimum, an extra day or two should be allowed between the presidential nomination and voting for vice president.

Another protection against a frivolous or disastrous choice would be for each presidential candidate to submit several names to the convention rather than a take-it-or-leave-it single name. This approach, favored by McGovern, would be better than simply throwing open the choice to the convention, which might disregard the essential ingredient of compatibility. The convention could even adjourn and let the party's national committee vote a week or more later on the recommendation or recommendations, providing even more time for a sober decision.

More radically, presidential nominees could run alone, recommending only after election the vice presidential choice, to be approved by a majority of the members of Congress. This idea was proposed in 1973 by Senator Robert P. Griffin of Michigan, a Republican, and would in effect follow the same procedure now called for in the Twenty-fifth Amendment to fill a vice presidential vacancy. The major advantage of postponing the choice until after the election is that it would remove purely and blatantly political factors that often enter ostensibly to enhance the chances of victory at the polls. The president-elect would be freer to choose the person he really considered best qualified to assume the presidency if it came to that.

In the case of divided government, however—the White House in the hands of one party, Congress in the hands of the other—this scheme could be an invitation to turmoil. Congress would be in a position either to block the president-elect's choice or to force him to select someone acceptable not so much to his own party as to the opposition, or someone who represented a politically neutered compromise. Such an outcome would foretell trouble even before the new president took office. Also, the voters would have no say, and would have no measure of the presidential nominee's judgment about the matter. That voters have often disregarded this yardstick is not a valid reason for getting rid of it.

The Twentieth Century Fund report concluded optimistically: "Ultimately, the price of a rash or overly 'political' nomination is paid in the coin of the electoral realm: on election day." Presidential nominees had come to realize, the report said, that he "who pays insufficient attention to governance criteria in choosing the vice-presidential nominee will suffer for it in the election." In this the report was woefully wrong.

In the end, good vice presidential selection comes down to two incontrovertible elements. First, the presidential nominee must make a wise choice. Second, voters must hold that nominee to account on Election Day if he fails to do so. All that can be done is to provide ample time for judgment to be exercised coolly and responsibly; then it is up to the citizens to assess that judgment in their votes.

In a very real sense, in picking a vice president a potential president is being selected, and the decision should be evaluated in these terms. Until selection of a running mate by a presidential nominee becomes a key voting issue in presidential elections, no amount of tinkering with the way the decision is made is likely to make much difference.

12 The Grand Facade

Today's presidential campaigns are like the famous movie scene in which Frank Morgan as the Wizard of Oz stands behind a curtain and spins wheels to produce great puffs of smoke and flame. In real life, the role of Toto the dog is played by the news media, pulling aside the curtain and revealing what is actually taking place.

The fact is that the presidential campaign that most voters see from Labor Day through the first Tuesday in November, and often during the primary campaign season as well, has become a facade, with the much more significant and influential campaign going on behind the curtain. The principal nominees, in an elaboration of the two-track campaign conducted so successfully by Richard Nixon and his strategists in 1968 and 1972, go through the traditional ritual of stumping from state to state, but they are actually seen and heard by a relatively tiny portion of the American electorate. What most Americans see and hear comes from television studios, occasionally in the live form of the candidate but more often in canned paid commercials—the second track of the old Nixon strategy.

Some candidates, in the manner of Hubert Humphrey in 1968, continue to travel on the first track, stumping state to state at a frenetic pace, wearing themselves to a frazzle. But the wiser ones now pattern their first track after the Nixon model, targeting television market areas and showing themselves in the flesh just enough to create the appearance of nonstop campaigning. At each place the campaign plane sets down, the candidate makes the same speech, to another audience to whom it sounds new. Then he climbs back aboard the plane and enjoys good food, drink, and conversation as the campaign party flies to the next stop, where the ritual is repeated.

Listen to James Carville as he describes a typical routine for Bill Clinton in 1992: "Let's say you do an event in Toledo. The idea that you really meet a Toledian is ludicrous. You go to the airport, there's an escort; you go in and go into the backstage, they bring twenty politicians back there, they bring some union people back there, you shake hands with them; you give a speech, you go to the rope line, you shake hands for ten minutes, they haul you away, you're packed on the airplane, you go to the next stop . . . There's no way a presidential candidate [in the general election] ever gets to talk to average people."

In 1996, President Clinton built a "bridge to the twenty-first century" several times a day, while somewhere else in America, Bob Dole talked about a tax cut plan he had agreed to advocate, against his own long-held belief about budget balancing, on the advice of his hired guns. Reporters covering the campaigns reached the point where they could recite key parts of the candidates' speeches verbatim as they delivered them. To keep them occupied, another prize tactic of the Nixon campaigns was used—the circulation of "position papers" on all manner of issues from which the press could write stories justifying their existence and expense accounts. The old-fashioned news conference was rare or nonexistent, though an occasional "press availability" occurred, usually a brief question-and-answer session on the run, more of a "photo opportunity" than a chance to explore key issues.

Meanwhile, campaign strategists and operatives were busy hatching the elements of the second track—television commercials exalting the candidate and, increasingly, castigating his opponent. The two tracks merged when the stumping candidate detoured to a television studio for a network or local interview or a "town meeting" peopled by supporters. Clinton was so confidently effective in this latter format that he even risked unscreened audiences, but Dole's "open" formats usually took place before the selected faithful.

Though they both claimed to be campaigning "all over America," they carefully stayed with the states whose electoral votes were up for grabs, or at least were within reach of the underdog. In September, for example, according to tracking by the Annenberg School for Communication at the University of Pennsylvania, neither Clinton nor Dole "delivered a major stump speech or aired a significant number of ads" in seventeen states.

On both tracks, reporters for both print and televisual media were held at bay. As with the Nixon campaigns of 1968 and 1972, spontaneity was avoided in favor of a carefully controlled environment protective of the candidate against hostile or merely risky questions and circumstances.

It was very different when candidates traveled by commercial plane rather than their own charters. In 1968, when Robert Kennedy decided suddenly to enter the race against President Johnson, there was no time at first to hire a charter, so Kennedy and a horde of reporters piled onto regular commercial flights. Kennedy would routinely sit with the reporters and hold running press conferences amid awed regular passengers who found themselves thrust into the middle of a presidential campaign—usually to their delight. By the 1970s, however, campaign entourages—staff and newspeople—became so large that not only were charter planes required, but often candidate and staff flew in planes separate from the news media. On the candidate's plane, there would be a few seats for selected reporters—usually television network correspondents, some cameramen, and reporters and columnists from the larger newspapers and newsmagazines. Between stops, you'd hear the clatter of portable typewriter keys pounding out stories to be handed to Western Union telegraph operators or dictated to the home office by phone at the next stop.

When reporters were not at work, we amused ourselves with writing irreverent campaign parodies of popular songs, spoofing the candidate and often singing them to him either face to face or over the plane's public-address system. Other times, we engaged in silly antics such as rolling oranges down the climbing plane's aisle at takeoff or, more daringly, standing on the slick plastic cards bearing instructions for evacuating the plane in case of emergency, and hurtling down the aisle as it took off. Gary Hart in 1984 was particularly deft at this exercise. A second aircraft, "the zoo plane," carting most of what the print reporters called "the animals"—television cameramen and other technicians, and the still photographers, a particularly raucous bunch—handled the overflow.

All these amusements were part of an easy and open relationship among the candidates, their staffs, and newspeople, which yielded stories and campaign analyses that transcended the routine and helped to alleviate the repetition and boredom of the campaign. Reporters had an opportunity to see and listen to candidates at their less guarded ease that is not usually available today, when candidates and their hired guns are ever mindful of the television camera, the boom microphone, and the ever-ready tape recorder.

Technology has affected the reporters as well as the politicians. The days of frantically pounding out stories on portable typewriters, after which one had little to do but eat, drink, and horse around until the train, bus, or plane reached the next stop and you could file your story, are mostly gone. Armed now with laptop computers and cellular phones, reporters busy themselves endlessly not only with writing their articles and transmitting them electronically but holding nonstop phone conversations with the home office. Did you get my story? Is it going on page one? Is it above the fold? If I'm not on page one, who is? Why are you changing my lead? What did the opposition lead with yesterday?

There does not seem to be as much carousing among reporters as there used to be on the campaign buses, trains, and planes, or after hours in the bars of overnight hotels along the trail. For one thing, candidates who routinely used to join reporters for dinner and a few jars of elixir afterward more often than not closet themselves with their staffs and stay away from the watering holes. For another, many of the younger breed of reporters do not seem to adhere as much as their elders to the axiom about all work and no play. The idea of relaxation for many of them seems to be to turn in early and then get up before dawn to jog. There's a story, possibly apocryphal, about a major daily newspaper sending a young reporter to New Hampshire about two months in advance of that state's first-in-the-nation primary. The first thing he did, the story goes, was not to check out the best restaurants and bars but to join a weekly bridge club.

The net effect of all these changes is that life on the campaign trail for both candidate and the news media has become an exercise much more of motion than of substance. Many daily newspapers are either canceling coverage of the candidates' daily stumping or moving reporters into the field to cover various states or to monitor the second-track campaign going forward in the television studios and on paid commercials. The "death watch" is diminished, and the "truth watch," of reporters viewing the television ads from which most voters learn about the candidates, is augmented.

Reporters assigned to cover the candidates can still assess their performance and analyze their behavior, but because they are sealed in a flying capsule throughout the campaign it is hard for them to develop perspective on the candidate and to assess his success or failure. They usually manage to see television ads only on the run—in their hotel rooms at night or early in the morning—so paradoxically the reporters who spend the most time with the candidates often see the least of the campaign as it is being seen by most voters. That is why serious news organizations must cover and report on both campaign tracks.

Active campaigning for the American presidency was relatively slow to develop in the early years of the Republic. Presidents from Washington to Van Buren were largely passive players in their own selection. The process was intended, as noted earlier, to be conducted in each state by the political elite, who knew the candidates and could make informed decisions.

The campaign that resulted in the election of the first Whig president, William Henry Harrison in 1840, was perhaps the first blossoming of presidential campaigning. Although General Harrison himself made few speeches outside his native Ohio, his supporters and allies organized massive rallies and parades where marchers warbled songs extolling the hero of the battle of Tippecanoe in the War of 1812. With John Tyler as his running mate, the slogan became "Tippecanoe and Tyler Too." Harrison was touted as a "log cabin" frontiersman like Andrew Jackson, taking on Van Buren, the aristocratic New York stuffed shirt. In what came to be known as "the Image Campaign," a record turnout of four out of every five eligible voters put Harrison in the White House, if only briefly. After delivering a marathon inaugural address lasting nearly two hours in which he pledged to serve only a single term, the sixty-eight-year-old Harrison developed pneumonia and died after only one month in office.

Succeeding presidential candidates, by custom or choice, essentially stayed on the sidelines during their own campaigns. In keeping with tradition, Lincoln remained home in Springfield and left the campaigning in his party to Senator William Seward and others. The Democratic nominee, Senator Stephen A. Douglas, however, broke with that tradition and campaigned vigorously, first across the North in early hopes of winning, later in the South, where two other candidates, John C. Breckinridge and John Bell, held sway but where Douglas labored to discourage secession.

With presidential nominees still often sitting out the campaign at home, as James A. Garfield of Ohio did in 1880, party-affiliated operatives regularly filled in on the stump, carrying the party's and the candidate's message, raising money, and masterminding the campaign. Candidates like Garfield preferred to stay on their front porches and receive visitors or write letters, and leave the heavy political lifting to the party men behind them who figured to profit from their election.

An exception was the Republican nominee in 1884, James G. Blaine, who ventured forth and had the unhappy experience of being associated with a New York minister who openly assured him that an audience of Republican clergymen "don't propose to leave our party and identify ourselves with the party whose antecedents have been rum, Romanism and rebellion." So much for the Catholic vote and Blaine's White House aspirations.

Presidential nominees were still staying home during the fall campaign of 1896, and the Republican candidate, William McKinley, was no different. But he was an effective public speaker and so a "front-porch campaign" was devised, wherein he invited a steady stream of party leaders and officials as well as assorted voting groups to call on him for a few words at his home in Canton. Meanwhile, his Democratic opponent, William Jennings Bryan, shattered the stay-home tradition by traveling 18,000 miles championing unsuccessfully the cause of free silver with his fabled line: "You shall not crucify mankind upon a cross of gold."

Bryan, however, did not have the field to himself, because McKinley's running mate, the irrepressible Theodore Roosevelt, jumped into the breach. He took to the stump with his customary energy against Bryan, as if he himself were the Republican presidential nominee, even referring to Bryan as "my opponent."

Roosevelt's own presidency saw the beginnings of the most profound developments for participation of average voters in the political process, with the emerging of state presidential primaries to select delegates to the national party conventions. This development eventually made the front-porch campaign a relic, by imposing new pressures on candidates to demonstrate their talents directly to those whose support they sought. Roosevelt himself, however, in 1904 essentially honored the tradition of the incumbent remaining off the stump, and he was easily elected in his own right in a dull campaign.

Roosevelt took to the stump again in 1912 as the Progressive Party nominee, with his successor, President William Howard Taft, this time playing the traditional incumbent role largely on the sidelines. The Democratic nominee,

Governor Woodrow Wilson of New Jersey, proved to be an effective campaigner as an intelligent and witty phrasemaker against the fiery Roosevelt. The campaign was notable chiefly for an assassination attempt against Roosevelt, who three weeks before the election was shot in the side of his chest in Milwaukee. With the bullet lodged in a rib, Roosevelt delivered his scheduled speech without medical treatment but then quit the campaign trail until a few days before the election, in which he ran second to Wilson.

In 1916, Wilson stayed off the stump until late in the campaign but finally jumped in behind the famous slogan "He Kept Us Out of War" and narrowly beat the Republican nominee, Supreme Court Justice Charles Evans Hughes. In 1920, Republican senator Warren G. Harding of Ohio, a bland man whose speeches consisted, as one wag put it, of "an army of pompous phrases moving across the landscape in search of an idea," reinstituted the front-porch campaign by addressing visiting delegations at his hometown of Marion.

Harding's successful campaign against former Ohio governor James M. Cox saw the first significant attempt to poll the American electorate in advance of the election. The weekly *Literary Digest* sent out eleven million postcards, the results of which easily predicted Harding's sweeping victory, unimpeded by a whispering campaign that Harding had what was then called Negro blood. The same publication predicted the election in 1924 of President Calvin Coolidge, elevated in 1923 upon the sudden death of Harding and running on the slogan "Keep Cool with Coolidge."

The election of 1928 saw one of the nation's most energetic presidential campaigners in Governor Alfred E. Smith of New York, the Democratic nominee, against Republican Herbert Hoover. Smith barnstormed the country, whistle-stopping by train and using radio to convey his extemporaneous remarks in a losing cause. But radio was a complement, not a substitute, for stump campaigning. Presidential campaigns still ran essentially on one track—the track that took candidates from state to state, mostly by train.

Radio took on a much greater significance with the candidacy of Governor Franklin D. Roosevelt of New York in 1932 and in three succeeding election campaigns. Armed with a brain trust of experts in public policy who had little political experience, Roosevelt crossed the country in his first presidential campaign, making twenty-seven major speeches based on their research and advice. His vigor in voice and appearance contradicted the whispers about his physical disabilities as a victim of poliomyelitis. That he was largely confined to a wheelchair was a fact kept hidden from the public, with the cooperation of the traveling press corps. Beyond that, Roosevelt's warm, mellifluous delivery and good humor were in sharp contrast to Hoover's flat, monotonous style. Still, FDR's campaigns also were essentially one-track affairs. Movie newsreels recorded aspects of them, but these did not approach the revolutionary impact that commercial television was soon to have.

Whistle-stop campaigning was the chosen method now for both Roosevelt and his Republican opponents, and huge crowds turned out to hear the president or simply to see the presidential car roll by. The *Literary Digest*, its sampling weighted toward traditional Republican demographic groups, widely missed the mark in 1936 by predicting a large electoral college triumph for Governor Alfred M. Landon of Kansas, snowed under by Roosevelt. FDR's masterful use of radio more than compensated for growing editorial opposition to him as he shattered the no-third-term tradition in 1940 and went one better in 1944.

More of a match for FDR was Republican nominee Wendell L. Willkie in 1940. Willkie visited thirty-four states, traveling about 30,000 miles and delivering 540 speeches in a growling, raspy voice with a vitality that was equal to Roosevelt's. With FDR's health suffering under the strain of his leading the nation in the war against German, Italian, and Japanese fascism, much of the active campaigning had been left to Vice President Henry A. Wallace. But as Willkie developed considerable appeal, Roosevelt embarked on "inspections" of national defense facilities that drew huge crowds, as did his open campaigning in the final weeks. In the end, he won comfortably with 54.7 percent of the vote and 449 electoral votes to only 82 for Willkie.

In 1944, the ailing Roosevelt limited his active campaigning to two dinner speeches and three public speeches, all of them broadcast on radio, and three other special radio "fireside chats." With the war progressing successfully, FDR again won easily over Governor Thomas E. Dewey of New York, winning 432 electoral votes to 99 for Dewey.

The upset election in 1948 of FDR's successor, Truman, marked the high point in effectiveness and public appeal of the whistle-stop campaign. Truman traveled 31,000 miles, mostly by train, reaching an estimated six million Americans with his down-to-earth style of the average man. On radio Truman seemingly was out of his class against the polished, precise Dewey. But Truman managed to cast himself as the underdog and challenger although he was the incumbent, and he prevailed, in spite of not one but two splits in his party that had Wallace running as the Progressive Party nominee and Governor Strom Thurmond of South Carolina heading a so-called Dixiecrat ticket.

Then came television. In 1952, the national conventions of the two major parties were covered by network television for the first time, revealing the political circus in all its positive and negative aspects. Speechmakers and delegates alike played to the cameras, but by and large the television audience was enthralled by this open demonstration of the democratic process in action. More than ever, there was a premium on how a candidate looked and acted, as well as on what he had to say. The erudite but not particularly photogenic Governor Adlai E. Stevenson of Illinois, the Democratic nominee, was eclipsed by his Republican opponent, the immensely popular national hero General Dwight D. Eisenhower, who easily carried the day, as he did again in 1956.

In the campaign of 1960, television came into its own as a dominant force in presidential campaigning chiefly as a result of the first televised presidential debates, between Democratic nominee John Kennedy and Republican nominee Richard Nixon. Kennedy was the lesser-known candidate, but his debate performances put him at least on a par with the more experienced Nixon and were a key factor in his narrow election.

Four years later, as noted earlier, forceful, negative television commercials that played on public fears that the Republican nominee, Barry Goldwater, was dangerously trigger-happy in the era of the nuclear bomb, helped Lyndon Johnson fashion an easy election to the presidency in his own right. And in 1968 and 1972, Nixon resurrected and then enhanced his political fortunes by devising the two-track strategy that elevated television to even greater importance.

Jimmy Carter of Georgia turned that trend on its head for a time, reverting in 1976 to the retail, handshaking style in the Iowa caucuses and early primaries with remarkable success. He was considerably helped by public revulsion about the slick politics revealed and widely condemned in the Watergate scandal that forced Nixon from office in 1974. Carter promised voters, "I'll never lie to you," and after Watergate they wanted to believe him. His opponent, Nixon's second vice president and successor, Gerald Ford, also seemed a stylistic throwback, but in their general-election confrontation, both of them used their daily appearances and speeches essentially as a means to draw time and footage on the evening television news shows. Meanwhile, they courted much larger audiences and each week fed them self-promoting television commercials costing millions of dollars.

In 1980 and 1984, Ronald Reagan and his handlers wanted to demonstrate in his daily travels that he had the vigor to be president and, in the second campaign, that he retained the vigor to keep the post for another four years. But the important part of the campaign took place in television studios, in personal appearances by the jovial Reagan or with carefully crafted commercials starring or lauding the old easygoing movie actor.

So it was also in George Bush's election in 1988 against the distinctly camera-unfriendly Michael Dukakis and the victories of Bill Clinton in 1992 and 1996. In each, the touring companies hurtled around the country on planes, the candidates waved at crowds and delivered their standard speeches, then climbed aboard for the next city and the same speech and routine all over again. Nixon's strategy of forbidding the spontaneous and isolating himself from the inquiries of his traveling companions in the press corps was relatively easy to emulate. Heavy Secret Service protection and cooperative party functionaries had little trouble keeping hostile individuals and hostile questions at bay. In 1992, the closely escorted Bush repeatedly finessed embarrassing and probing questions about what he knew about the sale of arms to Iran and sending the proceeds to the Contras in Nicaragua, and when he knew it.

Preconvention campaigning for the party nominations has, however, posed a more challenging task. It is much harder to avoid spontaneity in the face of shouting, demanding reporters when engaged in the retail campaigning of the early caucuses and primaries in smaller states. Most candidates either lack Nixon's icy discipline or are not temperamentally suited to keeping voters and the press at arm's length.

Still, it is every political consultant's objective, in the preconvention period as during the general-election campaign, to protect his candidate from unprogrammed events and situations behind a controlled facade of handshaking, speechmaking, and picture taking. This means the fewer news conferences the better, and then only when the candidate has something he wants to propose or advocate, not when the press corps is clamoring for a specific answer, or simply to get a crack at him after weeks of being held in check.

Increasingly, newspeople are criticized for focusing on "inside baseball"—reporting on the inner workings of the campaigns rather than simply telling what the candidates are saying and doing. But the latter is precisely what the consultants and handlers want, because they can tightly control the travel and the speechmaking so as to get out the message they want, undiluted and unchallenged by anyone who questions the candidate's veracity or consistency. The grand facade must be covered and reported, to be sure. But the press and television are doing themselves and the voters a disservice if they permit the elaborate traveling sideshow to be perceived as the main event, when the politicians and their aides are counting on the second track—television appearances and paid commercials—to do the major sales job on the candidate. That's why the news media must seriously examine what is done on that second track—behind the curtain that shields the great and powerful Oz.

13 Moments of Truth

Perhaps the single most significant development in the way Americans choose their presidents since the beginning of the Republic occurred on the evening of September 26, 1960. In Chicago, Senators Richard M. Nixon and John F. Kennedy faced each other, television cameras, and a panel of reporters, in the first of four presidential debates transmitted live to the nation's viewers. As matters turned out, Kennedy came off seeming more aggressive and confident, while Nixon looked wan and sounded defensive. Polls showed that most voters who had watched the debate clearly preferred Kennedy, while most who heard the debate on radio thought Nixon superior.

But it was the fact of the first Kennedy-Nixon debate itself, and the three that followed, that was the milestone. For the first time, scores of millions of Americans saw and heard the principal contenders answer questions about major issues, listening and watching with no press corps to filter the impressions.

The debates on network television were made possible by Congress suspending the so-called equal-time provision of federal communications law requiring that during a campaign all presidential candidates have the same access to the airwaves. The networks—which took turns in airing the debates, with CBS first, then NBC, and finally ABC for the final two—controlled the formats, as agreed to in negotiation with the candidates. Audiences for the four ranged between 65 million and 70 million (second only in television history to the final game of the 1959 World Series).

Voters, politicians, and press alike deemed the debates so critical to the outcome of the election that thereafter all party nominees considered participating in them or not strictly in terms of their potential political gain or loss. The conventional wisdom before the first of the 1960 debates had cast Nixon as the favorite, given his greater experience as President Eisenhower's globe-trotting vice president and his age (forty-seven to Kennedy's forty-three). When Kennedy won the election and fingers pointed to that first debate as the chief reason for his success and Nixon's failure, debates became in the eyes of presidential nominees and their campaign managers not only an opportunity but a prospective danger.

For that very reason, in spite of their considerable popularity, no debate was held during the next three presidential election campaigns. In 1964, President Johnson was so far ahead of Goldwater that he and his Democratic advisers decided he did not need to risk the uncertainties of debate, did not need to allow Goldwater the appearance of parity with a sitting president, and did not need to fear voter retribution for having skipped doing so.

In 1968, there was one memorable debate between Democratic contenders Senators Eugene McCarthy and Robert Kennedy during the California primary. But Nixon, once bitten in 1960, was twice shy eight years later, and did not debate in 1972 either. A rule gleaned from the wisdom of LBJ and Nixon, that an incumbent president should not elevate his opponent by sharing a debating platform with him, seemed on the way to being established. But when President Ford, having succeeded Nixon after Watergate, ran in his own right in 1976, he found himself far behind Jimmy Carter in the polls, so he disregarded the rule, hoping that a debate would help him close the gap. Instead, Ford in his second debate with Carter came a cropper.

The presidential debates in 1976 were sponsored and overseen by the League of Women Voters, who also instituted the first televised debate between vice presidential nominees—Bob Dole, the Republican, and Walter Mondale, the Democrat. And while it was impossible to determine what if any effect that debate had on the outcome of the election, the exchange also illustrated the pitfalls of the exercise.

Mondale, disciplined to a sharp edge for the confrontation, coolly answered questions, while Dole was at first casual and eventually bitter. In frustration, Dole finally lashed out. "I figured out the other day that if we added up the killed and wounded in Democrat wars in this century," he said, "it would be about 1.6 million Americans, enough to fill the city of Detroit."

Mondale immediately leaped on the remark, branding Dole as a partisan "hatchet man." If voters were assessing the two running mates, Dole certainly did his team no good that night.

In 1980, the presidential debates encountered storms as the League of Women Voters set out to put its stamp on them and establish further rules for participation. The Republican Representative John B. Anderson of Illinois, defeated in his party primaries, was complicating the situation by running as an independent, and the League unilaterally decided there would be three presidential debates. Anderson would be invited at least to the first, provided he achieved an average of 15 percent support in the major public-opinion polls, which at this time he was receiving. Carter, trailing in the polls against Ronald Reagan, was eager to debate him but balked at including Anderson, insisting he would not take on two Republicans. His campaign declared that the League had no franchise on presidential debates and invited other groups to sponsor one-on-one Carter-Reagan debates. Now the Reagan strategists, wanting to avoid debates as long as their man was ahead in the polls, did the balking, but eventually Reagan agreed to debate Anderson alone, in a confrontation that served chiefly to underscore Carter's intransigence.

By mid-October, the polls reported that Anderson's support was falling off sharply, which gave the League the rationale to exclude him from another debate. Also, Reagan's pollster found that the gap between Carter and Reagan was closing, so his candidate relented. Carter was confident he could best the old movie actor, and agreed to a single debate. His fate was sealed not so much by any mistake he made as by the fact that the debate gave Reagan a means to counter the fear that he was too old, too militant, and not sharp enough to be president. He presented himself as strong, controlled, and confident, compared to which Carter seemed testy. Reagan concluded with a simple but pointed question that threw the election back on Carter's record as president during the previous term: "Are you better off than you were four years ago?" On Election Day, the resounding answer was: "No."

By 1984, public pressure in favor of having presidential campaign debates was very high, and since Reagan was so far ahead of Mondale, he seemed to have nothing to lose by them. So Reagan agreed—but only to two. The League of Women Voters again sponsored them, but the candidates' strategists—especially the shrewd, hard-nosed James A. Baker III for Reagan—negotiated the key ground rules. This time Reagan sounded defensive and often confused in the first of the two debates, giving rise to immediate speculation that he had slipped mentally, probably as a result of his age (he was then seventy-three). But Reagan bounced back in the second debate, using his famed humor to dispel concern. Reminded of the huge pressures faced by President Kennedy in 1962 in the Cuban missile crisis, Reagan was asked whether "you would be able to function in such circumstances." He shot back with a mock-serious pledge: "I will not make age an issue in this campaign. I am not going to exploit, for political purposes, my opponent's youth and inexperience." Once again, the king of the one-liners had come through. That ended the talk about Reagan and senility, and he won reelection easily.

In advance of the 1988 campaign, the two major parties decided to move into the business of presidential debates themselves. The League of Women Voters was becoming too proprietary for the liking of parties and candidates, and so the Republican National Chairman, Frank Fahrenkopf, and his Democratic counterpart, Paul Kirk, created a bipartisan Commission on Presidential Debates. It decided that the two parties in 1988 would sponsor three debates between the major-party presidential nominees and one between their two running mates. Meanwhile, the League went ahead with its own plans. Each group announced it would hold an early debate in September.

But neither sponsor had the last word. Neither Vice President George Bush, the Republican nominee, nor Governor Michael Dukakis of Massachusetts, the Democratic nominee, was of a mind to let any outside group determine the timing, frequency, or panel composition for such a critical aspect of the campaign. By late August, an early Dukakis lead of 17 percentage points in the major polls had vanished and Bush was in no hurry to debate. Baker insisted that any arrangement would have to be negotiated between the candidates, and that under no circumstance would any debate be held as early as September. After intensive negotiations, in which the Dukakis camp said it wanted four presidential debates and the Bush strategists said they wanted no more than one, they agreed on two between Bush and Dukakis and one between their running mates. The new commission was to conduct the first presidential debate and the vice presidential debate and League of Women Voters the second presidential debate, but the League eventually bowed out, complaining that the parties were trying to manipulate the process, which certainly was true. Much back-and-forth went on over everything from the height of the podiums to be used to the composition of the panels, with the candidates insisting on vetoing certain suggested newspaper and newsmagazine reporters and television correspondents. So the commission jumped in and ran that one too, and that was the end of the League's often officious and self-important participation.

The first Bush-Dukakis debate was uneventful, with Dukakis the more aggressive and armed with details on a range of issues. But in the second, Dukakis was ambushed in a clever opening round of questioning by the moderator, CNN anchorman Bernard Shaw. Dukakis had a reputation as a cold, impersonal candidate, all facts and figures, and Shaw asked him point-blank: "Governor, if Kitty Dukakis [his wife] were raped and murdered, would you favor an irrevocable death penalty for the killer?" This shocking question, Shaw explained later, was designed to probe the emotional side of this very controlled man. But Dukakis answered as if only the important policy issue were involved, and not his feelings. "No, I don't, Bernard," he said, "and I think you know I've opposed the death penalty during all of my life. I don't see any evidence that it's a deterrent, and I think there are better and more effective ways to deal with violent crime." Then he went on to cite how crime had been reduced in Massachusetts without a death penalty for capital crimes. The crowd gasped.

This answer was a double whammy. First, it reminded voters of Dukakis' rather aloof attitude toward criticism of his prison furlough program. But, worse, it squared with the governor's image as a cold and emotionless efficiency expert. If he could not get angry about the idea of the rape and murder of his own wife, what would it take to get him exercised?" If Dukakis' candidacy wasn't cooked before then, you could have stuck a fork in it now.

Bush by contrast deftly fielded his opening question from Shaw, also intended to have shock value. Shaw quoted from the Constitution the clause that specifies that in the event a president-elect dies before he is inaugurated, the vice president-elect becomes president, and asked Bush what he thought of "that possibility." Bush replied evenly that he'd "have confidence" in Quayle, ticking off his qualifications as a former senator. After these opening questions and answers, Dukakis' slim chances of scoring an upset were gone and he lost the election.

Yet the question to Bush took on particular pertinence when Quayle stumbled on the campaign trail and gave a dismal performance against Bentsen in their debate. Asked what would be "the first steps that you'd take, and why," if he had to take over the powers of the presidency, Quayle floundered badly. "First I'd say a prayer for myself and for the country I'm about to lead," he said. "And then I would assemble his [the president's] people and talk." He repeated the qualifications he believed he had for high office, which he had listed earlier. Twice more when pressed on the same point, he fell back on chronicling his experience. "It's not just age; it's accomplishments, it's experience. I have far more experience than many others that sought the office of vice president of this country," he said. And then he offered his disastrous comparison with "Jack Kennedy" that haunted his political career thereafter.

In 1992, the Fahrenkopf-Kirk commission went ahead and planned three presidential debates and one vice presidential debate, stipulating that each of them would have only a single moderator, since it had been decided that groups of questioners were not conducive to direct exchanges and were prone to showboating on the part of the panelists. But again, while the horses could be led to water, they could not be made to drink. In this case, Bill Clinton was leading in the polls over the incumbent, and the incumbent needed debates. But Bush's strategists liked neither the single-moderator format nor the timing. They thought a panel of reporters would reduce the aspect of a direct exchange with the challenger, which they believed would benefit the glib Clinton. And as in 1988 they wanted late debates, hoping that voters by then would see the election more as a choice between two men than as a referendum on the Bush administration, which was struggling through a long period of economic recession. The Clinton camp, by contrast, insisted that no debate should be held later than mid-October, two weeks before the election. They feared that Bush might spring something in the final debate about which there would be inadequate time for reply. In mid-September the Bush campaign rejected the commission plan and instead told the Clinton people directly that the president was willing to debate "under the same terms and conditions" as had governed in 1988. Clinton's strategists refused.

By this time, in the minds of millions of voters, presidential debates were an institutional part of the election process. A dynamic soon developed—encouraged by the Clinton campaign—in which Clinton demanded debates and blamed Bush for ducking them. In a poll for *The New York Times*, 63 percent of voters surveyed faulted the incumbent. So Clinton went to the site that had been proposed by the commission for the first debate, Michigan State University in East Lansing, on the appointed day, saying he was there ready to debate. In the crowd, a student wore a chicken suit as others mocked "Chicken George" for refusing to face Clinton. Soon, more similarly attired students began showing up at rallies around the country—often with logistical assistance from the Clinton campaign. Bush finally relented.

By now, however, there was another problem. Earlier in the year, the Texas billionaire Ross Perot had declared himself an independent candidate, paying his own way, and he had risen swiftly in the polls. But as the national press corps delved into his past and raised more and more questions about his business practices and claims, Perot suddenly withdrew in July. In early October, however, he reentered the race, again with considerable support in the polls. The commission decided to invite him to the debates, and Clinton and Bush, not wanting to alienate Perot voters and still hoping to lure them, acquiesced.

Once again, the debates were critical in the campaign, especially the second one. For the first time, the commission decided to use a "town meeting" format, with local voters who claimed they were undecided as the audience. The single moderator, Carole Simpson of ABC News, stood among them at the University of Richmond and recognized questioners at random.

The decision to take questions from a live audience met with considerable skepticism from the press corps. Veteran reporters argued that average voters would pose obvious and simplistic inquiries that the candidates had already answered numerous times and to which they would give boilerplate replies. But they were wrong. Three voter-interrogators eschewed convoluted questions of the sort that reporters themselves, submerged in the arcana of the campaign, had often asked. Instead, they asked straightforward questions that went to the core of their personal worries.

The first wanted to know why both Bush and Clinton were "trashing their opponents' character" instead of addressing serious issues. The second asked what they had in mind "to meet our needs, the needs in housing and in crime and you name it, as opposed to the wants of your political spin doctors and your political parties," adding: "Can we focus on the issues and not the personalities and the mud?" The third inquired how did "the national debt personally affect each of your lives, and if it hasn't, how can you honestly find a cure for the economic problems of the common people if you have no experience in what's ailing them?"

President Bush, whom the news media often painted as aloof and aristocratic, seemed utterly confused by this line of questions. To the first, after Perot had deplored "the mud wrestling," the president astonishingly defended his criticism of Clinton's character, saying, "I believe that character is part of being president. I think you have to look at it." And besides, he said, Clinton had started the trashing by running the first negative ad, "and I'm not going to sit here and be a punching bag."

But Clinton commended the questioner, saying that he, too, had been "disturbed by the tone and tenor of this campaign . . . so I'm not going to take up your time tonight [defending himself against Bush's charges] . . . I'm not interested in [Bush's] character. I want to change the character of the country."

When the second questioner pressed the three candidates to "make a commitment to the citizens of the United States to meet our needs, and we have many, and not yours again," Bush hedged. "It depends how you define it," he said. "I mean, I think in general let's talk about the issues, let's talk about the programs. But in the presidency a lot goes into it. Caring goes into it. That's not particularly specific. Strength goes into it. That's not specific. Standing up against aggression. That's not specific in terms of a program. This is what a president has to do. So in principle, though, I'll take your point and think we ought to discuss child care or whatever else it is."

This was hardly responsive to the questioner's appeal. But Clinton, in his answer, was the soul of empathy. "I worked twelve years very hard as governor on the real problems of real people," he said. "I'm just as sick as you are by having to wake up and figure how to defend myself every day. I never thought I'd ever be involved in anything like this." He felt the questioner's pain.

The third question completely threw Bush. "Well, I think the national debt affects everybody," he began. "Obviously, it has a lot to do with interest rates." Simpson, the moderator, encouraged him to give a more personal response. The questioner wanted to know, she interpolated, "how has it affected you . . . personally?"

Bush struggled. "I'm sure it has," he allowed, tentatively. "I love my grandchildren . . . I want to think that they're going to be able to afford an education. I think that that's an important part of being a parent." He still wasn't sure of what the questioner wanted to know. "If the question . . . maybe I get it wrong. Are you suggesting that if somebody has means, that the national debt doesn't affect them? . . . I'm not sure I get—help me with the question and I'll try to answer it."

The woman tried. She told Bush of "friends that have been laid off from jobs . . . I know people who cannot afford to pay the mortgage on their homes, their car payment. I have personal problems with the national debt. But how has it affected you, and if you have no experience in it, how can you help us, if you don't know what we're feeling?"

Bush still seemed puzzled, and Simpson again stepped in to help. "I think she means more the recession," she explained, "the economic problems today the country is facing, rather than the deficit." A light went on in Bush's head, though a dim one. "Well, listen," he said, "you ought to be in the White House for a day and hear what I hear and what I see, and read the mail I read and touch the people that I touch from time to time." Incredibly, he went on talking about how economic hardship had affected *others*, as he had learned secondhand. He told of going to a black church in the Washington area where "I read in the bulletin about teenage pregnancies, about the difficulties families are having to make ends meet. I talk to parents. I mean, you've got to care. Everybody cares if people aren't doing well . . . But I don't think it's fair to say, 'You haven't had cancer, therefore you don't know what it's like' . . . But everybody's affected by the debt because of the tremendous interest that goes into paying the debt, everything's more expensive. Everything comes out of your pocket and my pocket . . ."

The president was beginning to get the drift by now, and the point he seemed to be making—that you don't have to be poor to appreciate the plight of poor people—certainly had some validity. Clinton, after all, had also talked about dealing with the problems of others as governor. But he had managed to sound personally involved, while Bush seemed not even to understand what the questioner was driving at.

When it was Clinton's turn to respond, at his theatrical best he stepped from behind his podium and walked over to the woman. "Tell me how it's affected you again," he urged. "You know people who've lost their jobs and lost their homes?" Not waiting for an answer, he went on: "I've been governor of a small state for twelve years. I'll tell you how it's affected me. Every year Congress and the president sign laws that make us do more things and give us less money to do it with. I see people in my state, middle-class people—their taxes have gone up in Washington and their services have gone down, while the wealthy have gotten tax cuts. I've seen what's happened in the last four years when, in my state, when people lose their jobs there's a good chance I'll know them by their names. When a factory closes, I know the people who ran it. When the businesses go bankrupt, I know them."

Clinton told the woman he had been hearing questions from "people like you all over America" over the previous thirteen months of campaigning in similar town meetings, "people that have lost their jobs, lost their livelihood, lost their health insurance . . . We've had four years where we've produced no private sector jobs. Most people are working harder for less money than they were making ten years ago." Though his personal life probably had not suffered any more than Bush's had as a result of the recession, Clinton painted a picture of himself as sharing in these typical American difficulties of the time.

Perhaps better than any previous debate had, the one in Richmond showed how well presidential debates, in this format particularly, could give voters a window into the thought processes of the individuals who sought their votes. So successful were the 1992 debates and the town-meeting format that the Fahrenkopf-Kirk commission modeled the 1996 debates after them. But there always remained the question of when and how the candidates would participate. In 1996, both Clinton and Dole had strong reasons to want to debate—Clinton because he excelled at it and Dole because he trailed badly in all the major polls—and both committed themselves early to doing so. The usual jockeying and negotiating resulted in two presidential debates and one between Al Gore and Jack Kemp.

The most notable aspect of the 1996 debates, which were not at all critical to the election outcome, was the decision of the commission to exclude Ross Perot, running as the nominee of a newly formed Reform Party. As in 1992, the commission had as a prime criterion that a candidate had to have a "realistic (i.e., more than theoretical) chance of being elected the next President of the United States." In 1992, the judgment had been made that since Perot had earlier reached 39 percent in some polls and would be spending as much of his own money as he wanted, he had that "realistic chance."

Other criteria for 1992 and 1996 included "evidence of national organization," such as ballot placement "in enough states to have a mathematical chance of obtaining an electoral college majority," "organization in a majority of congressional districts in those states," and eligibility for federal matching funds or independent ability to fund a national campaign. The commission also specified "signs of national newsworthiness and competitiveness," which would be determined on the basis of "the professional opinions of the Washington bureau chiefs of major newspapers, news magazines and broadcast networks . . . the opinions of a comparable group of professional campaign managers and pollsters not then employed by the candidates under consideration . . . the opinions of representative political scientists specializing in electoral politics at major universities and research centers . . . column inches on newspaper front pages and exposure on network telecasts in comparison with the major party candidates [and] published views of prominent political commentators."

This elitist circumstance rightly outraged supporters of independent and third-party candidacies, even though the commission also specified it would consider "indicators of national public enthusiasm or concern," such as "the findings of significant [undefined] public opinion polls conducted by national polling and news organizations" and "reported attendance at meetings and rallies across the country (locations as well as numbers) in comparison with the two major party candidates." Disregarded were the facts that polls were often erratic and undependable and crowd sizes were often meaningless. Mostly they were only a measure of how well a campaign had done its advance work, whether or not an event was held in a heavily populated area at a convenient time, and what the weather was.

The commission appointed a panel of academics to make the decision. In 1996, it decided Perot did not qualify because his polling numbers were lower than in 1992 and this time around he was limited in his spending by having accepted the federal subsidy. Perot's supporters screamed bloody murder. He desperately needed exposure with Clinton and Dole, to demonstrate that he belonged on the same stage with them. Perot was not the only casualty of the decision, however. His exclusion was bad news for everyone who believed that the electoral process already worked undue hardships on fledgling independent parties. Yet in the eyes of the commission, some candidates, as in George Orwell's *Animal Farm*, were more equal than others.

The decision, however unfair, did express the truth that multicandidate debates usually diminish the content by reducing the focus in depth on key issues. The commission specified that its goal was "to afford the members of the voting public an opportunity to sharpen their views of those candidates from among whom the next President of the United States will be selected," and experience had shown that the more candidates involved in a presidential debate, the less continuity of discussion resulted, with secondary candidates hustling disproportionately for airtime, even to the point of pulling outrageous stunts to get attention.

For example, in a multicandidate debate in New Hampshire in 1972—including such losers as Mayor Sam Yorty of Los Angeles and House Ways and Means Committee chairman Wilbur Mills—a Democratic activist-candidate named Ned Coll reached below the table and produced a toy rat to illustrate some irrelevant point. In 1980, the manager of Ronald Reagan's campaign in the New Hampshire Republican primary, John Sears, tried to turn a scheduled two-man debate between his candidate and George Bush into a multicandidate affair precisely because, he said later, there would be less time for each participant and hence would reduce the risk to Reagan. When a local newspaper, the *Nashua Telegraph*, withdrew its sponsorship over a dispute on participation, the Reagan campaign bought the airtime and promptly invited the other Republican contenders. Four of them showed up, and the affair became a circus.

As the other candidates stood around, awaiting chairs, Reagan began to make his case for including them. Bush, who was insisting on the two-man debate previously agreed on, sat stolidly, like a petulant schoolboy, staring straight ahead. In the end, neither Bush nor the newspaper would yield on including the other candidates, and the debate finally proceeded with just Reagan and Bush. But what they said got virtually no publicity amid the furor of the argument over participation. Bush looked foolish and Reagan went on to win the primary. Bush's attitude certainly hadn't helped him and, more important, the fuss enabled Reagan to reduce the two-man debate itself to a political footnote.

Debates during the primary season in 1996 once again demonstrated the diminished value of multicandidate exchanges. In Iowa no fewer than nine candidates took the stage for a Republican presidential "forum" sponsored by the *Des Moines Register.* Dole, the clear front-runner at the time, had only to keep his powder dry, avoiding undue contention. Meanwhile, the other eight jockeyed for advantage. With so many candidates sharing the ninety-minute program, more heat than light was spread in the studio and on the television screen.

All the contenders had been greatly outspent in television commercials by Steve Forbes at that point, and all but Dole were lagging far behind in the polls. So all but Dole pounded away at him, while Forbes, a Johnny-one-note, advocated a flat tax as an elixir for the country's economic woes.

Lamar Alexander, a former governor of Tennessee, called Forbes's flat tax "a truly nutty idea in the Jerry Brown tradition." He went on: "Steve, the only thing you've ever run is a magazine you inherited, and you raised the price of your magazine. Now what would you do with taxes?"

Pat Buchanan joined in, observing to Forbes that "my flat tax is a middle-class tax cut. Yours looks like one that was worked up by the boys at the yacht basin."

David Yepsen and Jonathan Roos, writing in the *Register* the next day, observed that the forum "illustrated that Dole, as the leader, is clearly profiting from all the quarreling among his challengers. While they each would like to take him on, they also can't let another challenger get too far ahead." Phil Gramm, dropping out of the Republican nomination race soon thereafter, deplored having participants in the debates who were "not real candidates" and got in the way.

It should be said that multicandidate debates can be more readily defended in the early presidential primaries and caucuses, when many people enter the field for a party nomination who are relatively unknown to the voting public. Voters have a chance to start sorting them out, but debates do give a distinct advantage to established candidates who know how to bob and weave, as Dole demonstrated in this one, remaining "presidential" as the others duke it out.

The sorting-out, however, doesn't always work as quickly as it should. In 1996, candidates who soon established that they had neither the popularity nor the acumen to be president—most conspicuously Congress' prize bomb-throwing loudmouth, Robert Dornan, Iowa businessman Morry Taylor, and former minor State Department official Alan Keyes—nevertheless persevered, cluttering up the landscape and the discussion.

Yet there is a built-in mechanism for eventually getting them off the stage, as noted earlier: candidates face a cutoff in the campaign subsidy provided under federal campaign law if they fail to win 10 percent of the vote in two successive primaries, and those who do so usually drop out. But the Steve Forbeses of the world, able and willing to pay their own way, are not so readily sent to the sidelines.

The presidential debates, however, are a different matter. It takes a major effort in organization, publicity, and personality for an independent or third-party candidate to be taken seriously. The presidential debates commission's criteria are justified, if not its suggestion that the grand jury be made up of pundits, campaign operatives, and political scientists, who seem to be as wrong as often as they are right in their prognostications.

The decision by the commission in 1996 to exclude Perot stuck a pin in his ballooning dream for a repeat performance of his 1992 surprise. However, he met most of the major new yardsticks established by the commission—on the ballot in enough states and organized in enough congressional districts to have a realistic if not overwhelming chance to win.

Who was to say he did not have such a chance? The advisers to the commission probably were right in saying he didn't, but in doing so they threw a very cold dash of water on all those voters who are saying increasingly that they are not satisfied with the existing two major parties and would like to have an alternative. After all, Perot in his obnoxious, know-it-all way did enrich the debate discussion in 1992, forcing Clinton and Bush to talk about the budget deficit, trade policy, and other issues the two principals might well have dodged.

Would it have done irreparable harm to permit Perot to take part in the first debate, in view of his performance in 1992 and the considerable public notoriety he still enjoyed, and then bounce him for the next one? Such a step would at least have given encouragement to the many crusaders in American politics who think independents should have greater opportunity for expression, not only the new Reform Party but also the Libertarian and other long-shot parties that represent serious political thought in the country, if not serious election prospects.

Another problem for presidential debates is that the major-party campaigns are still allowed to dictate whether there will be debates at all, how many of them there will be, in what format, and by whom moderated. Although after the last six presidential elections we like to think of the debates as having attained an institutional status, the fact remains that if a candidate or candidates decline to debate, the only sanction can come from voters at the ballot box.

Why not require participation in debates as a condition of the major-party nominees' accepting the huge federal payment that now, by law, pays for their general-election campaigns? Such a step doubtless would require new legislation, and probably would be strongly resisted by both parties, which would not want their nominees forced into uncertain events. But this requirement would assure regular debates every four years, could specify the number of debates and their format, and end the procedural circus that now marks every presidential campaign.

After the 1996 commission decision that excluded Ross Perot, my colleague David Broder of *The Washington Post* came up with some excellent recommendations for improving the debates. While noting that the two-party system "has served this country well and is worth protecting," he suggested that it was good "only up to the point that it does not conflict with other values important to the electorate. In an era when increasing numbers of voters are discarding old party loyalties, significant independent candidates have a claim on participation in the debates."

Broder proposed that Congress should amend the campaign finance laws to require that each party "takes responsibility for its nominee participating in debates under conditions to be set by the bipartisan commission." He suggested further "that the co-chairmen representing the major parties select a third co-chairman, who is politically independent, with the further requirement that all decisions be unanimous." This caveat would make it impossible for Republicans and Democrats to collude to maintain control, but it might create stalemates on controversial matters.

Concerning third-party participation, Broder proposed that the first debate each year be open "to any and all minor-party candidates who have more than five percent support in national polls or have ballot position in all fifty states." Subsequent debates would be limited to the major-party nominees and any others "who continued to achieve five percent in the polls." This threshold seems too low to me for the subsequent debates, if the objective is to give voters a clear choice between the candidates who have a realistic chance of winning or otherwise affecting the outcome of the election.

The Commission on Presidential Debates in 1996 struck on a wise formula when it got rid of journalist panels to pose questions, settling instead for a single moderator. Jim Lehrer of PBS' *NewsHour* conducted the debates with fairness, firmness, and intelligence. In selecting him, the commission eschewed the more famous television network stars such as Peter Jennings, Tom Brokaw, or Dan Rather, whose celebrity status rightly or wrongly was judged to subject the debates to inappropriate glitz. Over the years, the journalist panels have too often generated showboat questions or, worse, disjointed debates with questions hopping from one subject to another and back with little coordination.

Before the second 1988 debate between Dukakis and Bush, the panelists—Bernard Shaw as moderator with Ann Compton of ABC News, Andrea Mitchell of NBC News, and Margaret Warner, then of *Newsweek*—met to discuss what they could do to make sure all the important questions in the campaign would be posed. The format called for Shaw to start by asking one question of each nominee. The others asked him what his opening questions would be, so they would not be caught short in the event they had prepared similar questions. At first, Shaw said later, he balked, not wanting to tip his hand. But the others pressed him, so he told them, word for word, what he had prepared for Dukakis—the hypothetical question about whether he would favor "an irrevocable death penalty" for the rapist and murderer of his wife. The three women were aghast and tried to talk him out of it, but he held fast.

"I asked that question to probe, to see what was there," Shaw told me later. "My intent was not to roll a grenade across the stage." But a grenade was exactly what the question turned out to be, and it blew up in Dukakis' face. There is no guarantee that a debate without journalists will be free of such grenades. But Lehrer, though criticized in some quarters as too bland, should be the model.

The debate commission, explaining its considerations in selecting a moderator in 1996, specified that he or she probably ought to come from television, in order to be comfortable on the stage and in receiving the producer's instructions, which are fed to the moderator through an earpiece in the course of the debate. This seems reasonable and prudent, and it does not bar members of the print press, many of whom appear often or even regularly on television and are accustomed to these mechanics.

But the identity of the moderator and the issue of whether to have more than one questioner are secondary to assurances that the presidential debates do become institutionalized, with recalcitrant nominees losing federal campaign money if they refuse to participate. The presidential debates remain the best single opportunity for voters to hear the candidates express views directly and to size up their abilities.

14 An Accident Waiting to Happen

Of all the gripes about the way we Americans pick our presidents, none is more obviously justifiable than this one: that the process does not assure that the candidate who gets the most votes is elected.

Three times in the nation's history—four if you use a certain popular-vote calculation in the state of Alabama that would have given Nixon more votes cast than Kennedy in 1960—the will of a majority or plurality of the American electorate has been thwarted by the system. In 1824, Andrew Jackson won the popular vote by 37,000 ballots over John Quincy Adams; in 1876, Samuel Tilden had 251,000 more votes than Rutherford B. Hayes; in 1888, Grover Cleveland beat Benjamin Harrison by 95,000. In all three cases, the popular-vote winners were denied the presidency.

In the 1960 count, Kennedy was credited with all of Alabama's Democratic popular vote, although six of the state's eleven Democratic electors ran unpledged and in fact cast their electoral votes for Senator Harry F. Byrd of Virginia. Had the popular vote been allocated proportionally between Kennedy and Byrd as calculated later by *Congressional Quarterly* and its political editor of the time, Neal Peirce, Kennedy's national popular-vote total would have been reduced by 176,000 and hence his national plurality of 112,000 over Nixon would have vanished, with Nixon having a 58,000 plurality. Nixon, however, lost the electoral vote to Kennedy, 303 to 219, to 15 for Byrd. (Notably, when the Democratic National Committee later calculated the number of Alabama's delegates to the 1964 national party convention, it used the same figures that would have made Nixon the popular-vote winner in 1960!)

As recently as 1992 and 1996, with the third-party candidacy of Ross Perot muddying the picture, there were fears once again that a monkey wrench would be tossed into the archaic presidential selection machinery, resulting in a popular-vote winner being denied victory. It didn't happen, but the danger remained, as it does today.

The culprit is the electoral college, an anachronistic brainchild of the Founding Fathers dreamed up to satisfy the conflicting wishes of those determined to defend the predominance of the larger states and those who were protective of the influence of the smaller. This division was also responsible for the establishment of two legislative bodies, the Senate with two representatives from each state to protect the smaller states and the larger House of Representatives with a membership based on population. When it came to deciding how the president was to be chosen, the same division surfaced, along with a split over whether the legislative branch or the "people"—as yet undefined—should make the choice. Roger Sherman of Connecticut argued that the president "ought to be appointed by and accountable to the legislature only, which [is] the depository of the supreme will of the society." Elbridge Gerry of Massachusetts weighed in with a warning that "the people are uninformed and would be misled by a few designing men." And George Mason of Virginia argued that "it would be as unnatural to refer the choice of a proper magistrate to the people as it would to refer a trial of colors to a blind man."

But early proposals to have Congress select the chief executive were discarded out of concern that such a president would be subservient to the legislative branch. Also dismissed was the notion of direct popular vote, out of fears among the smaller states that they would become irrelevant in the process, that the president would be too powerful, and that, as Gerry and Mason held, the mass of voters would not be well enough informed about the candidates to choose wisely, opting instead for favorite sons in their own states and producing chaos and indecision.

A compromise was finally seized upon—a scheme first put forward by James Wilson of Pennsylvania and later modified. It was adopted with little debate or enthusiasm, partly because the Constitutional Convention wanted to get on with ratification of the whole process and because no immediate problem was foreseen. After all, it was widely conceded that George Washington would be easily elected as the first president.

As Neal Peirce wrote in his definitive book on the electoral college, *The People's President*: "The most basic reason that the electoral college was invented was that the Convention was deadlocked on simpler schemes like direct election and choice by Congress, and thus invented a system that could be 'sold' in the immediate context of 1787." Peirce quoted the constitutional scholar John P. Roche's description of it as "merely a jerry-rigged improvisation . . . [a] Rube Goldberg mechanism."

Under the scheme adopted, it was decided that each state, as noted in Article II, Section One of the Constitution, "shall appoint, in such manner as the Legislature thereof may direct, a number of electors" who would cast their votes for two individuals of their choice, only one of whom came from the electors' state, to serve for four years. Each state would choose as many electors as it had senators and representatives in the federal legislature. The individual with the most votes would be president and the person with the second most votes would be vice president. Nothing was said about the qualifications of the electors or how they were to be selected, other than to note that no member of Congress or anyone else "holding an office of trust or profit" in the federal government was eligible—an obvious way to prevent the appearance or reality of undue influence or bribery.

It was to be a strange college—more like a correspondence school. The electors would never meet in a body but rather would gather in each state, cast two ballots for president, and forward the results, sealed, to the president of the Senate for counting and certification before members of both houses of Congress. Gouverneur Morris of Pennsylvania said this would avoid "the great evil of cabal," since the electors "would vote at the same time" throughout the several states "and at so great a distance from each other."

Election of a candidate required a majority of the votes cast. In the case of a tie or failure of any candidate to achieve a majority, the names of the top five vote-getters would go before the House of Representatives, where each state would have one vote—another nod to the concerns of the smaller states. If there was a tie for runner-up, the Senate would select the vice president. This procedure indicated that in the absence of political parties, the original intention was for the electoral college to function principally as a nominating vehicle, selecting names that would be passed on to the House for decision. But with the emergence of political factions and eventually parties, candidates winning the necessary majority in the electoral college became the rule, not the exception.

As Alexander Hamilton observed in *The Federalist*, No. 68, the electoral college approach would assure that "a small number of persons, selected by their fellow-citizens from the general mass, [who] will be most likely to possess the information and discernment requisite to such complicated investigations," would make the selection. But "the general mass" in those days did not mean everybody. The franchise was generally limited to landowners in most states; hence those who picked the electors were themselves among the elite. Also, the way electors were chosen varied widely from state to state, with legislatures in some states and qualified voters in others selecting them according to a number of formulas.

The electors, Hamilton noted, would be persons "most capable of analyzing the qualities adapted to the station" of the presidency under conditions "favorable to a deliberation and to a judicious combination of all the reasons and inducements which were proper to govern their choice." Translation: The man in the street need not apply. This expectation of high caliber and judiciousness among the chosen electors was to fall far short of the mark over ensuing years.

Through this discreet selection, Hamilton contended, "tumult and disorder," "cabal, intrigue and corruption" would all be avoided, and "would be much less apt to convulse the community with any extraordinary or violent movements than the [direct] choice of one who was himself to be the final object of the public wishes." Translation: If the mob made the choice, it might lead to chaos.

But chaos resulted anyway after Washington decided not to seek a third term. His vice president, John Adams, was elected to succeed him, but Adams had to serve with a member of the opposition "party," Thomas Jefferson, as his vice president, as a result of the unintended consequence of the "double balloting" for president.

That election was marked by the vote of the first "faithless elector," a Pennsylvania Federalist named Samuel Miles, who, although chosen as a person who would cast his ballot for Adams, voted for Jefferson. An irate fellow Federalist wrote: "What, do I choose Samuel Miles to determine for me whether John Adams or Thomas Jefferson shall be President? No! I choose him to act, not to think." But whatever the intent of the Founding Fathers, there was nothing in the Constitution that stipulated that the electors were anything but free agents in their task, nor is there any further instruction today as to how they are to vote.

In the nation's fourth election, the electoral college tie between Jefferson and Burr, which threw the election into the House of Representatives for the first time, led to adoption of the Twelfth Amendment to the Constitution, providing for the separate election of president and vice president in the electoral college. It also reduced the number of presidential candidates to go before the House from the top five vote-getters in the electoral college to the top three. By 1824, eighteen of the existing twenty-four states had decided to choose electors by popular vote, with the remaining six by state legislatures, both methods using shifting formulas as practical political considerations dictated. As the popular vote spread quickly, state parties began to run their electors on statewide general-election tickets, and by 1836, all but South Carolina were doing so. After the Civil War, that state as well adopted the procedure, as did others as they entered the Union. Local political groups and kingmakers were also exerting more influence. For example, a collection of Tennesseans known as the Nashville Junto who had engineered a Senate seat for General Andrew Jackson pushed him for the presidency in 1824 and succeeded in 1828.

Although Jackson won the popular vote in 1824 he failed to gain an electoral majority, winning the votes of only 99 electors with 131 required. The election for the second time went to the House, to choose among the top three electoral-vote finishers: Jackson, John Quincy Adams with 84, and William H. Crawford of Georgia, Secretary of the Treasury under President James Monroe, with 41. House Speaker Henry Clay, who had actually run third in the popular vote ahead of Crawford, trailed him by four electoral votes and thus was cut from the list submitted to the House. On the very first ballot in the House, Adams won the presidency with the votes of thirteen states out of the twenty-four, the barest majority required, and also, it was reported in an anonymous letter to a newspaper, with a deal with Clay that made the latter Secretary of State. Clay denied the allegation but Jackson wrote to a friend: "So you see the Judas of the West has closed the contract and will receive the thirty pieces of silver. His end will be the same. Was there ever witnessed such a bare-faced corruption in any country before?"

In 1828, when Jackson ran again, only two states—Delaware and South Carolina—were still leaving the choice of their electors to their legislatures, a circumstance much to the favor of "Old Hickory," since Jackson was popular with the general public. After perhaps the most negative presidential campaign yet, he defeated Adams in the popular vote, 647,000 to 508,000, winning 178 electoral votes to Adams' 83.

Adams was vilified for his supposed deal with Clay in 1824, and his strategists struck back. They painted Jackson as a violent hothead and dredged up an old story about his having married his wife before she had been divorced from her first husband—which in fact had been an unintentional mistake rectified with a second marriage ceremony. Friends of Jackson responded with a charge that as minister to Russia Adams had helped bring about the seduction of an American girl by the Tsar, and as president had bought with public money a billiard table to put in the White House for his son. These allegations might have had little effect had all or most of the state legislatures, made up of men practiced in the hard world of politics, chosen the presidential electors. But with the popular vote now reigning in twenty-two of the twenty-four states, such charges seemed to resonate more pointedly. This phenomenon was to continue and grow, as more states came into the Union with political decisions made after listening directly to the voice of the people.

Twelve presidential elections and fifty-two years passed before the electoral-college vote again deprived the popular-vote winner of the presidency. In 1876, disputed electors in four states kept the Democrat, Governor Tilden of New York, a single vote shy of the required majority. He had run ahead of the Republican, Governor Hayes of Ohio, by 250,000 popular votes but extensive investigation in the four states—South Carolina, Florida, Louisiana, and Oregon—revealed fraud and corruption on both sides. In the Southern states particularly, there was widespread evidence of Republican manipulation and even purchase of black votes, and of Democratic intimidation and violence to curb that same vote. When the time came for the president of the Senate to count the actual electoral-college votes, as provided by the Constitution, the question arose whether he had the right to decide between two sets of electors, involving a total of twenty electoral votes submitted in the disputed states. The Constitution said only that in the presence of both houses he was to "open all the certificates and the votes shall then be counted."

In 1865, Congress had adopted a rule that if the electoral vote from any state was rejected by either house, voting separately, it would be thrown out. And in 1873, all the electoral votes of Louisiana and Arkansas and three from Georgia had indeed been rejected. But in early 1876, the Republican-controlled Senate had refused to readopt the rule for the next election, and the Democrats in control of the House after the election thereby were denied the right to throw out the disputed electors, which would have given Tilden his majority.

To deal with the dilemma, a joint committee of the two houses created an Electoral Commission of five senators, five House members, and five justices of the Supreme Court to decide among the twenty disputed state electors, unless overruled by both houses. Tilden needed only one of the twenty to win.

All the commission members had to swear under oath that they would "dismiss every consideration that would cloud their intellects or warp their judgments," including, obviously, partisan affiliation. The party breakdown of the commission was seven Democrats and seven Republicans, with the fifteenth member to be selected from among members of the Supreme Court by the two Democratic and two Republican justices already specified.

They were expected to pick Justice David Davis of Illinois, appointed by President Lincoln but generally regarded to be an independent. But before Davis could be named, a coalition of Democrats and independents in his home-state legislature inexplicably appointed him to a vacant seat in the U.S. Senate, taking him off the hook. A Republican, Justice Joseph P. Bradley, was named in his place and proceeded to vote with the Republicans down the line on all twenty disputed electors, awarding them to Hayes and making him the electoral college winner, 185 votes to 184 for Tilden. The Democratic House objected, but the rule said only both houses could reject a commission verdict, and the Republican Senate held fast. The experience offered ample grounds to reexamine the utility of the electoral college, but still it withstood complaints that it be eliminated or reformed.

In 1887, Congress tried to clear up the situation that had occurred in the Hayes-Tilden fiasco. It passed the Electoral Count Act, empowering the states to decide the legality of its electors and requiring a concurrent majority of the two houses of Congress to overturn a state's decision. But the electoral college continued to be an institution of dubious worth and fairness. Cleveland, seeking reelection in 1888, won the popular vote by 95,000 ballots but lost the electoral vote to Harrison, 233 to 168, amid widespread reports of vote buying and voter intimidation. When Harrison thanked Providence for his victory, Matthew Quay, the Republican Party boss in Pennsylvania, remarked, "Providence hadn't a damn thing to do with it." Harrison would never know, he said, how many men "were compelled to approach the gates of the penitentiary to make him president." But if the popular votes were disputed, the electoral count was not and the electoral college remained untouched.

The specter of more popular-vote winners but electoral-college losers continued to hang over the unaltered process. There had been other popular-vote close calls: Clay trailed James K. Polk by only 1.5 percent in 1844; Winfield Scott was only 0.1 percent behind James A. Garfield in 1880; James G. Blaine lost to Cleveland by only 0.2 percent in 1884. And in 1916, an even greater electoral-college folly was narrowly averted when Democrat Woodrow Wilson held a solid 582,000 popular-vote margin over Republican Charles Evans Hughes, but would have lost the election had Hughes won only 12 more electoral votes. The last state to report its popular vote, California, at the time had 13 electoral votes, enough to make Hughes president. After a slow vote count, Wilson carried the state by only 3,806 popular votes out of nearly a million cast. Had Hughes won less than two-tenths of 1 percent more of the vote, the clear popular will of the national electorate would have been thwarted.

In 1948, the cloud appeared again, when the presidential election between Truman and Dewey was threatened by the intrusion of two minor party candidates, former Vice President Henry A. Wallace running on the Progressive Party ticket and then Governor Strom Thurmond of South Carolina running as a States' Rights Party candidate. Thurmond, the "Dixiecrat" nominee, won only 2.4 percent of the popular vote but 39 electoral votes from the South. This alone was not enough to force the election into the House. Wallace, who collected about the same popular vote as Thurmond, had widely dispersed support and got no electoral votes. Truman, with a popular-vote bulge of nearly 2.2 million over Dewey, won in the electoral college 303–189. But this electoral vote was deceiving. In three large states, California, Illinois, and Ohio, Truman's margin was such that a shift of only 29,300 votes to Dewey in the three would have made Truman the loser; a shift of only 12,500 in California and Ohio would have put the election into the House. With the Democrats controlling 21 state delegations, the Republicans 20, and the Dixiecrats 4, the Southern group would have been in a position to tip the election.

The 1960 election, in addition to the intriguing issue of whether Nixon really won the popular vote but was undone in the electoral college, was notable for a scheme by six unpledged electors in Alabama to trigger enough defections from Kennedy in other Deep South states to throw the electoral-college majority to Nixon. About a month after the election, the six met in Birmingham and announced they would cast their votes "for an outstanding Southern Democrat who sympathizes with our peculiar problems in the South." Their position, they went on, "remains fluid so that we can cooperate with other unpledged electors for the preservation of racial and national integrity." And they chastised fellow Southerners who "ally themselves with a candidate who avowedly would integrate our schools, do away with literacy tests for voting," and "otherwise undermine everything we hold dear in the South"—clearly referring to Kennedy.

Two days later the six Alabamians met with eight unpledged Mississippi electors in Jackson and agreed to give their electoral votes to Byrd. The scheme needed 35 Kennedy electors to switch in order to throw the election into the House, and Mississippi's strongly segregationist governor, Ross Barnett, wrote letters soliciting support from six other Southern states. But in the end, the Kennedy electors held fast and the anti-Kennedy Democrats picked up only one more vote for Byrd, and that from a Republican in Oklahoma.

Still another electoral-college threat to the major-party nominees presented itself in 1968, when the independent candidate former Governor George C. Wallace of Alabama pointedly hoped to throw the election between Nixon and Humphrey into the House of Representatives unless they struck an unspecified deal with him. As Election Day approached, the front-running Nixon saw that Humphrey was closing the gap on him, that Wallace was registering 20 percent of the vote in the latest Gallup Poll, and that he might fall short of an electoral majority. To avert the prospect of having the election go into the Democratic-controlled House, Nixon transparently proposed to Humphrey that they agree, to avoid a constitutional crisis, that the winner of the popular vote be declared president.

Humphrey, understanding what Nixon was up to, replied that he would "stand by the constitutional process," confident that if the election did go to the House, he would be elected. Nixon, his ploy foiled, called Humphrey's position "a clear indication that he cannot win the popular vote and his only hope of winning is to get Mr. Wallace enough votes in enough states to deny the electoral college vote to Nixon." As matters turned out, Wallace ended with only 13.5 percent of the popular vote and 46 electoral votes, not enough to stop Nixon, who won the popular vote over Humphrey by only 0.7 percent but captured 31 more electoral votes than he needed for the victory. Asked by Peirce later how he would have handled the situation had Nixon failed to receive an electoral majority, Wallace replied: "Why would I want to lose control of the matter by throwing the election into the House where we would have no control whatsoever? No, the election would have been settled in the electoral college." In other words, he would have tried to make a deal with Nixon, "because we were violently opposed to Mr. Humphrey's philosophy and ideology."

In 1976, yet another electoral-college disaster was narrowly averted. Jimmy Carter beat Gerald Ford by 1.7 million votes, but a shift of fewer than 9,300 votes in Ohio and Hawaii would have given Ford the required 270 electoral votes. However, one Ford elector from Washington State, Michael Padden, proved "faithless," deciding before the official count to give his vote to Ronald Reagan on grounds that Ford was not strongly enough opposed to abortion. Thus, even had Ford won Ohio and Hawaii, he would have had only 269 votes to 268 for Carter, paving the way for wild dealmaking or the decision going into the House.

It is clear from all this that the possibility still exists for a presidential candidate to win the support of a majority or plurality of voters and be denied the presidency, especially when a third candidate of any appreciable strength is present. The fact that it has occurred only three times (or four if you accept the argument that the Alabama vote was misallocated in 1960) in forty-four presidential elections for which popular votes are available (none from 1789 to 1820) is hardly an argument for retaining this flawed process.

In practice, the electoral college has become a bad joke. The role of elector routinely has fallen to party functionaries and hacks as a minor badge of honor. In almost all cases, electors dutifully troop to their state capitals after the election and cast their ballots as the voters have instructed, although there is no stipulation in the Constitution that they must do so. Some states do have statutes explicitly instructing their electors to vote for the candidates to whom they are committed, but their enforceability is questionable.

The manner in which electors are chosen is haphazard, as is the way in which they are presented to the voters. Some states list the electors' names on the statewide ballot, others only the names of the candidates to whom they might be pledged. In the confusion, voters in some states have inadvertently cast ballots for electors for the presidential candidate they actually opposed.

More serious by far is the problem of the unit rule in allocating each state's electoral vote—the winner of the popular vote of any given state collecting all the electoral votes there. This winner-take-all procedure developed out of partisan considerations, with parties in power in particular states insisting on it. The stipulation in effect disenfranchises in the electoral college all voters who cast their ballots for losers in any state, even though their votes, when counted nationally, might be in the majority. Furthermore, millions of ballots are "wasted," in the sense that a candidate who piles up a huge lead in any state benefits in the electoral college no more than had he won the state by a single vote. This is true whether the state delivers fifty electoral votes or five, and discourages voting in states where a candidate is predictably an easy winner.

Beyond that, the electoral college has proved to have a strong "multiplier effect," giving the popular-vote winner a larger percentage of the electoral vote than he gets in the popular vote—an average of 10.1 percent more according to Peirce and Lawrence Longley in their book, *The Electoral College Primer.* Seventeen times from 1824 to 1996, candidates who have not won a popular-vote majority have been boosted to an electoral-college majority and elected.

When the electoral college fails to produce a majority for one candidate and the election goes to the House of Representatives for resolution, another major disenfranchisement occurs. Article II as amended stipulates that in voting for president, each state delegation has one vote—and this when California currently has fifty-two representatives and Wyoming one. Another potential nightmare is the possibility that the House, meeting on January 3 (as provided in the Twentieth Amendment), could not produce a majority in time for the presidential inauguration on January 20. In that event, the new vice president—whose own election most likely would have been forced into the Senate, where a majority of states also would have been required to choose him—would merely "act as President until a President shall have qualified." And if neither a president nor a vice president has been chosen by January 20, Congress would have the task of "declaring who shall then act as President, or the manner in which one who is to act shall be selected, and such person shall act accordingly until a President or Vice President shall have qualified." In response to this convoluted language, Congress in 1947 passed the Automatic Succession Act, which makes the Speaker of the House the President, with the Senate president pro tem next in line.

The solution to this craziness is obvious: abolish the electoral college and replace it with a direct popular vote for president and vice president. Almost since the beginning of the Republic, sharp criticism of the electoral college has brought demands for its reform or abolition. Proposals have ranged from eliminating the electors altogether in favor of a direct popular vote, to reallocating electoral votes by way of special electoral districts, congressional and at-large districts in each state that would eliminate the winner-take-all approach. In 1892 Michigan did pick its electors by congressional district, with two also picked at-large, and the delegation was split, nine votes for the Republican ticket, five for the Democratic, but then it abandoned the scheme. Maine has used it since 1972 without once splitting its electoral vote, and Nebraska has employed it in the last two presidential elections, also without a split.

To guard against minority presidencies, some have proposed that there be a runoff between the two popular-vote finishers if neither has a majority in the first election. Other reformers have suggested, with the interests of the smaller states in mind, that in addition to electoral-college voting by district there be two electoral votes allocated to each state, large and small alike. Still others have proposed that when a presidential election is forced into Congress, the House and Senate should vote in joint session, with each congressional district casting one vote and each state casting two at-large, representing its Senate seats, with a majority required for election.

The basic idea of keeping the electoral college and having the electors chosen by districts rather than statewide has only generated new arguments between Democrats and Republicans, between conservatives and liberals, between rural and urban areas, between North and South, over which would benefit and which would be hurt. States where one party dominates would still likely produce majorities for the same candidate in most districts, often resulting in winner-take-all situations, and voters who cast their lot with the loser would still be disenfranchised. Beyond that, the scheme is an invitation to gerrymandering of districts.

Also, if a candidate won a majority of a state's popular votes, he could still lose the electoral count there if he won them in fewer districts than his opponent did; projected nationally, the popular-vote winner could once again wind up being the electoral-vote loser. According to Peirce, "the district system would likely benefit small-state, rural conservatism and harm big-state, urban liberalism." In 1960, he calculates, Nixon, who lost to Kennedy by 84 electoral votes, would have won by 33 under a district system.

The most obvious way to break down the winner-take-all system within the electoral college is to allocate electoral votes proportionally to the popular vote. This straightforward approach, proposed many times in various forms, has been effectively killed by opponents fearful it would politically weaken individual states, strongly favor one-party states, and encourage presidential candidates to concentrate their campaigns on the biggest cities and most heavily populated states (which happens now anyway). Other critics fear that the proportional approach would make it easier for independent and third parties to win electoral votes, with the result being the formation of more minor parties at the expense of the two-party system. And as long as a majority of electoral votes was required for election, the danger of a popular-vote winner being denied the presidency remains and would even be enhanced.

In 1950, the Senate actually approved a proportional plan for allocating electoral votes in the form of a constitutional amendment to change the electoral college, but it was easily defeated in the House. In 1956, another plan that would have incorporated parts of the district and proportional systems came before the Senate but was strongly attacked by liberal Democratic senators Paul A. Douglas of Illinois and John F. Kennedy of Massachusetts, who called the proposal a "hybrid monstrosity" that amounted to a "shotgun wedding," and it was beaten back.

Kennedy at the time said "no urgent necessity for immediate change has been proven" because "no minority presidents have been elected in the 20th Century, no elections have been thrown into the House of Representatives, no breakdown in the electoral system or even widespread lack of confidence can be shown." Only four years later, he was to have a personal experience in which that confidence was shaken, if not in him, in many other Americans. As Peirce noted in his book, Kennedy's strategy of capturing the large industrial states of the North as a key to victory "would have been denied him under either the proportional or district plans that he was instrumental in defeating in the 1956 debate."

Kennedy did, however, try to resurrect another reform in the 1956 discussions, "the automatic system," which would abolish the position of elector but retain and incorporate in the Constitution the winner-take-all allocation of each state's electoral votes, and have the entire Congress vote if no candidate had a majority of the electoral vote. The proposal got nowhere, even when it was picked up by President Johnson in 1965. Johnson warned that "today there lurks in the electoral college system the ever-present possibility that electors may substitute their will for that of the people." But he defended winner-take-all as "an essential counterpart of our federal system and the provisions of our Constitution which recognize and maintain our nation as a union of states."

With this presidential impetus, hearings were held the next year by the Senate Judiciary Constitutional Amendments Subcommittee chaired by Democrat Birch Bayh of Indiana. But Bayh himself abandoned the fight, coming out instead for a direct popular vote. Anything less, he said, "would be like shifting around the parts of a creaky and dangerous automobile engine, making it no less creaky and dangerous. What we may need is a new engine, because we are in a new age."

The argument for abolishing the electoral college altogether in favor of a direct popular vote had been voiced as far back as 1816, when Senator Abner Lacock of Pennsylvania proposed it, saying no electors "should be employed between the people and their votes." But the counterargument of states' rights—and that small states would suffer in influence—prevailed, then and thereafter. It is no surprise that an early advocate of the direct popular vote was Andrew Jackson, the first presidential candidate who won the popular vote but was denied the White House by the electoral college. "It must be very certain that a President elected by a minority cannot enjoy the confidence necessary to the discharge of his duties," he said, in vain.

One reason that efforts to abolish the electoral college have repeatedly failed, according to Peirce, is the widespread belief that the constitutional amendment required for it could never be ratified by three-fourths of the states, as required, since so many states would fear loss of influence. To overcome this roadblock, it was suggested in the late 1960s that state approval of a direct popular vote could be achieved by having the amendment go through special state conventions rather than through the state legislatures, but that idea got nowhere either. Yet paradoxically a survey of state legislators done by Democratic senator Quentin N. Burdick of South Dakota in 1966 found that nearly 60 percent of those polled—from forty-four of the fifty states—favored outright abolition of the electoral college. And in response to critics who expressed fears that the direct popular vote would encourage splinter parties, it has been suggested that the presidential winner be determined by only a plurality rather than a majority of the vote, or in some proposals only 40 percent, with a runoff between the top two finishers if need be. That way splinter candidates who might otherwise make it harder for anyone to get a majority vote would less likely muddy the waters on Election Day.

Nevertheless, conservatives and states' rights defenders have continued to block efforts to abolish the electoral college. Meanwhile, more and more voters have shown a desire for alternatives to the two major parties. This is a development that could jam the machinery of the electoral college, throw future elections into the House, and enhance the possibility once again of electing to the presidency a candidate who lost the popular vote.

If ever there was an idea whose time has come, junking the electoral college and instituting a direct popular vote for president and vice president is it. For openers, most Americans are only dimly aware if at all that there is such a thing as the electoral college, and that they don't vote directly for president and vice president. And most of them do not know that the electoral college has at least three times put candidates in the White House who were not the ones a majority or plurality of voters had chosen, and could do so again. The arguments for the direct popular vote are numerous and persuasive. Whether a majority would be required for election, or a plurality, or a fixed percentage and a runoff between the top two vote-getters if that percentage was not achieved, the ultimate winner would clearly be the people's choice.

The arguments for the electoral college run from the specious to the ridiculous, especially in light of the Supreme Court's one-man, one-vote edict. If election districts must now be reapportioned to assure as reasonably as possible that no person's vote is worth more than another's, how can we endure a system that in effect disenfranchises millions of American voters when they do not vote with the majority in their state? Or that gives some states more voice in choosing a president than their populations justify? Or that leaves major-party nominees vulnerable to political blackmail by splinter-party candidates? Or that turns over to Congress the final choice in an already inequitable process?

What of the original intentions of the creators of this system—that electors would be the nation's wisest men, who know the candidates best and would bring their wisdom and knowledge to bear in choosing a president? The very notion that they should act and think independently was dismissed long ago, and for most of our history they have been mere instruments of the popular will, winning the derogatory appellation "faithless" when they dare to assert their independent judgment, as the Constitution nevertheless authorizes them to do. Far from being our elite, today the electors are more often than not political hacks given the task as a minor payoff for loyal service to their party—and given, to boot, a license to gum up the works.

Finally, what of the argument that decision by electoral vote obliges presidential candidates to campaign in every state, small as well as large, while a direct popular vote might encourage them to ignore the smaller ones? Candidates have long since drawn their strategies in keeping with the electoral map, concentrating on states with the largest cache of electoral votes, but these states also happen to be those with the biggest populations. In an election that could be decided by a mere handful of popular votes, why would the candidates be any more likely to ignore the small states than they do now? If anything, a direct popular vote would strongly encourage people to register and turn out the vote everywhere, because what would matter would be the total vote nationally, not which state it came from. Believing that your state is going to be an easy winner or a sure loser for your candidate would not be relevant, so in fact, the direct popular vote could help end voter apathy and restore health to the political parties.

Also, with a direct popular vote, the major parties would be less likely to look to the larger states for their presidential and vice presidential nominees as a rationale—often misplaced—for locking up those states' electoral votes. The state origin of a candidate, in any event, has become much less important in modern, televised campaign strategies.

On election night, too, results on a state-by-state basis, and a running tally toward the fixed electoral-vote total of 270 needed for election, would no longer distort television coverage of the election. Their elimination would discourage the use of exit polls—surveys of voters leaving their polling places whose findings now often persuade voters in Western states to stay home if they think their candidate has already won or lost. The incentive to vote late would in fact be enhanced and, along with it, voter interest in close races.

In all the millions of words that have been spoken or written against the electoral college and in support of the direct popular vote, none are more to the point than those of former Democratic senator John Pastore of Rhode Island. Rhode Island obviously benefits from the current system, but that did not deter Pastore when he debated the issue with Senator John Kennedy in the 1956 debate on electoral reform.

Kennedy, making the case for the system that rewards small states by giving large and small alike two electoral votes each, pointed out that "Rhode Island is over-represented in the electoral college today, based on its population." Pastore replied: "I say that when the people go to the polls the man who receives the greatest number of votes should be elected President of the people. He is the President of the people of the United States, and not the President of the states. It makes no difference to me how many electoral votes the people of Rhode Island have."

Kennedy then asked Pastore: "Would the senator do away with the two electors which his state has by virtue of the fact that it has two senators of the United States?" Pastore answered: "I would do away with the whole electoral college. I would do away with it completely. I would have the people elect the President of the United States on election day. I would not care where the candidates came from, whether they came from the North, the South, the West or the East. They are all Americans. We are all one country. I say let us vote for the best man. It is as simple as that. That is my idea of representative government. Everything else beyond that is a gimmick."

Gimmick or not, the electoral college remains in existence today, a "Rube Goldberg mechanism" that few Americans know about or understand, whose chief contribution to our political system is its way of making possible the installation of a person whom a majority of Americans don't want. This particular college should close its doors.

15 Whither the Parties?

For all the talk that the Democratic and Republican parties have become obsolete or even irrelevant, their dominance of the presidential nomination process continues. Between them Bill Clinton and Bob Dole won all 538 electoral votes in 1996. Since the evolution of the two parties as principal rivals, no president has ever been elected who did not swear allegiance to one or the other.

Independent or third-party candidates have bucked them from time to time, and once in a long while someone with substantial popular support. In this century there were Theodore Roosevelt in 1912, Robert La Follette in 1924, Henry Wallace and Strom Thurmond in 1948, George Wallace in 1968, and Ross Perot in 1992 and 1996, as well as several Socialist nominees including Eugene V. Debs and Norman Thomas and, more recently, Libertarian standard-bearers. But Roosevelt won only 88 electoral votes, La Follette 13, Thurmond 39, and George Wallace 46, all from the South; Debs, Henry Wallace, Thomas, and Perot none. The system is indisputably stacked against minor-party candidates, who are overwhelmed by the two major parties in terms of tradition, money, and the ability to attract news media coverage.

For all their shortcomings, the Republican and Democratic parties provide the mechanisms through which the principal presidential nominees present themselves to the voters: the state primaries and caucuses, and the national conventions. The national parties, linked with state and local affiliates, are major fund-raising vehicles. And they mobilize manpower across the country to work in behalf of their nominees.

Having said that, one must also add that the role of the major parties has diminished substantially, with new developments inside and outside the party structure. The parties had been losing their clout ever since government itself began to provide services to voters—from job placement and job security to welfare—that were previously bestowed by the parties. Especially in cities, party bosses who once wielded power through the dispensing of patronage and voter services largely went into eclipse. Also, as the old phenomenon of voting according to party loyalty began to fall away and ticket splitting became more commonplace, candidates learned they could be more independent of party affiliation, especially with the advent of television. Television enabled them to communicate directly with voters who could or did put them in office and keep them there.

The explosion of presidential primaries has put political power over candidate selection in the hands of voters, and it has done so at the expense of elected officials and party leaders. Few party bosses today are capable of delivering convention delegates as of yore, and candidates have less need to court them or to conduct their own campaigns through the party apparatus.

Television and the new technocracy of presidential campaigning have made candidates independent political entrepreneurs. "Television enables candidates to deliver their messages to the voters without filtering them through the parties," Joe Napolitan says. In 1960, he recalls, the Democratic National Committee selected the advertising agency to do commercials for the nominee before the latter was even chosen. "I can't imagine any candidate today letting the DNC or the RNC pick his ad agency," he says, or make any other personnel or strategic decisions. Routinely, the party nominees skirt the party machinery by employing skilled political technocrats themselves to craft and communicate their messages. They use professional fund-raisers and direct-mail specialists to solicit the huge sums of money required for competitive campaigns in the primaries; they hire pollsters to produce ratings that they hope will entice contributors; they hire television-commercial makers and strategists to chart their course.

In the 1996 election cycle especially, the national parties were reduced to being mere funnels through which soft money from major donors was passed on to state party organizations and special-interest groups to get around the federal limits on campaign spending.

One key reason for the diminution of the national parties' power in the presidential election process, as the former Republican National Chairman Frank Fahrenkopf points out, is the manner in which a tradition of neutrality in the primaries and the post-Watergate reforms have restricted what the parties can effectively do. The national party chairman and the apparatus at his disposal are not supposed to take sides in any competitive contest for the party's presidential nomination—although this rule has been stretched in the past when an incumbent is challenged. And once the party nominee has been chosen, campaign finance law prohibits any direct contributions from any source to the nominees who accept the federal subsidy.

For this reason alone, Fahrenkopf says, the party nominees must set up their own campaign organizations instead of running solely through the party apparatus. The financing system now gives the money to the candidates, rather than making the federal payouts "to the largest and broadest political organizations in the country—the national parties." Most of that money goes to media advertising, the bulk of it to television, and "the party has no say in that spending," he notes. No wonder that polls indicate a growing public impression that the two major parties are irrelevant, resulting in diminishing voter affiliation with them and in some quarters a clamor for new parties. After more than two hundred years of American political history, party politics is under fire.

The irony surely would not be lost on the Founding Fathers. In writing the Constitution, they made no reference whatever to the establishment of political parties. George Washington in his farewell address of 1796 specifically warned that "the spirit of party . . . serves always to distract the public councils and enfeeble the public administration. It agitates the community with ill-founded jealousies and false alarms [and] kindles the animosity of one party against another." The party structure, he said, "foments occasionally riot and insurrection," and he compared it to "a fire not to be quenched [that] demands a uniform vigilance to prevent its bursting into a flame, lest instead of warming it should consume."

Yet, from colonial days, the concept of party inevitably took hold. Landowners who elected each other to local legislative assemblies in essence comprised a sort of party in political opposition to the appointed colonial governors and other representatives of the British Crown, voicing their views at colonial caucuses and town meetings. Merchants and tradesmen joined forces for political advantage, as did small farmers and menial laborers. Even before the Revolution, clear factions had developed—loyalists to the Crown, known as Tories, and their restless critics, known as Whigs. And, after the war, rival political camps emerged—Federalists favoring a strong central government and Anti-Federalists seeking to restrain its power.

The selection of the first president went forward in the absence of any formal parties. General Washington of Virginia, everybody's choice, did not campaign for the job yet won the votes of all 69 presidential electors in that first election of 1789, with John Adams of Massachusetts running second, the second choice of 34 electors, far ahead of John Jay of New York, selected by only 9.

While neither Washington nor Adams belonged to any formal party, they did share the general preference for a strong central government that was manifested in adoption of the Constitution and embraced by the Federalists. (Over time, they evolved in name first into National Republicans and then today's Republicans.)

While there were yet no formal political parties with organizations reaching across state boundaries, there already were distinct factions determined by geography, economic interests, and ideology. Also emerging were political clubs, such as the Society of St. Tammany in New York, later to evolve into one of the most notorious of (Democratic) party instrumentalities.

By the 1800 election, congressional caucuses of Federalists and Anti-Federalists were taking the lead in nominating the presidential candidates, with the emergence of political parties a natural consequence. But such caucuses soon came under attack, especially in Western states like Tennessee that were moving more toward the popular vote.

With the presidency of a Tennessean, Andrew Jackson, in 1829 came one of the great foundations of party building—Jackson's energetic embrace of federal patronage, labeled "the spoils system" by his foes, who dubbed him "King Andrew the First." With this weapon, and his cultivated reputation as a man of the common people leading "the party of the people," he gave an identity to the Democrats that exists today, albeit in considerably eroded measure.

And Jackson's tenure also gave impetus to the creation of the Whig Party, an amalgam of National Republicans, Anti-Masons, and disaffected Democrats who had been pooling their resources in several state elections. Under the Whig banner, three presidential candidates ran against Van Buren in 1836, hoping to force the election into the House, where one of them—Daniel Webster, General William Henry Harrison of Ohio, or Senator Hugh White of Tennessee—might be named president. But Van Buren with Jackson's backing prevailed, becoming the first vice president since enactment of the Twelfth Amendment to be elected president, and the last until George Bush won the White House in 1988.

Around this time also, organized labor was beginning to weigh in as a political force. In New England, New York, and Pennsylvania, workingmen began coalescing to elect to local offices and state legislatures their own people or politicians favorably disposed to their economic wants and demands for labor rights. They were called Locofocos because when opponents turned off the gas lights on them at a Democratic convention in New York City, they lit friction matches of that name. They eventually formed their own third party but still found a welcome in the party of Jackson and Van Buren, though castigated as radicals by the Whigs.

Political factions, based in the earliest days primarily on regional interests, were more and more dominated by economic concerns that transcended geography. As the franchise was extended beyond landowners to a broader electorate, these factors reflected class values across state boundaries. Just as Democrats in the Jackson era proclaimed themselves the party of the people, the Whigs for better or worse were the party of business, banking, and the rich; that label clung not just to the Whigs but later to present-day Republicans.

National party conventions by now were a fixture of the political landscape, and with them came intraparty intrigue. In the celebrated convention in which the nomination was settled among party power brokers in a "smoke-filled room," Van Buren in 1844 was denied another chance, and, after nine exhausting ballots, the dark horse James K. Polk, a former governor of Tennessee, was chosen. In the general election, he defeated the Whig nominee, the venerable Henry Clay of Kentucky, in a campaign of mudslinging and vilification. Presidential politics was already becoming destructive.

The 1844 election also saw the emergence of a third party that affected the outcome. A group of Eastern anti-slavers had formed the Liberty Party in 1839 and at a convention in Warsaw, New York, had nominated James G. Birney, leader of the American Anti-Slavery Society, for president. His candidacy in 1840 was nondescript, but in 1843 he was nominated again, in Buffalo, and in the 1844 election Birney drained off enough votes in New York to deny the state, and the presidency, to Clay.

Another independent party emerged, the Free-Soilers, who opposed the extension of slavery to any state and favored free homesteads for public lands; they joined the Liberty Party in the presidential field in 1848, when delegates from eighteen states met in Buffalo and drew Van Buren out of retirement as their candidate. The two independent parties splintered the vote sufficiently to deliver the White House to the Whigs and their candidate, General Zachary Taylor. The historic significance of the election was that it marked the first time all states voted on the same day.

But the election of Taylor was the Whigs' last hurrah. Taylor died after only sixteen months in office and was succeeded by Millard Fillmore of New York. The Great Compromise of 1850, crafted by Henry Clay, which brought California into the Union as a free state, badly split the Whig Party. Franklin Pierce of New Hampshire, nominated by the Democrats on their forty-ninth ballot, beat General Winfield Scott, chosen by the Whigs on their fifty-second, in an electoral-college landslide, 254–42. In short order, the Whig Party was dead, replaced in 1854 by a new Republican Party.

Separate meetings of anti-slavery activists in Ripon, Wisconsin, and Jackson, Michigan—the cities still vie for paternity—gave birth to the new party. At the same time, the so-called Know-Nothing movement also sprouted in the East and South, fed by unrest over the tide of immigrants from Catholic Ireland and elsewhere in Europe. The movement, eventually calling itself the American Party, soon split over slavery and disintegrated.

With the conflict over slavery now generating talk of secession from the Union in the South, the Democratic Party in 1860 suffered a regional split that produced two Democratic presidential candidates, Stephen A. Douglas of Illinois for the North and John C. Breckinridge of Kentucky for the South. (The situation was further complicated in the South by still another party, calling itself the Constitutional Union and nominating John Bell of Tennessee.) The new Republican Party, rejecting William H. Seward, regarded as a radical abolitionist, turned to a man defeated earlier by Douglas for a Senate seat from Illinois named Abraham Lincoln, as the least objectionable of what was generally considered a mediocre field. Lincoln's manager, David Davis, whom Lincoln later appointed to the Supreme Court, helped the cause by (illegally) offering cabinet positions to leaders in other camps, and Lincoln was nominated over Seward at the end of the second ballot. Thus was the man many later considered the nation's political savior and greatest president produced by wheeling and dealing amid the atmosphere of the infamous smoke-filled room.

Douglas ran a strong second to Lincoln in the popular vote (1.86 million to 1.37 million) but a poor fourth in the electoral college, where the vote was Lincoln 180, Breckinridge 72, Bell 39, and Douglas only 12. Despite fears that the presence of four candidates would force the election into the House of Representatives, the North delivered the required electoral-college majority to Lincoln while the Southern states largely supported their two native sons, with party affiliation seemingly mattering little.

With the outbreak of the Civil War, the Republican Party accepted a temporary name change to the Union Party in deference to the many Democrats, mostly from the North and border states, who aligned with it. This development in turn led to the fateful decision to replace Lincoln's first-term vice president, Hannibal Hamlin of Maine, with former senator Andrew Johnson of Tennessee, a Democrat who was serving in 1863 as the state's military governor. With the war turning decisively in the North's favor upon the fall of Atlanta, the Lincoln-Johnson ticket won easily in 1864.

After war's end, the Republican Party eventually resumed its old name. The two-party system had survived the Civil War and with it so did the electoral college, though in a somewhat confused condition as states of the old Confederacy made their way back into the Union. Enactment of the Fifteenth Amendment enfranchising blacks weighed heavily in favor of the party of emancipation, making the election of General Ulysses S. Grant over Democrat Horatio Seymour of New York clear-cut in 1868, with thirty-four states participating. Virginia, Mississippi, and Texas, still under military rule, did not vote.

It should be noted that in all these battles the leading figures were all politicians associated with one of the major parties, either as officeholders at the federal, state, or municipal level or as strong party leaders, businessmen, and "bosses." Politics was a game played by insiders using party machinery.

Throughout this period, new third parties came and went—the Labor

Reform Party in 1872, the Greenback Party in 1876 and 1880, the Anti-Monopoly Party in 1884, the Union Labor Party in 1888, the People's Party in 1892 and 1896, the National Silver Party and the Prohibition Party in 1896—all to little effect. It was not until 1912 that a substantial third-party effort was mounted, behind former president Theodore Roosevelt, who fell out with his chosen successor, William Howard Taft, and bolted the GOP to form a new Progressive or "Bull Moose" Party. Roosevelt ran ahead of Taft in the fall but in doing so he split the Republican vote and enabled the Democrat Woodrow Wilson to be elected.

For the next eight presidential elections, the two major parties alone contested and dominated the political process. Even the notable challenge in 1948 from two splinter Democratic groups—the Southern "Dixiecrats" behind Governor Thurmond of South Carolina and the new Progressive Party behind President Roosevelt's spurned third-term vice president, Henry Wallace—failed to prevent a full term for President Truman. Twenty years later, in 1968, when former Democratic governor George C. Wallace of Alabama ran under the American Independent Party label, he won 13.5 percent of the vote behind Nixon and Humphrey, the best third-party showing since Theodore Roosevelt in 1912. And in 1992 and 1996, the Texas billionaire Ross Perot took the independent route, running without a party label in 1992 and mounting the most effective such candidacy in American history, winning 19 percent of the vote, then running as nominee of his own Reform Party in 1996 but winning only 9 percent. His showing did, however, assure the new party of $12.6 million in federal campaign funds for its nominee in 2000.

Through all these years, the Democratic and Republican parties toiled with cyclical successes and failures, as the parties navigated periods of dominance and strong machine politics into the television age, and then slipped into steady decline. One reason was that the parties didn't really master the sophisticated use of computers, for fund-raising and direct mail, as these new technologies arrived on the scene. "Between elections they sat around doing nothing," Bob Squier says, "when they could have been building up their ability to do these things and therefore making their party the place to go for technology." A new center established in his own Democratic Party was not staffed with high-caliber technicians. "It became a place you went to do low-cost, cut-rate television. If the parties had figured out that the technology was going to have this effect on them, they could have figured out those elements in it that could be wholesaled. They could have built up the capability within the party structure and parties would have been more powerful."

As far as presidential politics goes, it has usually been true that a party is significant only when it does not control the executive branch, or when an incumbent of a given party does not run for another term. Presidents routinely pull political power and strategy into the White House, relegating their national party and national committee to a service function. Presidents of both major parties treat their party functionaries and mechanisms with attitudes ranging from tolerance to contempt, often assigning an agent with no notable influence to oversee the party headquarters. This practice marked the presidencies of Kennedy, Johnson, and Nixon, and reached its nadir in the creation of the Committee to Re-Elect the President, the notorious CREEP, in the campaign of 1972, when the Republican National Committee was placed in the hands of a caretaker senator from Kansas named Bob Dole. The freewheeling, arrogant excesses of CREEP, under the direction of political operatives answering not to Dole but to former Attorney General John Mitchell, Nixon's de facto campaign manager, produced the Watergate break-in that ultimately brought about the first resignation in disgrace of an American president. Dole recalls that Clark MacGregor was "sort of chairman" at CREEP. "I was sort of chairman of the party too. We had a budget of about $4 million, they had a budget of $44 million."

Even the harsh lesson of Watergate has not ended the habit of incumbent presidents putting their reelection campaigns in the hands of separate entities, and nonincumbent party nominees do this, too. In the process, both major parties have been reduced essentially to vehicles for raising money and, markedly in 1996, for shuttling soft money to state parties for use in presidential campaigns in circumvention of federal restrictions.

Former Democratic National Chairman Paul Kirk says the Clinton campaign's practice in the 1996 campaign of subordinating the state parties "to the benefit of the national ticket and to the detriment of everything else the party was supposed to be doing" was destructive. "It was going that way anyway," he says, but the Clinton campaign "pushed it to an extreme. The White House was calling the shots completely." When an incumbent president neglects the interests of the state parties in pursuit of his own reelection, Kirk says, he fails to fulfill his obligations as leader of his party.

"The parties have become basically just banks—fund-raising mechanisms," says Ray Strother, "and they have very little effect on elections. Party identity has shifted so much. How you registered doesn't mean anything. You don't ask party registration anymore in polls. You ask, 'What do you consider yourself?' The party apparatus state by state is normally staffed and manned by people who've never been involved in politics and campaigns and have as little ideology as the people who are in the consulting business today."

Candidates, too, "have no loyalty to parties," Strother says. "The old guys I'd deal with would sit around and talk about the New Deal, talk about Democratic ideals and philosophies. Well, what is the Democratic philosophy now?" He notes the tactic Dick Morris advocated and Clinton practiced. "Dick Morris said that when you get into a campaign and your opponent has two or three issues that are better than yours, well, go ahead and adopt his issues. Say, 'Yeah, we agree on these things,' and get them out of the way. Clinton still does that; he's consultant-trained (by Morris)."

Morris readily acknowledges this approach when he says "that's my idea of triangulation: take the best of each and merge them. That's not an act of political morality, it's an act of political sagacity." While Morris may be the extreme example, his basic point—that one party or the other doesn't hold all the wisdom and judgment, and that candidates these days are better off out from under the party label, or at least downplaying it—is widely accepted.

Still, it is much harder in presidential campaigns than in state, local, or congressional ones to duck party affiliation. The entire nomination process is heavily party-oriented, though on the Democratic side particularly, candidates soft-pedal party ties and pitch their appeals not to the party's liberal tradition but to pragmatic, independent ticket splitters. Clinton's self-proclaimed identity as a "new Democrat" was a thinly veiled rejection of his party's traditional posture as a political entity focused on righting inequities against the most disadvantaged elements in the society, in favor of a new image as the party of the comfortable but worried middle class.

Among Republican candidates, there is much less blurring of party identity, as the conservative movement, and Ronald Reagan, went a long way toward raising the GOP out of minority status. But it still exists as the party functions have been widely usurped by armies of professional consultants who work outside party discipline and are driven by the desire to win rather than by any ideological fervor.

The fact that voters' identification with party is much weaker than it was in the past does not mean, however, that we are seeing the major parties' eventual demise in presidential politics. They are so institutionalized in the process that it would take a revolution in political thinking and action, for which there is no evidence, to alter the basic two-party system. For all the polls that indicate a growing public yearning for alternatives, and despite the successful creation of a Reform Party in 1996 and creeping public support for the Libertarian and other minor parties, nothing on the horizon suggests a breakdown of the status quo.

So the important question is whether the parties' role in the presidential selection process should be strengthened or altered, and if so, how. Haley Barbour, former Republican National Chairman, leaves no doubt of where he stands. "I believe that presidents come and go," he says, "but the parties are forever."

The last major effort at overhaul, begun in 1968 by the Democrats, intentionally or not delivered a body blow to the influence of party leaders and regulars. A proposal by Senator Harold E. Hughes of Iowa was approved at the Democratic National Convention that year for a review of delegate-selection rules that would assure more "meaningful and timely opportunities" for participation by all Democrats in the 1972 presidential nomination process. The reform commission finally produced delegate-selection changes aimed at "maximum feasible participation" of minorities, women, and youth in the process. State parties were required to include these groups in their convention delegations in numbers roughly proportionate to their populations in the states, and the unit rule—delegations required to vote as a bloc—was abolished.

With the issue of the Vietnam War inflaming the country and particularly the Democratic Party in 1972, the anti-war leader Senator George McGovern capitalized on the new rules he helped enact for the party and won the presidential nomination in a surprise over Hubert Humphrey. Many establishment party figures who ran as delegates for Humphrey lost and did not attend the convention. Liberals particularly proclaimed the arrival of "participatory democracy" in their party, but the price paid was the selection of a weak nominee who lost the election in a landslide to the incumbent Richard Nixon.

Under subsequent Democratic Party reform commissions, specific quotas for minorities, women, and the young were shunted aside in favor of affirmative-action schemes, and proportional representation at all levels of delegate selection was instituted to reflect voters' presidential preferences. A compliance review commission was established under the Democratic National Committee to monitor implementation of these rules. Other rules were also instituted: shortening the period for delegate selection through state caucuses and primaries from six to three months (early March to early June) with exceptions "outside the window" for the traditional kickoff caucus (Iowa) and primary (New Hampshire) states. To respond to complaints that many important elected officials and party leaders were shut out in the 1972 and 1976 delegate-selection processes, state delegations first were increased by 10 percent to accommodate them.

In advance of the 1984 convention, another adjustment provided that 14 percent of all delegates be chosen from among party leaders and elected officials. For the 1988 convention, the pool of these "superdelegates" was increased to allow virtually all Democratic governors, members of Congress, and members of the party's national committee to attend. These and other changes were intended to keep the selection process open without denying the party the wisdom of party leaders and elected officials.

The Republican Party had an ideological resistance to imposing rules on state parties and less interest was expressed internally about representing minorities and other groups. The party was generally more cohesive, and it continued to adhere to procedures that gave greater influence to party leaders and elected officials. No specific provision for superdelegates was deemed necessary to give the party's "wise men" (and women) seats on the national convention floor. The party was, however, obliged to go along with the Democratic shift toward more primaries for delegate selection simply because dates for primaries and caucuses were established by the state legislatures, and during this period most of them were controlled by Democrats.

The move away from the caucus-convention system to primaries in most states at least offered the prospect for greater voter participation in the presidential nomination process. But by 1996 it had created unintended consequences that resulted in a rush to judgment on the Republican side and a gross inflation of the influence of money. As noted earlier, the front-loading of primaries worked an undue financial hardship on all but the best-heeled candidates, and assured the same results for 2000.

The national parties, while much better organized as service mechanisms for state parties and candidates at all levels than in the past, now have little influence on the nominating process, certainly in comparison with the candidates' own organizations, with their paid consultants operating essentially outside the national party apparatus. The party chairmen have become little more than cheerleaders on the sidelines while the candidates and their free-agent political professionals play the game. And the single big party event, the national convention, is an essentially meaningless sham, orchestrated for television.

Once the presidential nominees are chosen, the national parties become even more subordinate to them and their hired guns. In the general election campaign—a short run, from the end of August through the first Tuesday in November—they and their leaders have only a service function. This they perform well, not only at the national level but in races for Congress and governorships as well, the Republican Party more effectively, by and large, than the Democratic. Both national committees write party position papers and prepare "talking points," and they send manpower and campaign paraphernalia to the states. Most important, they have funneled "soft" money, slated under federal law for "party building," to "coordinated" state campaigns.

In 1996, the parties bought millions of dollars' worth of "issue advocacy" television and radio advertisements, purporting to advance certain issues but clearly intended to bolster the candidacies of their national standard-bearers. As already noted, the Democratic National Committee ran such ads in key states after the Democratic loss of Congress in 1994, helping to arrest Clinton's slide in popularity and to resurrect his political fortunes.

But in terms of the parties' prime surviving function, that of selecting the presidential nominees, they have become essentially helpless. The procedure is a runaway train, with hired guns outside the formal party structure at the throttle.

One way the parties could regain influence would be for Congress to authorize free television time for qualified candidates, and to make the parties responsible for determining eligibility and time allocations. This alone would give relief from the fund-raising ordeal that so burdens presidential candidates today. Another way would be to funnel *all* campaign funds through them. With the current system of financing presidential campaigns—directly through the efforts of individual candidacies—the best-known candidates and the front-runners in the polls, who can raise enough money to run television commercials and finance polls, whose favorable numbers then induce more contributions, fatten their campaign treasuries while lesser-known long shots struggle to compete. It would be much fairer if all contributions for political activity in the primaries and caucuses were to go to pools distributed by the national parties. The parties would be strengthened, and could be enhanced, if they set conditions of fair campaign practices, such as prohibiting negative radio or television ads.

A major incentive in campaign giving would be eliminated, however: the contributor's hope of gaining access to or influence with a specific candidate. And the concept of general giving has been shown to be unpopular, since a paltry, ever-decreasing percentage of American taxpayers check off the box on their income-tax returns to allocate three dollars for the bankrolling of presidential campaigns. Congress could earmark general federal funds to go directly to each major party, from which candidates would draw in equal amounts.

Also, as Fahrenkopf suggests, Congress could stipulate that some of the federal money for the general election should go to the two principal parties rather than to the nominees, to pay for certain functions for which the parties are well equipped: polling and other research and grassroots organizing, for example. This assistance would help to restore the parties' political effectiveness and take away the fund-raising functions that, carried out in such excess in 1996, did so much to diminish their reputations.

The same funding scheme should be extended to other political parties if they reach a stipulated threshold of support. The system already is severely stacked against them, despite increasing public support for alternatives to the Democrats and Republicans. The two-party system, for all its inadequacies, is so entrenched that its defenders can well afford to tolerate the development of alternative parties without harming the existing hegemony. The surprising strength in 1968 of George Wallace and in 1992 of Ross Perot, two obviously flawed candidates, suggests that an independent candidacy launched by a more credible, well-financed individual—for instance a latter-day Dwight Eisenhower like Colin Powell—conceivably could give the current system a healthy shaking. Considering the low estate into which the two major parties have fallen, it would not be the worst thing to happen.

16 Time for an Overhaul

Perhaps the most distressing aspect of the American political system today is that nothing basic is likely to change before another presidential election has come and gone. For openers, the best and most qualified Americans may or may not be offering themselves for the presidency. And it is certain that every four years the process will deliver a number of mediocre self-selected candidates who don't have any chance of winning, and shouldn't have.

The political technocracy and the hired guns are clearly here to stay, with all their destructive characteristics: the pell-mell pursuit of victory, profit, and celebrity, often more in their own interests than in the interest of candidate or party, principle or philosophy.

"We have an industry here," says Charles Lewis of the Center for Public Integrity, "that is the last unregulated industry in America—the campaign industry. There is this whole group of experts, from the pollsters to the focus-group people to the campaign consultant people to the TV-buying people." And this "campaign industry" is only likely to get larger as it becomes more lucrative.

There needs to be a greater public awareness of what the paid political consultants do, how they do it, how much money they make doing it, and what the consequences of their actions are. "We know more about a toaster we're buying than the candidate we're electing," Lewis says. "If we're going to have this giant auction where millions and millions of dollars are raised and in the end we end up with a candidate, we need to know who these people are and who's behind them."

More probing news coverage can help, particularly the monitoring of paid television advertising, as is now widespread in the "ad watch" critics of many newspapers. The news media as well must strike a better balance between their examination of candidates' rhetoric, performance, judgment, and behavior, which is imperative, and the competitive pressures of around-the-clock news cycles, which too often lead to reporting first and checking later if at all.

A greater sense of responsibility and accountability within the community of political professionals is also needed. Efforts by the American Association of Political Consultants to enforce adherence to a code of ethics has not had much success. Candidates themselves must accept and assert more responsibility for what goes on in their names, instead of hiding behind the consultants or blaming them for questionable tactics.

This is particularly so in light of the epidemic of negative advertising. The policy of "anything goes," which so many of the well-oiled hired guns advocate, continues to pervade presidential politics. Negative tactics—from direct attacks on the character and integrity of opponents in television ads to exaggeration and misrepresentation of their records and positions—appall and disgust voters, fewer and fewer of whom go to the polls. If the system is so rotten and the participants so self-serving, they conclude, it makes no difference whether or not they take the trouble to vote.

Political consultants are well aware that among the most effective strategies is, as they put it, to "define your opponent before he defines himself." Recognition of this effectiveness has converted negative advertising from being a last-ditch, desperate tool of a prospective loser to being the opening volley in an all-out early attack on the opposition. In place of a longer, sober television presentation of a candidate's credentials for being president has come the thirty-second "attack" ad that does its work quick and dirty. In the hands of unaccountable "independent expenditure" committees especially, negative advertising has been brought to a high art. But this only feeds the public's sense that politics has become the functional equivalent of mud wrestling. The candidates in whose behalf these supposedly freelancing committees toil should not simply piously disavow their destructive handiwork; they should take concrete steps to discredit it.

"We're never going to get a perfect system," the reform activist Fred Wertheimer acknowledges, "but we have a track record of a presidential system that worked well just ten years ago, and we could get back to it if the will was there. This is a political-will question, not a question about nothing working."

Much of the will to restore integrity to our politics must come from the candidates; they must retain control of and responsibility for the ethical conduct of their own campaigns, keeping their hired guns securely to their roles as advisers and implementers. The candidates must oversee an environmental cleanup of the swamp of negative campaigning. They must do what they can to diminish the adversarial relationship between them and the press by becoming more accessible and informative, while at the same time guarding against elements of the press whose conduct blurs the line between responsible mainstream journalism and the routinely sensationalist practices of the supermarket gossip sheets.

But at the heart of what ails the presidential selection process today is the dominance of money. It is the essential, often determining element in any candidate's efforts to gain the White House. It poisons the political environment and corrupts the system, turning candidates, the parties, and their agents into groveling beggars and dispensers of favors and influence to special interests, foreign and domestic. "The idea of Harry Truman or Abe Lincoln going through this for two years—all these rubber-chicken dinners and cattle shows! It is so pathetic to watch," Lewis says. "I know there are people who think it's very exciting—our democracy at work, and what a great country. I'm not one of those people. I think it's demeaning."

The amount of money raised and spent climbs in each succeeding election cycle, but there should be less of it in presidential campaigns, not more. An increase in the limits on individual contributions would ease the backbreaking burden of fund-raising, but this improvement should be made within the context of sharp overall reductions. What is important is not how much money is spent, but that the candidates compete in relative equality. Beyond banning all soft-money contributions, the federal government should set a much lower ceiling on spending, and oblige all candidates to campaign under that ceiling. Free television time for the candidates is the best starting point. Congress should require television networks and cable outlets to give free time for all qualified presidential candidates, especially to counter negative ads run against them. It's about time the public got some payback for the broadcasters' and cable owners' use of the public airwaves, which were handed over in free broadcast licenses that generate untold millions of dollars to whoever leases them. Also, Congress should require a candidate who pays for television attack ads against his opponent to have his own name and likeness included in the ad, so as to identify him clearly with the charges.

President Clinton in early 1998 urged the Federal Communications Commision to require radio and television stations to provide free airtime to federal candidates, and FCC chairman William Kennard considered hearings on the issue. But Republicans in Congress quickly opposed the move, sponsoring legislation to cut off funds for any such FCC inquiry. Ironically, one of the sponsors was Senator John McCain, who was also co-sponsor of the stalled McCain-Feingold campaign finance reform bill. McCain argued that change in FCC regulations should be up to Congress, and unsurprisingly, the National Association of Broadcasters agreed, lobbying immediately to kill the idea.

David Doak, who agrees that the television networks should be obliged to provide free time for the candidates, at the same time warns that this change could lead to a proliferation of minor parties. "The Reform Party and everybody else will spring up to get the free time," he says.

Wertheimer argues that the most essential reform is not only banning soft money but also reducing the cost of television time. Most presidential campaigns now spend about two-thirds of all their money on producing and airing television commercials, which means that all other campaign activities are starved. Lower rates imposed by federal law on television stations would be justifiable, he says, in light of the fact that stations do enjoy free licensing, thanks to the federal government.

John Deardourff's suggestion that after the presidential nominees have been selected all paid television ads should be banned also would sharply cut costs. At the same time, the clatter of negative commercials would be stilled during the period when the election campaign and the debates draw heavy news coverage on their own.

With money polluting the process as it does, Congress should face up to its own responsibilities to reform the campaign finance laws. One irony about the whole campaign money mess is the fact that leading critics, such as Senator McConnell, say it is a mess yet adamantly resist reform. Part of the problem is obviously partisan politics—Republicans are much more successful at raising campaign money than Democrats are, and they want no serious changes. But another reason is that any proposed reform makes many members of Congress in both parties nervous, since the system, for all its faults, has worked for them. Banning soft money altogether in federal elections—for congressional as well as presidential candidates—would introduce the unknown into a known equation.

"It's an entrenched incumbent system," Wertheimer says, "with elected officials who have the power to make changes desperate to hold on to that system in the name of free speech. The 1996 scandal was as big as anything we've ever seen, because it was system-wide. Watergate [concerned] one president and one presidential campaign. In 1996 it was everyone—both parties, all the outside groups, Clinton and Dole themselves."

Something should be done to neutralize the advantage incumbents have in raising campaign money and granting access to special-interest contributors who want something in return for their money. One novel solution is offered by James Carville. "There's an awful lot of power in Washington," he says, "and human nature is that you can't mix money with that kind of power and not have a corrosive effect; it's inevitable." So, he says, money and power must be separated; a president or any other elected federal officeholder should be prohibited from raising even a nickel for his campaign or any other purpose and should be barred from speaking at or even attending any fundraising events anywhere. With such a scheme as this, Carville says, "an incumbent can't raise money for anything—not for the March of Dimes, not for whatever. He can't solicit, can't be around money. He can't backdoor it, discuss it, have anything to do with it."

Meanwhile, a challenger would be permitted to raise as much as he wanted; then the incumbent would be given a similar amount—or 80 or 90 percent of it—from federal taxpayer revenues. That way, Carville argues, there would be no inducement for a sitting president to grant special access to anyone who might otherwise wave a large campaign contribution under his nose.

Something also needs to be done to overcome the huge advantage that accrues to wealthy candidates, as a result of the 1976 Supreme Court ruling that the First Amendment guaranteeing free speech protects the right of any political candidate to spend whatever he wants of his own money. Doak calls this "the biggest problem we have to solve," along with protecting the candidates who have much less money to compete.

The runaway problem of "issue advocacy" also must be addressed by Congress if not by the courts. Lower courts have ruled that unless an advertisement explicitly asks viewers and listeners to vote for or against a candidate—"magic words," in the legal jargon—it complies with the law. Yet, "in every sense of the word," Wertheimer says, "they are candidate ads." Ads of this kind, as noted earlier, were instrumental in Clinton's comeback in 1995 after the Republicans' takeover of Congress the previous November. The McCain-Feingold solution to advocacy ads is a valid one: bar them from the airwaves within thirty days of a primary election and within sixty days of a general election.

On top of all this, Lewis says, "we have a neutered regulator that was captured by the regulated interests fairly quickly after its creation in 1978. The Federal Election Commission in March of 1998 [was] still discussing and pondering whether they could or should make soft money illegal. Soft money has been around for twenty years approximately, and we've seen huge abuses, [heard] so many stories about scandals. The idea that the regulator after all that was thinking about maybe making it illegal! I wonder sometimes what planet we're on."

The FEC is ineffective as the enforcement arm of the federal campaign finance laws in large part because of its decision-making rules and its composition. A commission vote is required to issue a subpoena, but the even split in commission membership—three Republicans, three Democrats—routinely produces stalemate, and it takes years to agree on penalties, usually watered down. At a minimum, Lewis says, the commission needs another, truly independent member.

"You've got to have tough enforcement and you've got to have a tough independent body to regulate the thing," he says. "We have it for food and drugs, for our health, for contaminated meat and consumer products. Why can't you have it for our electoral process? Is there anything more important in our democracy than how we choose our leaders? This is an area that clearly has been neglected, and it's done in collusion by both parties. Both parties are perfectly content. They have spent millions of dollars together in the past twenty years weakening the election laws. The accountants and the lawyers have found ways to drive fleets of trucks through the existing laws."

If the FEC is ever going to be effective, Lewis says, the agency "has got to be willing to prosecute if they [candidates and their campaigns] stray, and I mean really prosecute. And don't wait five years. Do it in a year, do it in six months." With computerized reporting of contributions and spending, he says, there is no reason it can't be done. "We have this wrist-slap mentality about election laws, [as if they weren't] really important. Everyone understands it's a sort of wink-and-nod exercise, that if you get into trouble, not much is going to happen to you. If you get in a jam, use your campaign money to pay [to get out of] it. Violating the election laws? It's like pulling the [Do Not Remove] sticker off the mattress."

The political campaigns in which voters have such lack of interest and confidence are themselves a mess—too long, too complicated, too costly, and weighted favorably toward the wealthiest and best-known candidates. As states jostle to have the earliest caucuses and primaries and all the publicity that goes with them, what up to the election year has been a marathon quest for campaign money becomes a mad sprint to collect national convention delegates. Would-be nominees with modest financial backing must win early or perish, especially when rich, self-financing opponents are jacking up the price of competing.

On the campaign trail, the candidates and their hired guns are driven single-mindedly to get television exposure, staging events for the cameras in empty "photo opportunities." News conferences, once a staple of presidential campaigns, are avoided like a plague because the hired guns are determined to avoid spontaneity and troublesome questions that might upset their carefully controlled strategies. The frenzied pace of the contest leaves little time between primaries and caucuses for the news media to keep voters abreast of what is going on.

At the same time, within the press corps, the relationship between many reporters and the candidates or other politicians becomes more and more adversarial—except when journalistic pursuit of celebrity makes them colleagues on television talk shows. As a result of the "gotcha" mentality in the news media, on one hand, and the quest for celebrity, on the other, reporters become just as much players in the game as referees or press-box analysts.

Our delegate-selection process today virtually assures that the party nominees will have been chosen long before the national conventions, which will continue to be idle exercises in party promotion and contrived demonstrations of unity and bliss. The roll call of the states, once an event of high drama, is nothing more than an opportunity for state party leaders and show-offs to grab their moment in the national television spotlight. The possibility that the political parties, national and state, might agree to some sensible formula for resurrecting the conventions as actual vehicles for selecting the nominees is slim.

To streamline the nomination process and give some relief to harassed presidential candidates, the period for raising money to qualify for federal matching should be shortened from twelve to six months before the election year, along with an increase in the contribution limits. Also, the front-loading of primaries and caucuses should be reversed, to allow candidates more time to make their case in individual states, and to give the news media more time to assess the results and better inform the public. As already noted, a sensible scheme would be to set five primaries and/or caucuses for every other Tuesday from March through mid-July, either on a regional or a random basis. Inducing the smaller states to hold their delegate-selection processes in the early weeks, and the larger states to hold off until later, would inject more suspense into the process, because it would take longer for any candidate to reach the majority of convention delegates required for nomination.

If some states were to send uncommitted delegates to the convention or resurrect the old practice of lining up behind a governor, senator, or other favorite son, there might even be the possibility of restoring the convention to its former decision-making power—and generating the sort of excitement the conventions now so conspicuously lack.

The selection of the vice presidential nominees continues to be a crapshoot, left to the presidential nominee to decide—by whim if he chooses—with little consideration most of the time for the fact that roughly one in five vice presidents has become president (including five of the last ten) and that the office is now a near-certain stepping-stone to presidential nomination. In seven of the last nine presidential elections, one or both of the major-party nominees have first served as vice president.

There is one obvious but essential solution to the haphazard choice of a running mate. The presidential nominee must take to heart the requirement that a vice presidential nominee must be qualified not simply to be vice president but also to be president. If the presidential nominee conspicuously fails to do so, he should be punished by the voters for potentially putting the country in the hands of a knave, a fool, or an incompetent.

Once the major-party national tickets are set, the fall campaign unfolds as an elaborate facade of feverish candidate activity across the country, with repetitious speechmaking and nonstop jetting around, while the more influential aspect of the campaign—reaching the great majority of voters—goes forward on television, much of it in self-serving, often negative commercials. Though the presidential debates give the voters their best clear look at the candidates, the question of how, when, and where they are conducted continues to create pitched battles between the major-party nominees. Conditions for the debates must be established and accepted by all candidates in advance, not left in the hands of partisan negotiators. An independent voice should be added to the Commission on Presidential Debates, which should facilitate the participation of independent or third-party candidates, in the first debate at least, who have qualified for ballot position in all states and have a demonstrated level of support. Participation should not be left to a subjective opinion about who has a "realistic chance" to be elected.

The election to the presidency of a person chosen by the American people continues to be imperiled by the anachronistic electoral college, which at least three times has denied the Oval Office to a candidate who has won the most popular votes. Despite many polls that indicate an overwhelming public preference for abolishing the electoral college and deciding on the presidency by direct vote regardless of what state the votes come from, there is still a chance of another minority-choice president. The electoral college should be scrapped. Without it, presidential candidates would concentrate on the states with the largest populations, which they do now anyway, but they would not be able to ignore totally other states as they do now.

In all this, the two big political parties continue to flounder, with voters less and less apt to identify themselves as party members and disregarding the parties' efforts to maintain unity and loyalty. Disaffection has, in fact, generated more and more interest in alternative parties. The major parties should be bolstered in the presidential election process by giving them a greater part in receiving and disbursing campaign funds to the qualified candidates, with a share of the federal allocation earmarked for use by the parties themselves for support functions they are well qualified to perform in the fall campaign. Simultaneously, it must be made easier for independent and third-party candidates to obtain ballot position in the states and in having their voices heard. The process is already—and unfairly—stacked against them.

The existing mishmash is clearly no way to pick a president in the oldest democracy in the world. Yet there is no great prospect that significant improvement will have been made by the time we elect the next president. That the whole presidential election process has become a captive of the politicians, the professional campaign consultants, and their moneyed backers whose interests are best served by the status quo is a disheartening conclusion, but a realistic one.

One politician who for obvious reasons has given much thought to what's wrong with the way we pick presidents is Lamar Alexander, who after failing in 1996 tried again but quit in August 1999 after a dismal showing in the Iowa straw poll. Much of his assessment can be put down as the standard rationale of a loser, but some of it is valid and pertinent. After withdrawing from contention in 1996, he compared the ordeal of running for the presidential nomination to "scaling a cliff for three years in the dark to earn the privilege of shooting one NBA-range three-point shot, i.e. the New Hampshire primary. It is like walking above Niagara Falls on a swaying tightrope as the wind blows and the crowd shouts, 'Fall!' "

Alexander complained that he and others like him were out there slogging around in 1995 but virtually ignored by the news media, which gave most of their coverage to "numerous Americans, estimable as they may have been, who had no intention of running [translation: Colin Powell] or couldn't win even if they did." He proposed that the news media start their coverage earlier and not just come in at the eleventh hour—an allegation valid for much but not all of the press. "If you guys were sportswriters, you would arrive during the last quarter of the Final Four championship and claim you have covered the entire basketball season," he scolded.

In August 1999, Alexander, dropping out for the second time, blamed the money, the accelerated process, and the news media's focus on the front-runner. Everyone jumped to conclusions too early, he said, on the basis of the hyped Iowa straw poll. "Money drives the whole process now," he said, with Bush and Forbes bringing their outsized financial resources to bear even as the news media proclaims the inevitability of Bush's nomination. And with a $1,000 limit on campaign giving, he lamented, "I couldn't raise a penny."

The kind of living-room campaign Alexander ran in Iowa was probably over, he said, buried by the avalanches of money inundating a retail campaigner like himself. If the truth be known, Alexander never caught on as an exciting, credible candidate, but if what he says is true, lesser-known candidates without a huge personal bankroll or a high-powered fund-raising operation need not apply from now on.

If the way we pick presidents is to improve to the point where confidence, interest, and participation are restored, there must be a much greater sense of public outrage at the status quo, and a much greater demand for change. For all the lamenting about the deleterious effect of money in politics, and all the voiced distress over the excesses of the 1996 campaign, particularly with Clinton renting out the Lincoln Bedroom and other crass practices, the fact is that the public really doesn't seem to give much of a damn. Polls continue to show that campaign finance reform is far down the list of problems that the average American worries about.

The whole money-in-politics scandal of 1996, Wertheimer says, "happened at a time the country looked at Washington and said, 'You guys are irrelevant. We're doing pretty well and the economy is okay, and that place [Washington] is a sinkhole, and we're not going to bother. We don't think you're going to do anything, and you're not capable of making real changes that mean anything.' Meanwhile, Clinton says, 'I haven't done anything wrong and besides, everyone does it,' and it sells. The public mood was out of synch with the scandal."

That mood continues. We have ample reason for pessimism as to whether any truly serious reform of campaign finance will occur, and indeed whether the whole disorderly process by which we pick our presidents will be fixed. As the game of presidential politics becomes ever more lucrative, much more time, energy, and expense is devoted by the candidates, the hired guns of all disciplines, the party leaders, and our elected officials to making the system work for them, instead of changing or streamlining it for the public good.

Members of Congress can ignore the need for reform with no fear of reprimand at the polling booth so long as the public remains disillusioned and turned off. And so our single most important act of public responsibility in a democratic society—voting for the national leader once every four years—continues to be exercised through a process crippled by antiquated rules and procedures, and preyed on by moneyed interests and an army of political mercenaries whose Holy Grail is winning at all costs.

It is, for sure, no way to pick a president. As long as the American people shrug their shoulders and don't clamor for some better way, we will be doomed to keep on without significant change—and getting what our collective apathy reaps.

BIBLIOGRAPHY

Bendiner, Robert. *White House Fever,* Harcourt, Brace, 1960.

Braun, Alan G., and Lawrence D. Longley. *The Politics of Electoral College Reform,* Yale University Press, 1975.

Broder, David S. *The Party's Over,* Harper & Row, 1972.

Burns, James MacGregor. *The Power to Lead,* Simon and Schuster, 1984.

Cohen, Richard M., and Jules Witcover. *A Heartbeat Away: The Investigation and Resignation of Vice President Spiro T. Agnew,* The Viking Press, 1974.

Davis, James W. *Springboard to the White House,* Thomas Y. Crowell, 1967.

Fallows, James. *Breaking the News,* Pantheon, 1996.

Germond, Jack W., and Jules Witcover. *Blue Smoke and Mirrors: How Reagan Won and Why Carter Lost the Election of 1980,* The Viking Press, 1981.

———. *Mad as Hell: Revolt at the Ballot Box, 1992,* Warner Books, 1993.

———. *Wake Us When It's Over: Presidential Politics of 1984*, Macmillan, 1985.

———. *Whose Broad Stripes and Bright Stars? The Trivial Pursuit of the Presidency, 1988*, Warner Books, 1989.

Halberstam, David. *The Powers That Be*, Alfred A. Knopf, 1979.

Hess, Karl. *In a Cause That Will Triumph*, Doubleday, 1967.

Laski, Harold J. *The American Presidency*, Harper, 1940.

Lewis, Charles. *The Buying of the President*, Avon Books, 1996.

Longley, Lawrence, and Neal R. Peirce. *The Electoral College Primer*, Yale University Press, 1996.

Mayer, William G. *In Pursuit of the White House*, Chatham House, 1996.

Morris, Dick. *Behind the Oval Office*, Random House, 1997.

Nichols, Roy F. *The Invention of the American Political Parties*, The Free Press, 1967.

Patterson, Thomas E. *The Mass Media Election*, Praeger, 1980.

———. *Out of Order*, Alfred A. Knopf, 1993.

Peirce, Neal R. *The People's President*, Clarion, 1968.

Pious, Richard M. *The American Presidency*, Basic Books, 1979.

Polsby, Nelson W., and Aaron B. Wildavsky. *Presidential Elections*, Scribner's, 1971.

Roseboom, Eugene H. *A History of Presidential Elections,* Macmillan, 1964.

Sabato, Larry J. *The Rise of Political Consultants,* Basic Books, 1981.

——— and Glenn R. Simpson. *Dirty Little Secrets,* Times Books, 1996.

Saloma, John S., and Frederick H. Sontag. *Parties,* Alfred A. Knopf, 1972.

Schlesinger, Arthur M., Jr., ed. *Running for President,* Simon and Schuster, 1994.

Wills, Garry, "The Real Scandal," *The New York Review of Books,* February 20, 1997.

Witcover, Jules. *85 days: The last Campaign,* G. P. Putnam's Sons, 1969.

———. *Marathon: The Pursuit of the Presidency, 1972–1976,* The Viking Press, 1977.

———. *The Resurrection of Richard Nixon,* G. P. Putnam's Sons, 1970.

———. *White Knight: The Rise of Spiro Agnew,* Random House, 1972.

Woodward, Bob. *The Choice,* Simon and Schuster, 1996.

INDEX